THE MOVIE BRATS

MICHAEL PYE
and
LYNDA MYLES

The Movie Brats

How the Film Generation Took Over Hollywood

Holt, Rinehart and Winston · New York

Copyright © 1979 by Michael Pye and Lynda Myles
All rights reserved, including the right to reproduce
this book or portions thereof in any form.
Published by Holt, Rinehart and Winston,
383 Madison Avenue, New York, New York 10017.
Published simultaneously in Canada by Holt, Rinehart
and Winston of Canada, Limited.

Library of Congress Cataloging in Publication Data
Pye, Michael, 1946–
    The movie brats.
        Bibliography: p.
        Filmography: p.
    Includes index.
    1. Moving-picture producers and directors—
United States—Biography. 2. Moving-picture
industry—United States—History. I. Myles,
    Lynda, joint author. II. Title.
PN1998.A2P9   791.43′0973   78–11901
        ISBN Hardbound: 0–03–042671–5
        ISBN Paperback: 0–03–042676–6

First Edition

Designer: Amy Hill
Printed in the United States of America
1 3 5 7 9 10 8 6 4 2

The chapter on George Lucas first appeared
in *The Atlantic Monthly*.

Grateful acknowledgment is made for use of the photographs:

Of Francis Coppola, courtesy of American Zoetrope. Of
George Lucas, courtesy of United Press International
Photo. Of Brian DePalma, courtesy of Wide World
Photos. Of John Milius, courtesy of Warner Brothers,
Inc. Of Martin Scorsese, copyright © 1977, United Artists
Corporation, all rights reserved. Permission of United
Artists and Martin Scorsese. Of Steven Spielberg, cour-
tesy of Wide World Photos.

To John, with love and thanks

Authors' Note

This book is a collaboration. Lynda Myles developed the idea of a cine-literate generation of filmmakers; Michael Pye prepared the historical, industrial, and sociological material. The readings of the films were developed jointly, over years of discussion, and represent a truly collaborative position.

Much of our material draws on our own conversations with filmmakers and their associates. Some derives from printed sources or interview transcripts which were made available to us. To make the distinction clear, we mark quotations from our own conversations with the present tense—"he says"; and those from secondary sources are marked with a past tense—"he said." Any published material from which we quote is listed in the bibliography.

Acknowledgements

This book depended on the kindness of friends—and strangers. Directors, producers, financiers, and associates generously gave us time and effort, often under impossible circumstances. We thank David Brown, Bill Clayton, Ron Dandrea, Brian DePalma, Gary Kurtz, George Lucas, John Milius, Walter Murch, Martin Scorsese, Ned Tannen, Richard Zanuck, and the Hollywood investigators of the Internal Revenue Service. David Golding, Alfred Hitchcock, Al Howe, Ed Sands, and Michael Deeley were helpful in the early stages of our research. In London we depended on the selfless support of the staff of the British Film Institute; we thank in particular David Meeker, and Gillian Hartnoll, Ann Walters and the staff of the library. We had generous help and advice from Michael Linden, head of the research department of the Motion Picture Association of America; the research departments of E. F. Hutton Inc. in New York, and the Bank of America in Los Angeles. At the London embassy of the United States the economic counselors helped us sort out our economic ideas, as did Malcolm Crawford of the *Sunday Times* (London). The libraries of the University of London, the London School of Economics, the Department of Corporations in Los Angeles, the Federal Communications Commission in Washington, the University of Indiana at Bloomington, and the British Independent Broadcasting Authority gave us invaluable help. We depended on the assistance of Christine Darby in Edinburgh, Angela Francis in London, Tammy Pittman in New York, and Virginia Santore in Washington for help in our research. Publicists smoothed our way constantly. In London we thank Graham Smith of Cinema

International Corporation, Donald Murrey of Columbia, John Fairbairn of Twentieth Century-Fox, Julian Senior of Warners; in New York, David Van Houten of Paramount, Jonas Halperin of Warners; in Hollywood, Louis Blane of Universal, and Joan Eisenberg of the *Star Wars* publicity team. While we were working on this book, friends were immensely supportive: we thank Neal Ascherson, Phil Hardy, Isabel Hilton, John Holm, Colin McArthur, Tom Nairn, Betty O'Brien, Walter Panzar, Chris Petit, Dave Pirie, Peter Wilsher, and Murray and Barbara Grigor. Michael Shaw and Anthea Morton-Saner at Curtis Brown, our agents, were our advocates and invaluable advisors. Ann and John Reihill generously gave us the address which signs this book; that made it possible for us to complete our work. And we thank our editors, Frank Pike at Faber and Jennifer Josephy at Holt, for their support and faith.

The Kipper House
Kinsale, Eire
March 1978

ONE

The Playground

The playground opens early. Mechanics push out the giant arc lights that simmer in the morning gloom. There is the muffled sound of carpenters, the slam of a door on a coffee van. A giant image flickers on the other side of a vacant hangar, and solemn men sit and debate how best to mix the sound that will match that image. This playground is a factory.

Studio executives pass the guards and put their glossy cars, carefully, into the parking spaces that are marked with their names. When each man quits the studio, his name will be painted over. This playground is no place for permanency.

On the fifty-fourth floor of the Bank of America tower on South Flower Street, men settle in their open-plan offices. They are blind to the dizzying view that stretches from ocean to mountains to the bleached, white bones of the Hollywood sign. They talk seriously of points and profit. They examine credit ratings and collateral. The bankers care about the playground because it is a business.

In Cincinnati a group of lawyers meet. They want to shelter their income from taxes. For that reason a banker in Los Angeles will advance money. From that money an executive will assemble his project. Carpenters hammer for it, stars act for it, writers invent for it, and directors shape it. The playground will come to life.

It is an extraordinary, a seductive, place. Our dreams were forged here. As you enter Twentieth Century-Fox, on Motor Boulevard off Pico, the playground offers you New York—lions and libraries, elevated railway and grand hotel foyers. At MGM the bleak hangars of the dream fac-

3

tory give way to a backlot where ruins stand; here is the house from *The Philadelphia Story*, altered for later films; and the railway station where Fred Astaire arrived in *The Band Wagon*; even the remains of Esther Williams's above ground swimming pool. This playground is a machine, an assembly line, a brokerage for artificial images. But it is also a sizeable part of the emotional reality of our past. It bred the images we share. We remember crying at the movies almost more than real tears. Our adolescent ideas grew on the models in the films we were offered. The playground helped shape our culture and our assumptions. What it produces is consumed on a mighty scale. The playground manufactures popular culture.

Once, there were giants here. There were Howard Hawks, John Ford, Orson Welles. They made films for men like Harry Cohn at Columbia. Cohn never fought against hyperbole. A plaque on Fifth Avenue still claims: "In Him Burned the Eternal Flame of the Creator." His cohorts remember him for the electrified chair he kept in his boardroom, wired to snap sleepy lunchers back to life or torment a minion.

There were men like Mayer, father figures to the industry; and Samuel Goldwyn, tangling his language picturesquely; and golden Thalbergs; and ambitious Selznicks; and Zukor of Paramount, Zanuck of Twentieth Century-Fox. There were moguls.

At the same time there was a machine for the moguls to operate.

This book explores the playground as it is now—as industry, as business, and as source of our dreams. It tells why the race of moguls died out, what happened next, and who took the power to form our fantasies.

The reality of Hollywood was once an esoteric theme. F. Scott Fitzgerald noted: "People in the East pretend to be interested in how pictures are made, but if you actually tell them anything, you find they are only interested in Colbert's clothes or Gable's private life. They never see the ventriloquist for the doll. Even the intellectuals, who ought to know better, like to hear about the pretensions,

4

extravagances, and vulgarities—tell them pictures have a private grammar, like politics or automobile production or society, and watch the blank look come into their faces."

Fitzgerald's audience can be forgiven. Glamour still clouds all the issues. An audience that watches *Jaws* will scream. At *Star Wars* they cheer. *The Godfather* leaves a sour, disturbing taste. *Carrie* revolts and fascinates and horrifies. *The Wind and the Lion* has a ravishing beauty. *New York, New York* dives between the exhilarating and the fearful. These films play on emotion and personal response. They contain the seeds of horror, love, fear, pleasure, revulsion, fascination. It is hard to connect them with the abstract, arid balance sheets of giant corporations— the conglomerates that have motion pictures as part of a division, the independent "majors" like Twentieth Century-Fox. Graphs and tables in economic analyses seem remote from the stirring in the head, the visceral shifts that film provides. Sometimes, it can seem better not to know how all those images appeared before us. The machine is treated like magic, better not to understand it, in case the power goes away.

It will not. Indeed, it is vital to examine the machine that makes popular culture. That machine is the necessary condition of the pleasure we take in cinema. If that pleasure has changed over the years, it is in part because the machine has changed. There is no very exact vocabulary for the link; but the film industry talks of movies as "product." The machine is what molds the product.

We plan to explore that process. We want to take you inside the "private grammar" of the movies—to see how deals are assembled, how films are made, who has the power and how they use it.

We begin with the great men of Hollywood. Some of them gain stature with distance—the studio chiefs who survived into 1946, the greatest year the commercial cinema has ever known, when more people paid more money, in real terms, to see film than ever before or since. We show why their command of the machine crumbled, and how the studios fell into the hands of new men—

agents, lawyers, accountants, salesmen. The talents of this new generation need be no less than those of a furrier like Adolph Zukor, who founded Paramount; bicycle salesmen like the Warner Brothers; a shipyard laborer like Darryl F. Zanuck; a would-be Episcopalian minister like Cecil B. DeMille; a trolley-bus conductor like Harry Cohn of Columbia; a glovemaker like Samuel Goldwyn; or a junk dealer like Louis B. Mayer, the front man of MGM. But the attitudes of the new men are very different. In Hollywood a cage of entrepreneurs has given way and left a corporate jungle. That first generation of filmmakers settled on Hollywood because it had decent water and was close enough to the Mexican border if writs arrived. The generation that has power today is in Hollywood only because the machine of filmmaking is there.

The structure of Hollywood looks deceptively like its old form. Six major companies, distributing the films they finance, are at its center; alongside is MGM, which now survives as a small production unit within a hotel company. Those six—Columbia, Paramount, Twentieth Century-Fox, United Artists, Universal, and Warners—are old names. But they are quite unlike the studios that bore the same names in the 1930s. Since film companies were forced by court decisions under antitrust law to sell all their theaters, the risk in financing and producing a motion picture has increased enormously. But while production is a gamble, distribution is not. Sending the films out to theaters is a steady source of income, if not profit. Every transaction involves a fee to the distributor, with a profit built into that fee. It follows that only the biggest companies, with that consistent source of cash from handling films, have the financial muscle to put up cash for steady programs of film. That is how the majors survive, the big studios whose names evoke past styles of film—MGM for musicals, Warners for gangster films, Universal for the horror of Frankenstein. But the major companies' relationships with filmmakers have changed radically. Once even a John Ford or a Howard Hawks had a contract and could be assigned to any film at the studio's whim. Now filmmakers more often work to organize their own films from their own ideas. Studios have power, but it is only the power to say no. No longer are they tyrants who can mold or wreck careers. They are no longer originators or creators.

The old guard wanted to create; but time and death took them away. Unhappily for Hollywood, they lived long enough to make fatal miscalculations. They failed to see the scale of social change in America after the Second World War or to understand that social shifts would also alter the role movies played in people's lives.

The new filmmakers understand that change intuitively. It shaped them as they grew up. Their films satisfy the social, economic, and class needs of groups the old moguls might never have recognized as potential audiences for their product. For as the charts of power in Hollywood have changed, so too has the ideology of the industry—the system of ideas which lies, implicit and concealed, within American film. This is the other part of the private grammar of film.

We believe the machine, the industry, the ideas, and the product are indissolubly linked. And we believe this is clear from the work of the men who, at the end of 1977, stood unchallenged as the powers within a new Hollywood. They inherited the power of the moguls to make film for a mass audience. And they know the past of cinema like scholars; they grew with it and through it. In their world anything can refer back to movies. Knowledge and power and spectacular success all make them the true children of old Hollywood.

At the core of this new generation are six men. They, and their associates, have made films more successful than any others in history. They knew the history of Hollywood from the late night television movies and the corner theaters; and because they chose to learn it at film school; and because they have sought out, analyzed, and enjoyed film of every kind. Their influences live on through their films. They are rare because their ideas have proved to be commercial; and the hollow studio system is grateful for that. They fill a need. Therefore, they have power.

The six directors form a tribe, with shared gods and idols. Their careers, their films, even their private lives overlap. These men are: Francis Coppola, first of the film school graduates to make a feature film and later the director of *The Godfather* and *Apocalypse Now*. It was Coppola who served as patron to the young George Lucas and produced his *American Graffiti*; later, Lucas was to make *Star Wars*. On that space fantasy Steven Spielberg had planned to help out as a second unit director, devising ways for intergalactic storm troopers to seethe with green steam as they died. In the event he was too busy with his own fantasy, *Close Encounters of the Third Kind*, a film on which rode all the fortunes of a major studio. The gamble was not as outrageous as it might have seemed; Spielberg was also the architect of *Jaws*.

At the Burbank studios he shares an office bungalow with his shooting companion John Milius, a classmate of George Lucas in the film school of the University of Southern California. It was Milius who wrote the original version of Coppola's *Apocalypse Now* and the horrifying story of the wreck of the *Indianapolis* in *Jaws*. As a director in his own right, Milius has made the epic *The Wind and the Lion* and *Big Wednesday*. With him as producer is Buzz Feitshans; and Feitshans appeared, in 1972, as editor of *Boxcar Bertha*, the first Hollywood film by Martin Scorsese.

Scorsese is part of the tribe's New York group. In that city he made *Mean Streets* and *Taxi Driver*. He shared university classes with Brian DePalma, maker of *Obsession*, *Carrie*, and *The Fury*. Here the links crisscross. DePalma works regularly with Paul Hirsch as his editor; and Hirsch helped cut *Star Wars* for George Lucas. Marcia Lucas, wife to George, was editor on films by Martin Scorsese—*New York, New York, Alice Doesn't Live Here Anymore*, and *Taxi Driver*. It was Francis Coppola who first suggested that Scorsese might be the right director for a major studio project. The man who wrote *Taxi Driver*, Paul Schrader, also wrote *Obsession* for Brian DePalma and drafted *Close Encounters of the Third Kind*, later written again by Spielberg. Francis Coppola's film *The Conversation* and George Lucas's *American Graffiti* share an extraordinary sense of the power of sound, generated by a shared sound editor, Walter Murch. At the end of *The Conversation*, its central character is left miming despairingly to a record of Georgie Auld playing saxophone; in *New York, New York* Auld was again the player behind the star. The writers of Steven Spielberg's first feature film, *The Sugarland Express*, made their first feature film under the protection of George Lucas. They had been at school with him. The circle constantly turns around and around.

"We are the pigs," George Lucas says. "We are the ones who sniff out the truffles. You can put us on a leash, keep us under control. But we are the guys who dig out the gold. The man in the executive tower cannot do that. The studios are corporations now, and the men who run them are bureaucrats. They know as much about making movies as a banker does. They know about making deals like a real estate agent. They obey corporate law; each man asks himself how any decision will affect his job. They go to parties and they hire people who know people. But the power lies with us—the ones who actually know how to make movies."

John Milius remembers Hollywood as it was in 1967, when he first tried to break into the movie business. "There were walls up in Hollywood then, and the place was very cliquish. You had to know Frank Sinatra or something. Sure, the studios were making more movies, which was good, but the studios also had real power. Heads of production had muscle. And they were more socially conscious—movie deals were made at parties. The Hollywood you read about all existed then. There were parties for people on the A list and for the less important ones on the B list. Now all that has gone. That sociability only exists in television. The only people I see socially are Steven Spielberg and a few friends I go shooting with and a few surfers. If George Lucas lived down in Los Angeles, I'd see more of him. Occasionally, I see Marty Scorsese. But we've dismantled the social establishment.

"Nobody in a studio challenges the final cut of a film now. I think they realize the filmmakers are likely to be around a lot longer than the studio executives. Now, power lies with the filmmakers, and we are the group that is getting the power."

It has taken pain and patience to gain power. These six directors—sharing projects, exchanging ideas, sometimes presenting each other with shares in profits on their films—did not always have the luck. They arrived through sheer determination. They all loved film. They wanted to make film. Only Spielberg and DePalma missed the experience of full-time film school, Spielberg because his grades were not good enough. All of them share a basic cinematic literacy and a set of influences and ideas that come from films, and these things are used in subtle forms in their own work. In the work of Martin Scorsese alone it is simple to trace the influence of a staggering range of filmmakers— Raoul Walsh, Robert Bresson, John Ford, Luchino Visconti, George Cukor, Jean-Luc Godard, Samuel Fuller, and François Truffaut. The conventions in a film like *Star Wars* derive from the classic films of Arthurian legend, the movie equivalent of chivalric romance. Before filming, Francis Coppola consciously reexamines the films of masters like Alfred Hitchcock or Ingmar Bergman. Steven Spielberg's wonders, which sparkle across the screen in *Close Encounters of the Third Kind,* derive from animated films as diverse as Disney's *Bambi* and Chuck Jones's immortal *Road Runner.* Brian DePalma plays, knowingly, with the plots and methods of Hitchcock films such as *Psycho, Vertigo,* and *Rear Window.* John Milius takes his sense of honor from Japanese cinema. In business, he says, he keeps to a personal code of Bushido.

Cine-literacy also means a close knowledge of film technology. George Lucas and Francis Coppola pay particular attention to sound; their sound editor, Walter Murch, is a vital part of their films. Brian DePalma revived a disused film convention, split-screen, and pushed it to its furthest limits. The special effects in a film like *Jaws* require meticulous story-boarding, drawing the action frame by frame almost like an animated film. It required a sophistication of technique that comes late to most directors, but that was fully formed in Steven Spielberg at the age of twenty-seven. Yet this generation is always careful to maintain a critical distance from its own work and from the film world. "The more powerful you become," DePalma says, "the more you have to avoid insulating yourself. That is the problem in Los Angeles all the time."

These six directors share a distaste for the superficial social round of Beverly Hills and the old Hollywood. George Lucas lives quietly in a suburb of San Francisco, within driving distance of Francis Coppola's mansion. Martin Scorsese and Brian DePalma keep their bases in New York, like sanctuaries. "Never, never live in Hollywood," DePalma says. "I hate this insulated universe where film is the most important thing." John Milius and Steven Spielberg live physically close to the ancient mansions of stars in the canyons above Los Angeles; but they stay aloof from the world below. They keep perspective by staying away from the obvious restaurants, the agents' parties, the specious glitter that fills the gossip columns of the trade papers. They know that Hollywood is an invention, a firework display designed by press agents and promoters.

But they cannot wholly escape even the destructive side of that artificial Hollywood. They, too, have a product to sell. That is another part of the great and continuous tradition. There are burdens that go with the pleasurable debt they acknowledge to the filmmakers of old Hollywood, and there is the duty they feel to help along the next generation of filmmakers. Francis Coppola has already discharged that duty through George Lucas, and, later, through the American Carroll Ballard and Wim Wenders, one of the brightest young German directors. Spielberg acts as an insurance policy on films for Universal; should his young protégés fail, Spielberg contracts to complete their films. George Lucas has sponsored his former University of

Southern California classmates Hal Barwood and Matt Robbins as directors: "I didn't have to stand up and do the deal, like Francis did for me," Lucas says. "I am an insurance policy, like Steven at Universal. If the guys can do it on their own, it's that much better."

In that tradition Coppola, Lucas, DePalma, Milius, Scorsese, and Spielberg are true movie brats, true children of Hollywood. They despise the present form of the industry. They mistrust its corporate managers. They know the house is empty, but they remain alert to the ghosts. They are the heirs to the grand tradition of American cinema.

This is how they came into their inheritance—what they made, and how they made it.

TWO

The Playground Opens

Look down the road. Green lawns, neatly matched, flank the identical houses. New families have begun to settle into their homes. Dreams that survived both the Depression and war are beginning to come true.

Down this road, and thousands of other suburban roads that sprouted new homes and new communities in the years after World War II, is the center of the world for the families that live here. Their neighbors are likely to be their friends; they will see each other often. Their families are newly started and likely to expand. Fathers delight in their babies. Mothers invite the next-door wife to coffee. They go to church on a Sunday morning, to show themselves as members of a community. As soon as the war ended, and production had picked up again, they bought a radio set. Now the family has pets, a car, a television set.

The suburbs that grew in the 1940s and 1950s were for people who could build their universe around hearth, home, and the small, nuclear family. Often, they had traveled long distances across the country, far from parents or other relatives, to set up house. The misery of the Depression and the isolation of the war years held them back from marriage and house-building. Now homemaking became their obsession, all the more if they had suffered real deprivation during the black years of the 1930s. The new suburbanites wanted certainty. They believed it was possible. America would grow ever richer. With those riches, class would become irrelevant. There would be enough for everybody, and it would be easy to tolerate the fact that some had more than others. Everybody would have the goods to show their status, the machines to do the work, the tools to help improve the home, and space for living.

Women had ruled families in the Depression years, and their daughters went to work during the war years doing jobs that had traditionally been reserved for "stronger" men. Now they had a chance to marry and raise children, and they joined the massive migration to the fringes of cities. Their husbands could study under the GI Bill. There was money to spare in the postwar boom; there were also the goods to buy as assembly lines changed from guns to radios, washing machines, and even televisions. Leisure time was full.

Work, now that it was plentiful, ceased to be the mainspring of life. It became a necessary evil, not a moral imperative. Home came before work, private life before the duties of office, factory, or shop. Before our eyes, down this quiet suburban road, American social values are shifting profoundly. Middle America is coming to birth. And, with its birth, old Hollywood is doomed.

There are conventional explanations for why the old studio system of Hollywood was undermined. In part, they are true. In the 1940s American courts decreed that the major film companies must sell their chains of theaters. Without a guaranteed outlet for their product, the studios entered a new game: each film constituted a risk. Not only might it fail with the public; it might fail even before the public had a chance to pass judgement. It could be a flop with the theater owners.

And as the companies took a greater risk on each production, they watched the raging force of television stealing their audience and wrecking their business. That, at least, is the customary explanation. But it will not do.

The divorce between studios and theaters took time; in itself, it cannot account for the Hollywood panics that various scholars place in 1946, 1948, or 1950. The court decisions had been expected since 1933, with the first antitrust cases in the motion picture industry. The Justice Department, seeking scapegoats in bleak economic times, started to pursue the studios more actively in 1938. The first principles of the final divorce—that independent theaters should be allowed to book what they wanted, rather than taking every film a studio made on pain of being allowed none at all—was conceded in 1946. The consent decrees that signaled the end of the cozy arrangement by which companies could take a profit on making, distributing, and showing a film were ratified between 1948 and 1950; but they did not become wholly effective until 1959, when MGM emerged from the Loew's theater and hotel chain as a pure production and distribution company. The companies found ways to soften the blow, including informal agreements on theater chains booking from studios other than their original parents. The old studio system proved resilient for almost two decades, from 1938 to 1958, under the pressure from antitrust lawyers. But finally, the cartel was smashed. Each film became a gamble.

Then came television. In cities where television stations were started, cinema attendance slumped. In cities where there was no television, it either rose or dropped only slightly. The close correlation between the rise of television and the decline of film has been taken as an explanation of what happened to Hollywood. But it can be misleading to assume that statistical correlations, however neat, mean that a trend is explained. It leaves the basic question outstanding: why did America want television in preference to film?

We know that, out in Middletown, they went on reading the fan magazines and gasping at the revelations of Hollywood private life. They watched feature films on television with avid attention. Americans did not suddenly reject the stars and the content of film. Indeed, they remained avid consumers. What they no longer needed was the social act of going out to the theater. In part, the need declined as the trouble of getting to a theater increased: suburban life, by definition, was lived away from the downtown theaters, and young families hampered social life. But something more radical was happening. The peculiar value that Americans were learning to put on the home meant that entertainment had to be shared within the family, at the hearth. In the early 1950s showpiece houses were designed with the television replacing the hearth; the design was open plan, and the TV set was mounted on a swivel so that anybody could continue watching from the kitchen, living room, or dining room. The young and educated, the main audience for film, were concentrating their attention on home and marriage. Television, cunningly, offered shows in which the star seemed to visit your home, addressed you confidentially, and made the experience of television a social act around the hearth. More important, sitting in a darkened cinema did not help place you in a community, as going to church did. It did not symbolize family. It did not, like spectator sports, offer a focus for male sodality away from the family. To the families in suburbia, the cinema served no purpose.

Television took time to establish itself. In the immediate postwar years it was radio that sold spectacularly. Fancy East Side bars in New York sold their wares by promising free television. A *Variety* editorial in 1946 challenged the set manufacturers to decide whether television was to be "for snobs or mobs." The cheapest set on the market then cost $279.95 and "the other models," *Variety* reported, "cost running into the $2,000 and upwards category and are strictly class production." In 1948 Harry Truman achieved what no man could do later: he won the presidency by barnstorming the country and ignoring suggestions that he should use radio or television.

That same year the Federal Communications Commission froze the expansion of the networks. No new stations were to be licensed until "interference problems" were sorted out. War in Korea extended the freeze. Economic effort was needed for something other than the manufacture of consumer goods. Major cities—Portland, Oregon; Portland, Maine; Little Rock, Arkansas; Austin, Texas—had no television at all. Few cities had more than one station. Only New York and Los Angeles had a real choice of programs; each had seven stations. Under all those handicaps, it is not surprising that the production of TV sets did not rise steadily. It progressed by hiccups. In 1947 the industry turned out 178,571 TV sets; the next year production was almost at the 1 million mark; in 1949 it was 3 million; and in 1950 there were 7.5 million new sets on the market. The rate of production dipped in the early 1950s; it was not until 1955 that more sets were made than in 1950.

In 1946 one home in every five thousand had television. In 1947 the number of sets had doubled; one home in twenty-five hundred was equipped with a set. In 1948 the figure changed dramatically: one home in two hundred fifty had a set. It was spectacular growth, but it was growth from virtually zero. Television was not sweeping the nation, as some thought. The Sears, Roebuck catalog does not carry a television advertisement until 1949; the set cost $149.95 (with indoor antenna) or $15.50 down and $7.00 monthly. Before that, the sets had a limited mass market. Yet in those three years, while television was establishing itself, the number of tickets sold at cinemas began to slump alarmingly. To the rulers of Hollywood, the slump was inexplicable.

There never was a year like 1946 for the American film industry. More than 4,060 million people paid $1,692 million to go to the movies. Flush with money after the war, and with few consumer goods to buy, Americans attended movie theaters. Families were not yet started; couples were courting, not raising children. Demobilization took time, and captive GI's took films as their form of temporary escape from the camps. The tensions of war were uncoiling, and entertainment was a priority. Until the massive coal and rail strikes at the end of 1946, America was infatuated with the movies.

But by the next year admissions had slumped by 10 percent. Theaters sold 403 million fewer seats. Yet in that same year fewer than 200,000 TV sets were sold, and not many Americans would have been able to find a fix of television to satisfy their craving for entertainment. In the front office of film companies, executives could look at the raw figures of cash taken at the box office and stay optimistic; seat prices rose to mask the fall in audiences. But the disastrous change continued. In 1948 only 3,422 million tickets were sold, which was a drop of 242 million from the previous year. Yet only 975,000 TV sets had been sold. Hollywood was in trouble, but television was not yet strong enough, or generally accessible enough, to be the prime cause.

In later years economists examined the figures for the growth of television and the decline of the movies. They found a direct correlation. For on the most sophisticated economic tests—allowing for the likely decline in movie-going even if television had not grown—the two phenomena seemed linked. But the link is not, in fact, cause and effect. The economists did not consider the nature of the cities which first had television, and where movie theaters suffered most. Television companies went first, unsurprisingly, to the expanding cities with suburban streets and a suburban style of life. The audience potential was enormous; the cities were the largest in the United States; the prospects for advertising were good. Most of the target cities for mass migration in America in the 1940s were also cities with television stations; the only major exception was Tampa, Florida, where the city offered a refuge for the retired as much as a new way of working and living for young families. New migrant populations spread into suburbia; their locations, families, and aspirations all made it likely that downtown movie theaters would face problems, and television would prove attractive. Television's growth did not maim the movies. Social change accounts for the fate of both media.

Movies were losing their share of the nation's spending on recreation. Even when families went out, they did not go as often to the movies. In 1946 almost twenty cents of every dollar spent on recreation in the United States went to movie theaters. In 1950 the figure fell to twelve cents of every dollar. Not until 1974 did Americans pay as much money to see movies as they did in 1946, and almost three decades of inflation made the apparent recovery an actual slump. Of every dollar spent on recreation in 1974, a mere four cents went to the movies.

As leisure habits changed, television did not appear to movies as a hated rival all the time. It was not always the drawing room monster to be abused, satirized, and kicked. "The major Hollywood companies," *The New York Times* reported on May 2, 1948, "are gradually, but nonetheless purposefully, acquiring TV interests." MGM bought into a Los Angeles television station. Twentieth Century-Fox did a deal with the R. J. Reynolds Tobacco Corporation to provide Movietone News five nights a week for television. If the movie moguls were restive and queasy about the new medium, they still sought compromise.

For the two media were not always enemies. In 1929 the fledgling CBS network, established to challenge the monopoly of the National Broadcasting Corporation and its monstrous parent, Radio Corporation of America, was struggling to survive. It had severe credit problems. A major company bailed it out by buying a 49 percent stake from a cigar magnate's son called William S. Paley. The main reason for the deal was the major corporation's faith in the future of television; and it sold its interest in CBS only when the courts and the Justice Department ordered it to do so. The savior of television in 1929 was Paramount Pictures.

Hedda Hopper was a shrewd woman beneath the gross hats and the acid manner. On May 31, 1950, she led her column with a solemn warning about television: "This is one medium," she wrote, "that I don't believe Hollywood can give the old runaround; so we might as well take the TV producers by their hot little hands and co-operate." Dutifully, the rulers of Hollywood trembled.

According to *The New York Times*, they had reason. In 1951 the *Times* found that since the war 51 cinemas had shut their doors in New York, 64 in Chicago, and 134 in the south of California. Almost all television cities were reporting a slump in moviegoing; sometimes the loss was as high as 40 percent. But the moguls did not look far enough. While moviegoing was on the decline, so were other social activities like eating out and other inner-city pastimes like borrowing from the New York Public Library. Television was only one symptom of the change.

There are signs that the old-timers did sense that change, even if they found no answer to it. In April 1946, startlingly early if orthodox Hollywood historians are right about the impact of television, Louis B. Mayer of MGM ordered a sizeable cut in the costs of each film made by the studio. If necessary, films must be shorter or a shade less ambitious. The reason was a cool calculation that 1946 was a year of miracles for the movie box office that would never come again. MGM thought the market for film in the United States and Canada was at the saturation point. The market overseas was snafu'd by other countries' postwar protectionism.

In the same year Darryl F. Zanuck at Twentieth Century-Fox made a vital decision. His studio would make no more B pictures, the cheap lower half of the bill for theaters out of town. From now on, Fox would offer only gloss and glamour and glory. At Universal and Columbia, then both makers of low budget films, studio executives reviewed their strategy and came to a similar conclusion: they started to make more expensive films. The reasons were not as simple as they seem. Logically, the divorce of studios and cinemas meant theaters could avoid buying "programmers," films whose sole virtue was the time they filled the screen. Logically, the antitrust actions would make the film industry more competitive, and put the big money with the big films. But the studios were not following logic which was quite that simple. Universal made its decision to make more expensive films while it was actually negotiating to acquire a theater chain of its own.

In 1946 the studios also took the first blow of the antitrust cases. They were banned from price-fixing, formula deals, and franchising arrangements—the arrangements by which an independent theater out in Nebraska could be tied to one studio, for its hits and its disasters, by simple blackmail. Either the theater took all the studio's films or it would get no films at all. That comforting arrangement was abolished, and the industry faced change.

Wall Street knew what was happening. Amusement shares began to slide at the start of June 1946. Miners and railmen went out on strike. The box office bonanza of the early part of the year began to falter. Trust breakers were active. Shares began to sink a full two weeks before television blooded itself on June 19. On that night NBC showed the Joe Louis–Billy Conn heavyweight fight in New York, Washington, and Philadelphia. For the first time, television offered a spectacle film could not offer—a big fight —on the night it happened. ALL SHOWBIZ EYES VIDEO NOW, screamed a *Variety* headline. "Top showbiz names, heretofore regarding TV skeptically as still a novel toy, are expected to jump on the video bandwagon . . ." Yet cinema and television were not yet seen as deadly enemies: television was used in the home and, to *Variety*, it was "radio's Frankenstein monster."

Hollywood fought back with special effects and grander stories and wider screens. Into the late 1950s the filmmakers were either hired from television or encouraged to make films that television could not possibly encompass. Either way, the logic was to provide such splendor on the screen that the traditional movie audiences would be enticed back to the theaters and away from the television screen. It was false logic. The traditional movie audiences were now the homemakers of Middletown. There were new audiences for film—younger, better educated, more mobile, and more affluent. By 1976 they were the audiences that filmmakers knew they needed. The Motion Picture Association of America, in its economic review of 1976, describes the new moviegoers: "Mature young people," it says, "are an important 'swing' segment that can make a movie a hit—if they get what they want, which is diverting entertainment. There are more people with less constricting freedom of choice in what to do with free time. They are more mature. They are better educated. And they are covering more territory—on wheels. The out-movement to non-metros [that is, migration from big cities] should be watched, and, when justified, acted on." That same message, ironically, should have reached Hollywood in the 1940s and 1950s.

For the war represents the last period when Hollywood was certain which films it should make. Film chiefs believed they had a duty to keep up morale. After the war it is easy to detect common themes—the pessimism of the *films noirs*—but difficult to imagine that the studios pursued those themes as a strategy to attract audiences. The filmmakers became distracted by the apparent threat of television, without realizing how much their traditional audience had slipped away. They looked at content, but not at the social role which television and cinema play in people's lives. The change in audiences and attitudes made it possible, indirectly, for the children of Hollywood to make careers as filmmakers. Directly, it helped make their films successful. The hit movies mirror society. Consider the careful, almost archaeological, attention to suburban detail in Steven Spielberg's *Close Encounters of the Third Kind*; and the idealized adolescence of George Lucas's *American Graffiti,* the golden past of the first generation of American children reared in the life-style of suburbia, with suburban aspirations and fears. The children of Hollywood understood, intuitively, the changes we describe here. That is why it was they who inherited from the moguls' panics in the 1940s and 1950s.

Hollywood, meaning the American theatrical film industry, suffered other blows in those years. The brutal advance of television actually helped disguise some of the other damage; it seemed to explain everything.

Studios connived in the disgraceful hounding of suspected Communists, Leftists, and even "premature anti-Fascists." John Wayne rode out on screen as a heroic investigator for the House Un-American Activities Committee. Harassment, exile, misery, and uncertainty followed for many liberal voices in Hollywood. Trash, purporting to be anti-Communist, was in general supply. Safety was the watchword in everything. It was a massive loss of face for the industry.

More immediately threatening were the changing attitudes of the banks that had learned to support Hollywood in the boom years. There is no helpful equation between how much cash a bank has available for lending and the amount it is prepared to gamble on films. It would be convenient if banks lent more when they thought the industry was strong and cut film lending the moment credit became tight; it would form a logical relationship between film finance and the general economy. Unfortunately, it is true only when banks are under great pressure or have cause for great alarm. In ordinary times banks lend most heavily to workable companies when those companies are doing least well and need the money most. When corporations are flush with money, they need banks least.

Nor has the industry ever had a simple credit-rating at those few institutions that are heavily committed to filmmakers, such as the California-based Bank of America. Decisions are made on an ad hoc basis. They depend on collateral like any bank loan; and a film is not collateral in itself. No star is, literally, bankable. The function of a popular star is to interest a major studio in a project. The studio will then guarantee a bank loan or provide the money, based on its own judgement of how well the film may do. The bank then looks hard at the distributor.

In the 1940s, they did not like what they found. One minor company, PRC, collapsed. So, very nearly, did the major United Artists.

United Artists was the company founded by Charles Chaplin, Mary Pickford, and Douglas Fairbanks. It never owned soundstages and a studio. Its business was supporting, financing, and marketing the product of independent producers. In the wonder year of 1946, UA managed to plunge into the red. Stockholders were told there was no money available for investment; the company could no longer shelter the independent producers who by now had the chance for homes at many of the other major studios. Pickford and Chaplin were at each other's throats, exchanging acid remarks and legal documents across the country, alternately announcing and denying that their stake in UA was for sale. Their only common ground lay in the alleged duplicity of David Selznick, their partner in UA, who had allegedly double-crossed them by shipping his projects, stars, directors, producers, and expertise over to the rival studio, RKO. It cost UA $2 million to buy themselves out of their contract with the absent Mr. Selznick.

The company had ill luck on its films. Charles Chaplin was savagely attacked for his sexual tastes and his leftist sentiments; when *Monsieur Verdoux* was released in the United States it was a financial disaster. Mary Pickford had quite uncharacteristic lapses of judgement culminating in the last, unhappy appearance of the Marx Brothers in *Love Happy*. That film was distinguished only by its final sequence in which a cash hungry producer sold advertising space in the backdrop in front of which Harpo was clowning.

The position of United Artists was desperate. In 1948 the banks decided on strategic withdrawal. Bankers Trust pulled out, Security First National demanded guarantees of $1 million each from Pickford and Chaplin before it would advance another cent. Without the guarantees it threatened a "film financing holiday." In fact, it financed no films for any studio in 1948. Bank of America started to demand 100 percent guarantees on all funds advanced to independent producers, effectively ending the era of banks putting risk capital into films. And besides Bank of America there was, as George Bagnall, vice-president of UA said, "no other real source for bank money." Out of the game went Bank of Manhattan, Irving Trust, Guaranty Trust. Their confidence was not helped by UA's wrangles with its prime producers. Howard Hawks was threatening to withdraw his masterpiece *Red River* because UA was unwilling to guarantee the $1 million by which he had overrun his budget. Howard Hughes was still embarrassing the company with his profitable but scandalous Jane Russell picture *The Outlaw*. ("How," asked the salacious advertisements, "would you like to tussle with Russell?")

The scandals came just as the slump in cinema attendance could no longer be disguised. Indeed, private estimates that circulated among bankers and studio chiefs suggested the slump was even worse than it proved to be. The private surveys suggested a drop in ticket sales of 25 percent between 1946 and 1948; actually, the drop was a smaller, but still very damaging 15.9 percent. Bankers and senior film executives were taking a more gloomy view of the movies than either the researchers—Audience Research Institute guessed the drop was around 14 percent —or the trade papers—*Film Daily*, optimistically, estimated a drop of only 5 percent. With antitrust cases coming to settlement, and the troubling prospect of television, film no longer seemed a sensible investment.

Worse still, the banks had less money to invest. The postwar boom was cooling off. America's passion for consumer goods was fading. Money was tight. Using a crude measure of bank liquidity—that is, the cash available and uncommitted—it seems likely that the banks' resources dropped between 1946 and 1948 by 11 percent. Even if the movies had looked like a good investment, the money might not have been available.

The wind turned cold between 1946 and 1948. There were bankers' doubts, corporate disputes, a slide in ticket sales that the studios thought privately was even worse than it was, the antitrust actions, and television. That was a frightening mixture at best. There had also been hefty pay settlements after the war which were inflating the cost of making the films that fewer people paid less to see. (One architect of those pay deals later abandoned his trade union role for politics and changed his course sharply: he was the onetime president of the Screen Actors Guild, Ronald Reagan.)

Had these factors been the only problems, Hollywood might have saved itself. There had been times that were almost as bad. The end of a boom could actually help ticket sales: the Depression had helped mask a slow decline in box office takings. Individual companies had been close to bankruptcy before. United Artists itself had weathered near disaster in the late 1930s, when it was bailed out by the interest of a British consortium headed by Sir Alexander Korda. But this time the problems were more fundamental; and there was, as yet, nobody in Hollywood who could see or understand them fully.

Suburbia represented a change of mind on a national scale. Before the Second World War suburban growth had been steady, interrupted only by the Depression. Even when immigration into America was drastically cut back, American suburbs remained the dream of millions; and millions moved to them from their port of entry in the 1920s. The difference after World War II was the attitude of the people who moved to suburbia. Those neat roads and identical lawns and carefully nurtured babies were a symptom of how they felt. Suburbia, unlike the cities, was an institution, a way of life created and changed for the newly affluent survivors of the war.

Margaret Mead saw the change and chronicled it in the 1950s. She saw that Americans had traditionally seen leisure as something that must be earned, and earned again. Leisure without effort was idle luxury, and immoral. In contrast, work was a moral good.

The Depression years suspended people's choice. No work, no cash, certainly no spare cash for pleasure: all that meant no right to play. At the same time, couples were postponing marriage and children. They could not afford them. Going back to work and earning money were the only morally proper ways to earn pleasure and happiness. It is as though America lived by an equation: work is equal to joy.

War smashed that. War workers seemed to make almost too much money. Soldiers suffered, not just on battlefields, but also from boredom overseas and too little time on leave. Families waited, aching for peace and privacy. They worked for their happiness; but the work did not produce joy. The old equation no longer worked.

"The generation which has married since the war has responded to these conditions," Mead wrote, "by shifting the balance from work and good works to the home. The home, in which one was once allowed a limited amount of recuperation and recreation in return for working hard, has now become the reason for existence which in turn justifies work at all."

That change proved far more important than the mass movement of human bodies to suburban communities. That was easily enough explained. War work brought labor to the cities. Boom times after the war allowed millions to trade in their dreams for marriage, bricks, and mortar. In 1946 millions of soldiers, sailors, and airmen were dispersed across the nation to take up lives that had been rudely interrupted by more than ten years of economic troubles and warfare. At last they could have families. Meanwhile, rural blacks fled the grinding poverty of the South for the tempting riches of northern manufacturing cities like Detroit. City growth became explosive.

Slowly the political boundaries of cities changed to match their ever-expanding physical boundaries. That helped to disguise the true extent of suburban growth. If you allow for the change in city frontiers in the 1950s, and the reclassification of suburban areas as urban when the neighboring city wanted its property and income taxes, then American suburbia was growing forty times as fast as the inner city in the 1950s. If the change were only a matter of bricks and mortar, it would be a dubious concept. Geographers often show signs of wariness at the word suburbia if it means only new houses outside old cities. We know metaled roads were blasted out from the cities, car ownership expanded at a staggering rate, and new homes mushroomed. But the key to understanding "suburbia" lies elsewhere.

Suburbia was a chosen, designed style of life. It was not inherited, although it reflects attitudes and aspirations that were deeply influenced by generations past. It is important to understand what is cause and what is effect. The neat suburban streets were what people wanted; the new environment did not determine the wants and

29

needs and nor did television. Housewives still listened to radio extensively while doing housework. During the Depression, women found themselves at the center of their home; and took responsibility for the home in wartime; and were often deprived by economic hardship of the education they deserved, or the chance to use it. They chose to be homemakers instead. Still, they expressed a fierce belief in homemaking as a proper activity for a woman. Their children also valued the security of a home; later, they took out more retirement plans, more insurance policies, and bought homes earlier than previous generations. The shadow of the Depression helped reaffirm, in richer times, the old values of home, hearth, children, and church.

In the home, television was most popular with the lower working-class families who may have lost the cinemagoing habit in the 1930s through simple lack of money. But even in the 1950s, television did not dominate their leisure time. The usual image of a passive, bloated America settling over a TV snack before the TV set and talking of nothing but television is not supported by any of the contemporary studies. A third of most people's leisure time was spent on crafts—sometimes painting or artistic pursuits, more often do-it-yourself work to improve the sacred home. In 1950 spending on leisure was dominated by do-it-yourself equipment and sport; together they took almost forty cents of each dollar spent in people's spare time.

Films were an occupation of more educated, more affluent people. They appear on lists alongside playing bridge, membership of the local Rotary Club, going to the theater, growing flowers, giving dinner parties, and "serving the community"; while, down the social ladder, people list playing poker, going to the zoo, fishing, watching television, growing vegetables, and do-it-yourself hobbies. By the late 1950s the pattern was set: blue-collar workers thought playing with children, seeing friends, and visiting family were all activities infinitely more significant than going out to a movie. Television was a favorite pastime because it interfered least with the pleasures of the home; it became one of them. The same pattern still held in 1970, when the United Auto Workers Union calculated the standard of living for 60 percent of the American working class: it fell below the level where a man might expect to "take his wife to the movies once every three months."

Hollywood took no notice. The nexus of home and hearth did not seem significant. The overlords of the film business were blinded, perhaps by the clear appetite of the same working-class families for fan magazines, star gossip, and a vicarious sense of glamour. If only the screen were larger, the stars more splendid, and the color more dramatic; if ancient Rome and ancient Egypt could be seen at the cinema, and never on television; if spectacular classic shows and musicals and books could be brought to the screen, then people would again want the cinema. But they did not. When they wanted entertainment they turned on the television; they could easily watch a movie, talk, and deal with children all at the same time. Churches thrived because people went there to show their community feeling; interestingly, they did not go to take part in devotions, because actual religious practice dropped in suburbia as attendance at church stayed healthy. Cinemas had no such social role to play, except for one group, the young. As churches served their parents, cinemas became useful to the generation of the children of Hollywood. There you could escape parents, be part of the pack, and play out and confirm your social role. Cinemas were useful again.

Imagine the year in which *American Graffiti* is set—around 1962. Out of suburbia came the "superkids." For them, home was a place to escape. They found their life with their contemporaries, not within their parents' community. They had the cars, the freedom in dating, the money, and the constant contact with the opposite sex to build what amounted to a separate way of life. Their banner was rock 'n' roll culture, provider of both fantasy figures and father figures; they were in revolt against those very suburban certainties that were, as *American Graffiti* shows, certain to engulf them in their turn. They would go to any entertainment that seemed to be provided especially for them. They were loaded with pocket money. They would take as well to movies as to any other activity away from their homes.

It took the main film world a long time to latch on to their importance. When it did, the revelation owed much to the makers of cheap exploitation movies—the men who eventually became the patrons of the children of Hollywood.

Samuel Z. Arkoff was a lawyer from Iowa who had set up business supplying filmed programs to television. James H. Nicholson was a West Coast theater manager. Together, with four employees, $3,000, and hope, they formed a company called American Releasing Corporation; two years later, when they began to produce their own films, the company became AIP—American International Pictures. Their first feature film production was *The Fast and the Furious*, a drag-racing film to appeal to any teenager who had ever crashed the gears on the public highway. It was a typical product. AIP, supreme among the smaller film companies, the so-called "minimajors," helped invent the beach party film, the drag strip racing film, and the Edgar Allan Poe cycle of horror films. In Roger Corman, a graduate of the Twentieth Century-Fox mail room and a onetime student of Oxford University, they found their ideal source—as producer, director, and entrepreneur—of the material they needed. Corman's genius lay in finding substance and resonance and wit inside the conventions of the exploitation film; he gave to AIP horror, atomic mutations, crab monsters, the melting of Monsieur Valdemar, and the duels of ancient magicians; gangsters at slaughter, Hells Angels at play, and drug-takers on trips. He invented wasp women, men with X-ray eyes, premature burials, creatures from haunted seas and Viking women with sea serpents, buckets of blood, teenage cavemen, wars of satellites, and little shops of horrors. His were the teenage dolls, the sorority girls, the undead, the horrid, the swamp women. Sometimes his material was gross and wild: atomic mutations that once were your brother, the last woman left on earth. Sometimes they amounted to idealizations of teenage culture—the blanket party at the beach, illegal racing of hyperpowered cars on the highway, and the roaring beat of rock 'n' roll. They horrified, stimulated, and excited, like headlines in a tabloid newspaper. They made couples at drive-ins scream and cling to the safety of one another. At the same time, the films were always more substantial than their audience thought. Americans, often curiously blind to the strengths of their own culture, resisted the idea that their cinema could be important; with Corman, they had to struggle with associations of dates, Cokes, and hamburgers even to find the films. European critics saw the power of their images and began to take notice of the latent talent involved in their production. But that phase lies ahead, with the first films of Francis Coppola and Peter Bogdanovich and Monte Hellman. Now we must examine why it made sense for Arkoff and Nicholson to dive, head first, into the business that every major studio was abandoning.

"In this age of specialization," announced the press officers of AIP, "our objective was to release selected products through selected distributors for specialized audiences." That is: they found a gap in the market and filled it.

Small cinemas were desperate for product in the early 1950s. The alternative was cold, empty cinemas, with dark screens. Yet they lacked the power to bid for the likely "hit" films; it was before the time when pornography would offer them a brief escape from financial trouble, and Hollywood was not turning out the low budget black and white pictures they needed. Indeed, the majors had finally had the sort of panic that is reflected in the number of films they issued. The break came later than might be expected. In 1946, the wonderful year, American film companies released 400 films, of which 383 were new. (The high point of sound feature film production seems to have been 1941, with 497 new films; reliable figures go back only to 1930 and the early days of sound.) Four years after the best year in cinema history, 1950, Hollywood was actually offering more films, 473 in all, of which 425 were new. This spectacular increase was commercial lunacy, the market those films shared was declining in money terms, let alone real money terms, while the cost of producing films was rising. Something had to give.

In 1952 the slump became visible. There were only 386 films released, of which 353 were new. From then, the graph zigzags downward. In 1954 there were only 294 new films, and reissues soared as two minor studios went into their death throes. Republic was the last authentic survivor of the long tradition of cheap filmmaking that grew up around Gower Gulch in Los Angeles; the district became known as Poverty Row. Republic ended its career of serials and Westerns and occasional attempts at prestige in February 1959. RKO went out of distribution in 1957. Both tried to revive their fortunes by reviving old films. Neither succeeded. When the boom in reissued films died down, the weakness of the minor studios began to hurt the cinemas even more. Monogram, another relic of Poverty Row, changed its name and image in 1953 to emerge as Allied Artists. Screen Guild became Lippert Pictures and disappeared in 1955. Even the major studios were severely restricting the number of films they made. In 1959 there were only 254 films on offer, and only 236 of them were new. That figure is half the number of films on offer in the bleak year of 1950.

The majors' central problem was a taste for clinging to old formulae. It was no longer easy to predict what films would do good business—but the studios insisted that they knew how. As Samuel Arkoff wrote later: "The oddity is not that the film industry is not understood by those outside it, but that those that are inside the industry also do not understand it; and that there are more dreams and make-believe and just plain ignorance in their beliefs about their own industry than exist outside it." Hollywood did not stoop to cater for younger, brighter audiences who might like the sensational, the gruesome, and the suggestive. AIP stooped with enthusiasm. They started with black and white double bills, topped by certain successful titles—*I Was a Teenage Werewolf, Hot Rod Girl, Runaway Daughters, Twist All Night,* even *I Was a Teenage Frankenstein.* The titles came first, then the theme, then the writer, director, and stars. Their sensationalism earned them the predictable scorn and hatred of Parent Teacher Associations across America. Children were being corrupted. Violence was being shown to them. Sex was being suggested to them. Something must be done. Arkoff and Nicholson, characteristically, fought back by releasing Roger Corman's extraordinary fantasies based on stories by Edgar Allan Poe. Suddenly, AIP films were respectable; they made adolescents sit down and read the books of Poe. Libraries stacked the books alongside lurid publicity for the film. AIP had done its most subversive act: it made schools and libraries into part of its sales force.

What they sold were technically not B pictures, those films made for the bottom half of a double bill. If films were designed for a double bill, they supported one another, not the product of some other studio. When one instalment of a saga—say, *Student Nurses*—had run its course at the top of the bill, it would return after a discreet interval as support to another instalment—say, *Private Nurses.* Each film was kept in circulation as long as possible, because the audience might suddenly change. The Edgar Allan Poe films were first greeted with ecstatic references to the (elusive) influence of Ingmar Bergman, but later began to attract a late night audience, which valued their aura of high camp.

When film moved inexorably to color in the early 1960s, costs soared. The main reason was that television sales depended on shooting in color. Even newsreel film became all-color in the 1960s; monochrome television was dead. AIP clung to the principle Arkoff had used in his early career: nonunion labor. As a television producer he had worked with nonunion crews because no formal agreement covered the new hybrid of film for television; the rules covered only live production and the filming of live programs from the screen. In film he followed the same road. The result was an apparent exploitation of young talent. But there was another side, especially with Roger Corman. When craft unions put up barriers to new entrants—"even the focus-pullers were over fifty," said one jaundiced observer—Corman and AIP offered the only chance for new talent. Corman, in particular, made generous use of that position.

Because their only conditions for filmmakers were title, a budget, a selling line, and a theme, AIP's product was extraordinarily mixed. It ranged from utter trash to the sophistication of Monte Hellman's contributions to the American New Wave, such as *The Shooting* and *Ride the Whirlwind*. The company kept to its fairground barker methods; the audiences at *Blacula* were offered bay leaves as protection against the black vampire when local shops failed to produce the more usual remedy of garlic. It seems to have had a peculiar talent for spotting the end as well as the start of trends. Major studios were swamped in the late 1960s with vague, unsaleable protest films by bright, young, and overindulged directors. AIP had already abandoned films about rebellious youth when students were first beaten in Chicago and later murdered at Kent State. Bullets made the theme too real; and their young audiences wanted escape at the cinema. In the same way, AIP made only one film whose sole theme is drug experience— *The Trip* by Roger Corman. Drugs alone were too commonplace to attract their audience. Instead, there were demons, horrors, gangsters, and bikers. AIP kept itself in the fantasy business.

From 1963 to 1973 AIP averaged twenty films every year, welcome manna for the empty cinemas. Their protégés began to spill into mainstream cinema, especially those who had worked for Roger Corman, like Peter Bogdanovich, Francis Coppola, and Martin Scorsese. Even when Corman went his own way with a separate corporation, New World Pictures, AIP still encouraged young filmmakers like John Milius. Studio heads kept a careful eye on their roster of new talent to counteract their own deficiencies. For as AIP took up the market that had once been reserved for Poverty Row, the major studios were edging toward collapse. The machinery of dreams was hopelessly tangled in debt and share-dealing profits and paper promises. Still, the studios persisted with the "nice," the "dignified" films that Arkoff so despised. Sometimes, that sort of film was a monumental success. More often, it lost everything. The banks were starting to notice, and to calculate the odds.

"The worst thing that ever happened to this business was *The Sound of Music.*" The diagnosis belongs to Alfred Hitchcock. In his dark, faintly Cockney voice it sounds properly ominous. It is also very shrewd. "That film," as Hitchcock says, "stimulated everybody into making expensive films."

Hollywood megalomania was nothing new; it had simply never been resting on so rocky a financial base. Filmmakers often turn to the cult of the spectacular when a new competitor emerges to disconcert them. It was a worthwhile gamble in the days of D. W. Griffith or Cecil B. DeMille, but it was perfect nonsense in the 1960s. It was a weak strategy against television. Too much capital was at risk on the public's taste for a single project. If the public rejected the film, there would be no return; and meanwhile, the cost of one spectacular ate up the studio's resources for making other films. This is important for reasons other than the odds against success, although only one film in ten makes money. It matters because the major film companies live from the fees they charge on distributing film—that is, marketing it and physically arranging its shipping around the country. That is where their certain profit and their flow of cash lie. Several films that are moderate successes may generate far more than a profit on production; they are bound to generate a profit on distribution as well. One major film that fails is a total loss.

Its cost will probably be borrowed from the bank, at size-able interest rates, and the major will pay its debt more slowly because it has fewer films from which to earn; and it will be handicapped for a while in making new product. The big failure is a catastrophe. Distributing more, having more chances of success, and controlling production costs on the big films would seem logical. Hollywood was seized by the cult of the spectacular—the $18 million musical like *Dr. Dolittle*, or *Star!*—and would not see it that way.

"Film by film," Frank Yablans told us when he was head of Paramount Pictures, "this business is nothing but a craps game. It's only worth calling a business if you have the flow of product." That was the retrospective wisdom of the early 1970s. Earlier, Hollywood forgot. The structure of the studios had been weakened by the death or retire-ment of many of the first autocratic generation of moguls, and by the internecine struggles that tore studios apart in the 1950s—Twentieth Century-Fox—and in the 1960s—MGM. The basic mistakes of the 1940s and the awful combination of economic problems were also hurting. The one wise move of the 1950s was to end the resistance of movie companies to making film material for television, and selling films to television. Columbia had pioneered in the late 1940s with its own subsidiary, making film series for television; but some less wise studios held out until 1955. Television kept the machine at work: network fees usually covered production costs so that sales to stations that took syndicated programs and sales overseas were pure and sizeable profit.

Then came a boom. Its basis was the war in Vietnam. It had not yet turned into a sour economic disaster. It was still stimulating production and consumption. It is a bitter fact that the first years of war, whatever the motives or morals involved, are good for many people who stay at home. They give employment, make money, and help make credit easier to find. David Brown, then head of stories for Twentieth Century-Fox under Richard Zanuck as head of production, remembers the boom all too well: "In the euphoria of the mid-1960s," he says, "the idea of borrow-

38

ing to increase profits seemed very attractive. But then interest rates went up. Still, the financial people encouraged us, and the bankers were happy." As we shall see, it was a shallow happiness; and at least one banker had fundamental doubts.

At Bank of America, Al Howe had long been the leading banker for any independent producer. He maintained a careful distance from the film industry and tried to see it always in strict banking perspective. "If I discover that one of my men believes he knows which film will make money and which will lose," he told us, "I say that he has 'gone Hollywood' and I fire him." Now he took his slide rule to the industry as a whole. He calculated that the annual worldwide box office for film was worth perhaps $2,000 million. Of that, the cinemas kept $1,400 million, and the film companies took $600 million. Once the studios had knocked off their distribution fees, of perhaps $180 million, and their distribution costs, of perhaps another $180 million for making prints and advertising, there would be $240 million left, from all the world, to cover the cost of actually making the films. Howe thought even this figure was overly generous. Much of the worldwide take at the box office would stay with overseas distributors. His final calculation showed that American film companies could expect to bring back around $200 million from all their films in a year like 1967.

Then the quiet Mr. Howe put in his knife. "During most of the 1960s," he wrote in the *Motion Picture Journal*, "seven major American motion picture companies assumed production risks each year exceeding $50 million each, and all other U.S. companies and risk-takers probably totaled another $50 million, a total of about $400 million. Thus the expense of making the product exceeded the market return by something like two to one, and something had to give."

Given that banks, stockholders, treasurers, stockbrokers, and investors are not usually blind and stupid, the obvious question is this: how could the motion picture industry contrive to be strangling itself so quietly? The answer is complex. Hollywood's other businesses, and its occasional monstrous hits, helped to hide the weakness of the industry as a whole. In 1965, for example, the industry could congratulate itself on the success of *Mary Poppins* and *The Sound of Music,* on the wry *Goldfinger* in the James Bond series, and in the stylish George Cukor version of *My Fair Lady.* It seemed that family entertainment could still pay. Relatively expensive family entertainment, with the "production values" that only money could buy, dominated the charts of the films that took most money at the box office in that year; there were war films, innocent Westerns, and tastelessly confected all-star spectaculars like *Those Magnificent Men in Their Flying Machines.* All would have been well if the films involved offered anything like a reasonable return on the capital employed to make their sequels, imitations, and replicas. But costs were soaring faster than income, and the hits seemed golden, certain. All that was needed to make the accounts balance was another hit like the last one, even though it would cost more. The road to wrecking was clear.

Blindness caused by the glitter of hits was only one factor that hid Hollywood's decline. The other happened on a Sunday evening in September 1966. More than 60 million people across the United States settled down to watch a film on television—David Lean's epic of the war in Burma, *The Bridge on the River Kwai.* The staples of American television—"Bonanza," "The Ed Sullivan Show" —paled alongside the attraction of a movie that had first appeared in theaters nine years before. The significance of the sale was twofold. First, the books of Columbia Pictures showed the film at a nominal value of one dollar. This is the film industry convention for valuing a movie that is past its prime years of earning in theaters. It remains a real asset: it might be revived. It cannot sit in the books at zero for that reason. But nobody has hopes that it will ever make substantial money again. Now, suddenly, a one-dollar asset had been sold to ABC television for $2 million. Wall Street took another look at film companies. One had just received a colossal and uncovenanted bonus; and the others had comparable films. Perhaps films were a real asset to a company after all, just like the studio land and machinery. Perhaps film shares were attractive after all.

There is a catch, of course. Television sales do little more than make most films break even. Networks are made to take bad films with good films in order to make sure that most of the books balance. Hit films are the ones that command huge prices from the networks; and an expensive film has to be a popular success before it can be sold expensively to television. If it fails, it fails doubly—fails to cover its cost in the theaters, and fails to deliver the bonus from television sales on which entire production programs were now to be based.

Hollywood saw only salvation. The figures were astonishing. When RKO left the film business in 1955, it had broken the industry convention by selling its entire library of 750 features and 1,000 short films to television; the price tag was a mere $15 million. Even assuming the shorts were given away, the average price for a feature could not be higher than $20,000. Ten years later, a single film could be worth one hundred times as much. Network appetite for the big blockbuster film began to grow, and it helped to justify the Hollywood instinct about what people wanted.

The studio chiefs can be forgiven a sigh of relief when the *Bridge on the River Kwai* deal was announced. The state of the theater business was parlous. RKO Theaters, built on the great Orpheum, Keith, and Albee chain with the help of Radio Corporation of America, now had only 68 houses left. It was forced to share its billing within a conglomerate that also owned anthracite mines in Pennsylvania and textile mills in the South. Stanley Warner Company, the theater side of the old Warner Brothers empire, now nestled alongside the Playtex bras and Sarong corsets which made 70 percent of its profits. Only 242 theaters remained. Paramount, which once had 1,400 houses, now had only 425. Most ignominious, the theater side of the company that once salvaged the newborn CBS was now a subsidiary of another network, ABC.

That was the position in 1964. It explains why Hollywood had developed its business relationship with its apparent archrival, television. In that year, long before the *River Kwai* deal, films made especially for television accounted for almost a third of the studios' revenue, more than $300 million. More and more, any actor who wanted work had to head for television. Film for cinemas accounted for only 24 percent of the income of members of the Screen Actors Guild in 1971. The rest came from television, which is not surprising. But 42 percent of all the money screen actors earned that year came from television commercials. Pushing Coke, selling detergent, and smiling a sweet-breathed smile were jobs paying almost twice as much as appearances in fully fledged movies. Those television jobs did have the effect of holding a pool of labor in California that would otherwise have dispersed. They helped keep Hollywood ticking over.

Indeed, the companies appeared to thrive. The illusion was dangerous. In the 1960s the new companies, the conglomerates that brought together firms in any business, were attracted to films. Hollywood offered a gambler's chance, a glamorous business and the same sort of tax advantages that went with zinc-mining and oil-drilling, where the more you use an asset, the less it is worth, very fast. Conglomerate managers had the capital and the resources to prop up the companies at their weakest moments, such as the crises of Paramount, before it was absorbed by Gulf + Western, a conglomerate that began life with a manufacturer of car bumpers in Grand Rapids, Michigan. The conglomerates liked the difference in the business. When a factory produces a car, it always needs the steel, labor, plastic, chrome, and glass, not to mention the assembly lines and the power and the plant. All those are essential for every car produced, and for every sale. But the cinema business depends not on selling strips of celluloid, but on selling cinema tickets. Once the film has been made (which is like designing a car) and promoted (which is like the expensive launching of a new model) there are relatively low running costs. The theater carries the cost of collecting the revenue; and while prints have to be renewed, advertising has to continue, office staff have to be paid, and prints have to be sent around the country, the studio pays out relatively little. If it has a hit, therefore, the percentage of profit is colossal and accelerating in proportion to the original costs; and, compared with retooling for a new Ford, a film can be made relatively cheaply, and with a good many chances in a year of making a profit.

That was how the conglomerates saw the film business. Gulf + Western bought Paramount; Transamerica, an insurance group based in San Francisco, bought United Artists. Universal had already been sold to MCA, Jules Stein's show business empire; the studio came as a fading partner to the American end of Decca records. Warner Brothers had sold to an investment operation called Seven Arts, originally a Canadian tannery. Columbia leaned, as had Warners in the 1950s, on the supporting arm of Wall Street investment houses; the most prominent was a secretive, substantial house called Allen and Company.

The studio that suffered most was MGM. It became the only surviving major to leave the business of film distribution. It cut back severely on its production. Its vast studios became a rental facility. After a devastating stockholders' fight in 1963 over the efficiency of the management, MGM shared the depression and uncertainties of the industry in the late 1960s. It also became a marked target. It had sizeable land holdings, but it also had a series of film flops. It had a stock market quotation with considerable value for any would-be entrepreneur and a glamorous name, perhaps the most glamorous of all the old Hollywood names. It became an obvious vehicle for a neat piece of share dealing. Kirk Kerkorian, an investor who had been associated with hotels in Las Vegas and with an airline, now bought heavily into MGM. He put in new management, saw the new management fail to deliver the promised bonanzas in the early 1970s, took the company out of the distribution business, and trimmed its production. Then Kerkorian used MGM's name, assets, and share quotation to float a vast bond issue for the MGM Grand Hotel, back where Kerkorian started, in Las Vegas. The film tradition survived only in the paraphernalia and the flak of a glossy gambling resort. The publicity called Grand Hotel "the coming attraction of our time." The publicists evidently failed to see the irony in their sales talk. "The mystique of Garbo," they wrote, "touches you as you enter the lobby . . . a two-story suite as grand as the one named after Dr. Zhivago . . . a Café Gigi . . . a Ziegfeld Room. . . ." In the cinema "soft lounges and cocktails go with the best films ever made. When did you last see Garland, Astaire, Tracy, Bergman, or Gable?" Back on lot two, behind the MGM studios, the rot and the sun were bringing to dust the remains of those films; Ashley's house from *Gone with the Wind*, the station set where Garbo reached town in *Ninotchka*, and where Astaire settled for being "by myself, alone" in *The Band Wagon*. Only a hitch in zoning regulations prevented the entire backlot from becoming Culver City's second hypermarket.

The studios that had no protectors fared worst. Just as the story of United Artists' disarray in the 1940s is a key to understanding why film companies suffered then, so in the 1960s the scapegoat was Twentieth Century-Fox. Fox was led to believe that money was plentiful, that hits like *The Sound of Music* pointed the way forward; and its management never paused to think that the business was, in its essentials, rotten.

The ironies are complicated. Since World War II, two factions had battled for Twentieth Century-Fox—the Zanuck faction, headed by Darryl F. Zanuck, and later supported manfully by his son Richard as head of production and David Brown as story chief; and the Skouras faction, led by the Greek shipowner Spyros Skouras, who took the studio into debt to launch the splendor of CinemaScope on a receptive world. In the 1950s Skouras had edged Zanuck out, and Zanuck was an independent producer in Paris. The banks caught up with Fox, and Zanuck was called back in 1962 to a studio that was in dire trouble. Richard Zanuck was installed as head of production; "the son," said wits with long memories, "also rises." Economy measures had to be severe. Zanuck junior remembers: "When we arrived, we were down to counting the janitors."

But then came *The Sound of Music*. It was, as Richard Zanuck says, "a phenomenal success." It also proved a disaster for Fox executives because their logic now went very expensively awry. They reckoned that Julie Andrews was now a superstar, and a glittering musical would make money with her: since she was such a success as a virginal governess, she would now play Gertrude Lawrence in *Star! The Sound of Music* had made millions from family entertainment with children; therefore, a musical with animals like *Dr. Dolittle* was bound to return its $18 million negative cost with a handsome profit. *The Sound of Music* was a Broadway success; *Hello, Dolly!* must be worth as much. More borrowing, at steeper interest charges, was needed to produce these three elephantine failures. Borrowing other people's money to increase your own profits—"leverage," to Americans, "gearing" to the British—was a device fashionable to excess in the 1960s.

"We researched *Dr. Dolittle*," Richard Zanuck says. "We knew *Hello, Dolly!* had done forty million dollars on stage before we bought it. *Patton* cost eleven million and the banks thought we were crazy. That was the only one that came off." Twentieth Century-Fox made mistakes, which is the nature of the film business. But the studio was making spectacularly expensive mistakes on other people's money; which was the particular nature of the film business in the 1960s. "Then," Zanuck says, "we ran into technical default on our loans. Now the bankers had made a packet out of Twentieth Century-Fox for forty years, and they still do not know anything about the motion picture industry. What they had in mind was the crash of the Penn Central." In short, the unthinkable was happening in America. Giant corporations were going bust. Penn Central, a railroad, had gone to the wall. Zanuck continues: "We brought in the Stanford Research people, trying anything to save money. We began to think we were working for the bankers; and nothing we could do was right."

Before Twentieth Century-Fox could collapse, Richard Zanuck had been thrown out of his studio, much like his father before him. He took David Brown to Warners; later, they formed a producing team which operated from Universal and made films like *Jaws* and *The Sting*. That sort of success must have seemed infinitely remote as he packed up his office at Fox and prepared to drive away for the last time. The last thing he saw would be the gigantic, hideously expensive New York street sets from *Hello, Dolly!* They represented a gamble which would have been so logical, if the stakes had not been so high, and the stake money had been his own. "Years later," Zanuck remembers, "the security men still had orders not to let me past the gates. I was the biggest individual stockholder in Twentieth Century-Fox, and the only time I could pass the gates was for a stockholders' meeting."

Banks are traditionally the villains of Hollywood, the organizations that dampen creative zeal. In fact, as we have seen, the bankers were remarkably tolerant with twenty years of gross mismanagement across the industry, years in which Hollywood failed to read the clear signs of change. Despite the fatal flaw, that era can seem attractive. George Lucas expresses a widely held affection for the moguls' time, when a Darryl F. Zanuck had real power at Twentieth Century-Fox, years in the 1930s when Zanuck could innovate, make snap decisions, and create projects of his own. Lucas despises the new corporation men. But at least these new power brokers have faced the basic problem that the moguls left untouched: how to change the nature of the product they were offering. By training, the new men might be agents or lawyers or accountants, aliens in the world of film art and show business. But their very training taught them the elementary logic of the business. Hollywood had to change if it were to hope for survival.

Unlike the early moguls, the new men were not risking their own money; they were concerned about keeping their jobs. They lacked the technical knowledge that past producers shared. Their ignorance now distances them from the filmmakers. But it also makes them dependent on the filmmakers, on being offered ideas from directors, writers, and producers who are younger, who know the art and craft of film, and who know a world outside the studio machine and have some instinctive sympathy with the new, cine-literate generation that comprises the majority of film audiences. They proved the generation who most needed the children of Hollywood, who had the least riding on the success of earlier generations of friends, and who had no choice but to take a chance because all the studio certainties exploded in the 1960s.

All they needed was the ideas, the talent, and the money. Conglomerates saved the balance sheets of some studios. Other majors were ready to release whatever good, independent productions they could find. But who would pay to make a movie? It was a pressing question for studios such as Columbia, which from 1973 was always interested in independent film; its own financial straits were appalling. Banks arranged a $120 million revolving credit to keep it in business. A flow of product was the only chance of making money; but there was no money to make the product. Banks were cagey. Even majors, Universal particularly, showed suspicion of theatrical film. Companies were destitute. Managements had changed. Who would put the money on the table?

The unsung, unwilling hero who saved Hollywood from despair was the American tax inspector. He alone made it worthwhile for individuals to invest in motion pictures, with the certain knowledge that only one in ten films ever makes its production costs back. Loss could be as worthwhile as profit, and investing in film began to make sense.

Hollywood had a long, uneasy relationship with the Internal Revenue Service. In the 1940s stars became independent producers for a simple reason. If a James Cagney took a fee for a performance, and earned his share of the eventual profits, he would be taxed on income; the income tax rates rose as high as 90 percent. If he became a corporation, and made the film himself, his earnings would be taxed at the corporation tax rate, around 60 percent. But if he made the film as a corporation and then sold the final product to a studio for a profit, that profit—the same money as his earnings before—would be counted as a capital gain. Cagney, or any other star in his tax position, would have sold an asset for more than it cost; and, on the difference, he would pay tax of only 25 percent.

The Hollywood inspectors of the Internal Revenue Service think that advantage was exploited. "In the 1950s," they say, "we had independent producers and stars who held the copyright and title in films. It didn't mean a thing. They did not put up one cent of their own money. The studio provided all the capital in return for the right to distribute the film for, say, seven years. The profit was split between studio and producers, usually half and half although we've seen deals in which 75 percent went to the producers."

Now, the tax game begins. Without ever writing a check, or risking money, a producer would try to treat the entire production cost of the film as though it were his capital investment. If, for example, the film cost $5 million to make, the producers would write off one dollar of the film's value for every dollar the film brought back to the distributor. Nominally, all they had done was to license the distributor to sell the film; they owned it. Actually, ownership was a rather academic point. The studio had bought the product, and the producers had not spent anything. Still, when the film had been depreciated to zero—that is, the distributor had recouped everything—and the film sat on the books at some nominal amount, the producer could exchange stock in the film for stock in the major corporation. If the film then went on to make a profit, that profit could be treated by the producer as a capital gain on selling the film as an asset. He ended up with cash in the bank, shares in the major, and a very moderate tax bill. It was becoming expensive to work for a simple fee.

The tax men watched with polite skepticism while revenue law gave producers an almost irresistible reason to go independent. In 1962 the tax men started to fight back. The law allowed taxpayers to take a credit on investment. Hollywood said a film was a tangible asset and a commercial investment; it was money at risk with a chance of profit. The tax men demurred. Hollywood's champions in the courts were first Red Skelton, whose production company settled a claim out of court; and then Walt Disney, the most persistent litigant, who won in 1968 a case concerning the company's tax returns for 1962. The Supreme Court would not hear the case; Disney filed again. The tax men thought the pause might mean victory. After all, they knew what neither the court nor Mr. Disney knew. They handled cases where tax claims were dubious, based on inflated film budgets or downright fraud. They knew that money from criminal sources could easily be made to appear respectable if it was put, without questions asked, into the production of a film; any money the film made would then be washed clean. They knew all that, and they were unsympathetic to Hollywood's troubles.

But they lost. In 1971 Wilbur Mills, using his powerful position on the House Ways and Means Committee, mentioned casually that film qualified for investment credit. Senator Long agreed. There was no formal court decision. Politicians spoke, and the tax men obeyed. Between 1971 and 1973 there remained a fierce lobby for investment credit on films; section 50 of the 1976 Revenue Act laid down that films were indeed investments, like any other. Investors could take a 10 percent tax credit on their investment, provided they were backing a film made in the United States and their money was genuinely at risk. "Filming abroad," says Ned Tannen, head of theatrical films for Universal, "became a scare city."

The battle over investment credits was at least over a principle: whether film, like an oil well, an office tower, or a zinc mine, is to be considered as a tangible asset. The issue of tax shelters is subtler. At their worst, tax shelters involved actual fraud, as much for taxpayers as for the Internal Revenue Service. At their best, the shelters provided producers with the money for "marginal films," "the ones," as Ned Tannen says, "which usually become the hits."

The problem for film producers was to offer a private investor some reason to hand over his money, when nine in ten films never make a profit. If a man chooses to put all his savings into a restaurant in Fort Lauderdale, he will probably make himself an income, possibly make himself a capital gain, certainly be the owner of an asset—buildings, equipment, goodwill—which he can later sell, or use as collateral to raise money from a bank. If the seafood is good, and he is spared violent chefs, insolent waiters, bad management, bad marketing, or bad pricing, he can invest in the expectation of making some money. His investment is, in part, protected by the assets he has. But a film offers him no such advantage. A bank, offered a film as collateral, would laugh. Few films make profits. Once a theatrical release is finished, the film could perhaps be another *Bridge on the River Kwai*; just as likely, it will disappear. If it never finds a distributor, which is possible, it may disappear at a much earlier stage in the game. Imagine the man who put money into a restaurant, and then discovered that the restaurant had crumbled, the land had flooded, the business had never been worth anything, and no customer had ever come in. That is the nature of investment in a single film.

But there was a way to use tax legislation to find money for movies. Brian DePalma's *Obsession* and *Carrie*, for example, were both made on the same principle: lawyers, accountants, and professional men all wanted to shelter their income from income tax. That is, they wanted to defer their tax bills. Films allowed a man to do just that, provided his income was more than $50,000 a year. They offered, in the grudging words of an IRS training manual, "a tax-free Federal loan."

Films made on tax shelter money usually carry this credit: "Production Services by . . ." What happens is that a partnership gets together to put up part of the budget of a film; but the partners do not actually own the film.

The partnership might be involved in, say, a $1 million project. There might be twenty-five members—friends from the golf club, fellow members of the local Rotary Club, a city's top accountants—and each would write a check for $10,000. The partnership finds $250,000 or a quarter of the film's budget. The rest comes from banks. Either the producer or a distribution company guarantees those bank loans. To the partnership they are "nonrecourse loans"; that is, no member of the partnership is personally responsible for repaying them. The producer promises to repay the loans out of income from the film. But each partner, in for $10,000, claims to be gambling $40,000— his cash, plus a proportion of the loan that helps make the film. The extra $30,000 is his "leverage."

Because he does not actually own the film when it is completed, nor does he officially have a share of it, he is allowed to write off expenses as they occur, and that can be fast. In a single year his check for $10,000 may buy him a tax deferral on $40,000, which, with tax at 50 percent, is a profit. In theory, he will eventually have to pay tax as though he only put $10,000 at risk. If he does not have to repay his share of the bank loan when it falls due, the IRS could pursue him. In practice the loans rarely fall due for eight to ten years; and the American tax man simply does not have the sort of audit system that would allow him to check that kind of discrepancy. A man might never have to pay tax on that extra $30,000 he only seemed to risk on making a film.

In a strictly legitimate tax shelter, like those for *Obsession* or *Carrie,* investors do not expect to make money. But they do have incomes large enough to be worth the trouble of sheltering. That was not always true. Fraudsters sometimes sold off film, frame by frame, to people with incomes too low to benefit from a shelter; they might have been power company workers, urged to buy a frame of some grandiosely titled footage of college basketball. The film was a fake; it never existed as more than a strip of raw 16mm stock. The deal is a fake: the apparent film-maker simply walks off with the cash, leaving the investors poorer, and with a sizeable problem in explaining their investment to the tax man. It was a cruel fraud that played on the fashion for sheltering income.

The cynical abuse of the system was bad enough to persuade Congress to outlaw it in December 1976; only investment credit remains to make the life of film producers a shade easier. The shelters that the IRS has prosecuted are an awful tale of low cunning in the film world. Some deals were built around investors who were willing to buy a piece of a completed film, knowing it could only lose money on its American release. They would promise to pay the cash due to the film's overseas owners out of American income and put down some minimal amount that would satisfy the overseas owner. It would be better than nothing. Then, by projecting income or inflating the purchase price they would claim substantial tax deductions. The promoters took their cut, and the investors would grow rich, if they were rich enough to start with.

In one notorious case, investors bought American rights to a Japanese film about the man who devised the raid on Pearl Harbor. "Not," as the IRS dryly says, "the sort of film that will play Peoria." The purchase price was supposed to be $800,000, but only $180,000 had to be given in cash to the film's overseas owners. The rest was on a nonrecourse note, only repayable if the film earned dollars in the United States, and there was no basis for legal action against an individual even then. "Only three copies of that film ever existed anywhere in the United States," the tax investigators say, "and the only income they ever reported was $13 negative income from Seattle, Washington." Until the IRS caught up, the investors were claiming to have lost $800,000, and staving off a sizeable part of their tax bills. The scheme fell apart only when the distributors went bankrupt.

Hollywood itself, far removed from this sort of squalid juggling, came to depend on tax shelters in the 1970s, along with money from any other source with ready cash. It was a convenient way to increase funds available for production, even for companies with conglomerate parents to look after them. It expanded the range of risks and made profit more likely. A producer like George Litto could hardly have launched *Obsession* without those Cincinnati lawyers who wanted to put off paying taxes. A corporation like Columbia needed to take substantial amounts of product from the shelterers. The studio would have a share in profits, if there were any; and, more important, it would keep films flowing through its distribution machine, earning the standard 30 percent distribution fee. The tax man was, accidentally, responsible for keeping the machine running.

Reasonably, the Internal Revenue Service did not feel their indulgence should stretch to a later development. Before tax shelters were ended, it could be useful for a major company to assign copyright and production credits in a television film to a group of would-be tax shelterers. The studio kept real control and simply faked the credit lines on the movie. The investors paid a relatively small fee—pure profit to the studio, whose costs were already covered by the network's fee for the film—and in return, they claimed a tax write-off on the entire production cost of the film. Nominally, the shelterers might be buying, say, foreign theatrical rights, just to make the contract seem respectable. In practice, the money they provided was often used for production. And even the biggest of the companies might be prepared to change a copyright line to help the shelterers as thanks for their cash.

In general, film makes a marvelous racket. It is hard to prove how much a film cost. It is often difficult to prove how much of a film's profit ever returns to its investors. "Distribution," says Alfred Hitchcock, "is a freemasonry like the kitchens of a restaurant. They have deep dark secrets. I have never yet been able to discover how much it costs to distribute a film."

The tax men faced a more difficult challenge as they attempted to clean up the worst abuses in the film business. They had to learn a skill that even Bank of America, with all its experience, regards as akin to witchcraft: the prediction of a film's success or failure. The tax men's training manual (3147–01 February 1976) lays down these guidelines: "Verification of the reasonable fair market value of the film is one essential and critical point in determining whether the organization of the partnership for tax purposes has substance as well as form. This fair market value is the basis for which depreciation, investment credit, and gain and gain or loss is computed on disposition of either the film or the partners' interests." Some criteria are simple: there must be independent appraisal, no unreasonable restrictions on the film's distribution to make sure it loses money, and a clear relationship between the fair market value and the price paid. That is where the problems begin, for the tax men are told to look for those intangible basics of popular appeal. Criterion 2 for judging a scheme is its "potential for audience acceptance (well-known story or star, favorable review of negative, etc.)." Few studio heads would like to make that sort of prediction in real figures.

"What film schools spawned," says Gary Kurtz, producer of *Star Wars* and *American Graffiti*, "was film schools. That, more than anything else." In the early 1960s, while Hollywood was rocking under its various waves of trouble, it must have seemed like that.

Three schools proved the most distinguished: the University of Southern California (USC), the University of California at Los Angeles (UCLA), and New York University (NYU). Their histories and traditions were very different. USC's film program had been set up between the world wars, supported by the film industry with ends of film stock and spare equipment and professional backing. UCLA taught film within a less industrial context; the course was and is run within its theater arts department. And NYU was the maverick, operating far away from the immediate hope of employment on feature films and producing people most likely to make rough, streetwise documentaries or go off to work in the New York television machine. Few people went to film school, even to the supposedly professional USC, with serious hopes of becoming directors, producers, or writers of any substance in theatrical film. When some succeeded, it was largely because of the industrial changes that we have sketched. At the time, their aspirations were strictly limited. "I thought," George Lucas says, "I might be a ticket-taker at Disneyland, or something."

It was a period when pressure on film school places was not yet acute. By the 1970s it was as hard to enter graduate film school as to find a place in medical school. Making the great film had replaced writing the great novel as a general dream. "But back in 1959," Gary Kurtz remembers, "it was very difficult to find enough students at USC when you were working on a student project. You had to beat the bushes to find them. I found myself shooting three movies just because there weren't enough cameramen on campus." Francis Coppola has spoken of his own disappointment in UCLA, despite the encouragement and support of the director Dorothy Arzner. Other students seemed more interested in focal lengths of lenses than in the substance that would make their technique useful. Most other observers agree that UCLA tended to encourage its students to make more personal, more private films that were heavily influenced by the styles of theater. "UCLA trained people for making protests on film," according to John Milius, a graduate of USC. "They were concerned with taking drugs and making experimental films. At USC, we were a private school, an elitist school that trained people for Hollywood. We were very much concerned with making the Hollywood film, not to make a lot of money but as artists." Walter Murch, a classmate of George Lucas and John Milius, admits that USC became known as the "soulless technocrats of film. But UCLA was just producing drug-induced frenzies of a totally uninteresting personal nature." The schools were certainly rivals; the only safe deduction from what Murch and Milius say is that the schools had different slants, and that rivalry was intense.

Film school was not a vocational course in the 1960s.

"I never had any idea I would work in the movie industry," says Walter Murch, the distinguished editor. Nor were the film school students always impelled by ambition. "I got to film school," George Lucas says, "on a fluke." Martin Scorsese arrived at NYU because his grades were not good enough for Fordham, the Jesuit university. He drifted toward courses on film history and found his vocation as a filmmaker confirmed only after he had made his first short film; before that, he still had the grains of a calling to the priesthood. Brian DePalma joined film classes by accident; he began as a physics major at Columbia University, changed to fine arts as he became interested in theater and film, made his first film because sophomores were not allowed to direct theatrical productions, and drifted into formal film classes when he could. Even Francis Coppola, the only man to present a full-scale Warner Brothers feature film as his master's thesis, was a theater director as an undergraduate; he deliberately delayed moving toward film, although making sophisticated home movies had been an obsession during his childhood and adolescence. Coppola made his first feature, *Dementia 13* (British title: *The Haunted and the Hunted*), in the low budget and nonunion orbit of Roger Corman. Perhaps the first UCLA film graduate to make a feature for a major studio was Brian G. Hutton, whose *Fargo* (Brit.: *The Wild Seed*) appeared in 1965. By the 1970s the position of film schools had changed beyond recognition. Instead of polite indifference, the major companies now keep a watchful eye on the potential talent there. "We know exactly who's there," Ned Tannen says. "We're on top of that situation hourly."

Even if film school did not mean jobs in the film industry, it was a vital formative influence for the filmmakers who emerged in the late 1960s and early 1970s. They had not come from Broadway and the theater, like an older generation, nor had they come from television, like the '50s recruits. They had learned film as film. "It was enormously important," John Milius says, "to me and George Lucas and people like Matt Robbins and Hal Bar-

wood. Steven Spielberg doesn't realize how important it was, because although he never went to film school he was drawn into that group which basically started at USC. We all worked on each other's films and nothing has changed. We still make films in much the same way. We all talk about them just like they were student projects. I don't know if it was the film school as such or the meeting of this group of people who became very involved and enjoyed the experience of going to film school. There was obviously some sort of magic in that class."

What film school offered was an experience of films that was simply not available anywhere else on the West Coast. There was discussion, enthusiasm, ideas—and the material on which to base them. While Martin Scorsese was being taught to revere the European masters like Bergman, even at the expense of American cinema, the USC film classes were fascinated, variously, by Republic serials, Japanese cinema, the tone poems of the National Film Board of Canada. For George Lucas, reared in a one-cinema town in northern California, it was a chance to learn the range and potential of film. He dates from that time his fascination with the "pure" film, with image and created environment rather than narrative flow or social comment. It remains one of his weaknesses when he tries to tell a story like *Star Wars*. But at USC it was a series of revelations: documentary material from filmmakers like the Maysles Brothers (the fathers of postwar cinema-verité), Leacock, and Pennebaker (the maker of the Bob Dylan classic *Don't Look Back*); experimental material from the San Francisco school of avant-garde filmmakers like Jordan Belson. "We were being exposed to a lot of movies you just don't see every day," Lucas says. "And that class was open-minded; we weren't bigots. We'd always listen to each other's interests." It led to ambitions that were not simple, material ambitions. "We wanted to be like John Ford, Howard Hawks, Orson Welles," John Milius says. "But we never thought we could be. I think the most successful student up to then had become an assistant editor after twenty years."

Film schools also taught technique. The directors of the 1950s had taken their style and their wishy-washy liberal ideas from television or theater; such technical grounding as they had was derived from live television drama with electronic cameras of strictly limited range. "Film got very competitive then," Gary Kurtz says. "Even the newer directors were not always fully aware of the technical side of film. And the technical people became antagonistic toward directors not well enough versed in their craft." The graduate filmmakers, by contrast, knew the range of a lens, the capacity of a microphone, and the uses and limitations of a brand of editing table. Francis Coppola could work as film editor, sound recordist, and dialogue coach before he began to write and direct. In place of the narrow experience the old studios offered, the new filmmakers had been given a thorough grounding in the basics of their craft. It is no coincidence that sound should be so crucial to films like *The Godfather* or *Star Wars,* or that the editing of *Taxi Driver* or *New York, New York* should be so idiosyncratic. Coppola, Lucas, and Scorsese all know the basic technology and grammar of film well enough to take it for granted and transcend it; like DePalma and Spielberg, and the less obviously proficient John Milius, they have a technical range that few of the ex–television directors could command.

Their interest in pure questions of how film works is best shown by the influence of a man whom Milius and Lucas both cite as crucial: Herb Kossower, professor of animation at USC. Animation is elemental film. Everything that appears on the screen must be put there by conscious design; it is not like a street scene, or even an actor's performance on a soundstage, where the best things may be products of serendipity. It teaches how sound and image connect, how images cut together, and what minimum detail is needed to make a point or maintain a story. It teaches "bounce," the quality of movement in film. When John Milius left USC his only serious job offer was as an artist for animated films. When George Lucas made *Star Wars,* the debt to his basic animation training became obvious. And when Steven Spielberg, an outsider in this group because his grades were not good enough to take him into USC, made *Close Encounters of the Third Kind,* he constantly referred back to sources in animated film, from Disney to Chuck Jones.

The exchange of ideas and suggestions about film is constant; and the ability to debate movies is endless. Spielberg's film scholarship is astounding; Scorsese still does nighttime homework by watching films on television with the sound off. But that does not mean that this generation of filmmakers imitates, quotes directly, or reproduces old films. Even where a director deliberately adopts a historical style—as Scorsese did with his pastiche of musicals from the late 1940s and early 1950s in *New York, New York*—he is playing with the grammar and style of film as a Joyce played with language, or a Pound with literary sources, or an Eliot with elaborate systems of reference through different cultures. When directors steal sequences, they do so by using film clips and acknowledging them; the quotations often appear on TV sets within the film, or as clearly sign-posted prologues. The fashionable critical game of ascribing certain parts of a film like *Star Wars* to direct imitation of an earlier masterpiece like *The Searchers* misses the point. True, both films share a burned homestead, and a dead, avuncular couple. But any links are subtler than they might appear. During film school, sometimes during their adolescence, and certainly in adulthood, these directors were steeped in film and film culture. Influences are often unconscious, using the devices that are half-remembered and half-ascribed. The films are the product of true, loving students of film.

These students had rich technique. They had impressive knowledge. What they lacked was a union card and a job. Francis Coppola moved smoothly from UCLA to a lucrative writing job, by way of the Samuel Goldwyn writing award in 1962. Gary Kurtz, after working briefly on a prologue for Coppola's cheap Gothick melodrama *Dementia 13,* shot in Ireland, went back to making films for the United States Air Force on drink and marital problems and secret movies for the Hughes Organization on cryogenics, the study of low temperatures. George Lucas made a living by teaching classes of navy personnel how to take photographs. Martin Scorsese beat back his shyness, and clowned for classes at NYU. Brian DePalma took a writing fellowship at the predominantly female Sarah Lawrence College and kept himself alive by selling scripts that were never made into movies. John Milius worked as a story assistant at AIP. For other film school graduates, there were few choices: they could found another film school, work for the audiovisual division of a university, make industrial film or commercials, or spend their time writing or teaching to no great effect. Much talent probably sank without a trace. But some filmmakers did have the will to keep trying. They knew there was always, and only, one man to whom they could turn.

"The ace in the hole," George Lucas says, "was Roger Corman." The major studios were in no position to take risks; they lacked the capital, and when they had it, they preferred to concentrate on the gigantic film, the super-spectacular. Only when *Easy Rider*, a relatively cheap, anarchic film of an acid trip across America, became an enormous success were the studios prepared to admit untried talent; the experiment was a disaster, and the studios went into retreat. There was only one man prepared to use students on real film projects, allow them to shoot footage, record sound, direct dialogue, cut film, and, when they had proved themselves as assistants, direct films. That was Corman.

None of Corman's crews had orthodox union contracts; he was able to employ people without union cards. He paid badly. He brought Paul Bartel, a bright New York underground filmmaker, out to the West Coast to make a film for $5,000 and no cut of the profits. That was as late as 1974. The film was *Death Race 2000*; and, a week after it opened, Corman's publicity machine was claiming a box office take of $4 million. But he gave opportunities when nobody else would. "Some of the film students," as Gary Kurtz says, "thought they were being exploited. I always thought the experience was more important." That sentiment would be shared by the graduates of the school of Corman, including directors, such as Jonathan Demme and Jonathan Kaplan, who were emerging in mainstream studio-produced films in the mid-1970's.

Corman had an almost guaranteed outlet for anything he made through the television side of AIP. Provided a film ran more than seventy-seven minutes, it would almost certainly end up either syndicated around minor league television stations or sold as part of a package to individual stations or networks. Padding films to the required length became a minor industry for eager film students.

Corman's production remained within the exploitation category, with its strict rules about plot lines that could be sold in a single slogan; that clear sense of market gave him a chance to back films much richer and stronger and more adventurous than the slogans would suggest. Exploitation gave him the rolling fund he needed for productions; his early days as a filmmaker—six weeks after Sputnik was launched, Corman's *Battle of the Satellites* was on the screen—had taught him the frustrations of waiting for money to come back from individual productions. By allying himself with AIP, and by observing their ground rules, he could keep projects constantly on the go.

It was a cheap, hand-to-mouth style of filmmaking. It forced filmmakers to pare down their ambitions, devise techniques that depended on great cinematic literacy, and shoot fast and to the point. If the central ideas and images are strong, the films acquire extraordinary resonance. Corman's works are to film in general as journalism is to prose in general; at best, more evocative, more direct, more disturbing, and more muscular than the more proper, highly valued literary qualities.

"Corman knew a lot of film students had good ideas and were very inexpensive," Gary Kurtz says. "He knew there were always shortcuts. And he knew that by gambling a very limited amount of money he had a chance to make quite a bit. A lot of these films never appeared on the screen; they were sold direct to television. Sometimes, when we were working on them, we weren't even sure what the project was, because there would be no title. We'd just be shooting the filler material—people in corridors, odd fragments of sex or violence, cars or something. Anything to reach the right length for TV."

Often, the authorship of Corman productions is totally unclear, and the credits offer very few clues. Kurtz was involved with a dubious shocker called *Blood Bath*, whose genesis was not unusual. It began when Corman wanted to make more than one film on a trip to Yugoslavia. He devoted a few days to shooting stock footage, and then handed the results to film students in Los Angeles with a rough plot line about a demented artist who boils his models in wax to produce the ultimate in hyper-realist sculpture. The result was quite unreleaseable and had to be reshot. Corman set the project aside for a while, and then decided the film might work if the demented sculptor was also a vampire. Stephanie Rothman was now director, and Kurtz, who had performed almost every other salvage operation on the project, became director of photography. They had only a week in which to work. None of the original actors was available. The Dubrovnik waterfront had to be recreated in the equally picturesque but very different surroundings of Venice, California. Every time the artist appeared, there now had to be a dissolve through oil to a quite different man with fangs. Every time there were shots of nighttime Venice, the lights had to be carefully controlled in case anybody recognized the place. "It was," Gary Kurtz remembers, "the I-remember-a-great-shot-let's-try-something-like-that school of filmmaking. While we were working in Venice, I remembered some material in Carol Reed's *The Third Man*, in the streets of Vienna, and I used that as a way of disguising where we were really filming."

Even on films which Corman signed as director, there would be many units working simultaneously. Sometimes, the richness of talent was almost absurd. *The Terror* was a compound of the Gothick ingredients that Corman has always enjoyed: Boris Karloff as a Baron, a castle lit by lightning bolts, a witch, a heroine, menace, and Jack Nicholson as the hero. Corman himself made the interior shots. Meanwhile, four other units worked on exterior sequences. Every time that Jack Nicholson pounded along the beach, he was being filmed by Gary Kurtz and directed by Monte Hellman, one of the more significant members of the American New Wave, who was encouraged by Corman beyond the point of profit and was never properly used by mainstream American cinema. Simultaneously, Francis Coppola was running another unit. New Hollywood assembled around Corman and gratefully shot his filler material.

"It was," Gary Kurtz says, "the only way to get a background in theatrical film. The studios were simply not prepared to offer you the training they once did." Anyone who was alert to the student grapevine could find chances of work on nonunion pictures of some sort; Coppola himself worked on some nudie films before making his first full-length feature through Corman. But it was the Corman connection that nurtured talent. Corman gave Coppola his first serious chance; that, indirectly, helped Coppola to the position where he could act as patron to George Lucas. Peter Bogdanovich made his first, and most satisfying, film, *Targets,* for Corman; it was made, typically, with a few days which Karloff owed Corman on a previous contract. Gary Kurtz learned the business of film production under Corman, while working on the two Monte Hellman Westerns that Corman sponsored. (He is not credited as producer on the films, although that is what, in fact, he was.) Martin Scorsese made his first Hollywood film, *Boxcar Bertha,* for Corman. Jack Nicholson also learned his trade as a writer and an actor under Corman. Only the great machine at Universal/MCA, constantly pouring forth film for television in series, serials, and features, has had a comparable importance; there Steven Spielberg found his first contract and made his first films. If we add the activities of AIP, then the importance of the Arkoff, Nicholson, and Corman alliance becomes even more crucial. AIP financed and produced the first film directed by John Milius, *Dillinger*; and it released Brian DePalma's first substantial commercial success, *Sisters* (Brit.: *Blood Sisters*). All this suited the film school graduates well, and not only because it gave them work. The methods were cooperative, collective, and disciplined by limited resources, but they allowed some rein for individual style and experiment.

To reach Corman, a student had to be fast to hear about a job—as stills photographer, substitute editor, and even translator and writer on those Eastern bloc epics that Corman would buy cheaply and doctor for the American market, adding dubbed voices and a handful of shots to establish some Western context for the action. One such film was a sentimental Russian space fantasy that Corman wanted to convert into a monster film. On the credits that film, *Battle Beyond the Sun*, is directed by Thomas Colchart. It is not a name the film books list. Colchart never worked again. He resumed his real identity, Francis Coppola.

THREE

The Children

Francis Coppola

Born 1939 in Detroit, Michigan, to Italian immigrant parents; raised in New York, where father was professional musician. Took B.A. in theater arts at Hofstra University, Long Island, in 1959; later, took Master of Fine Arts at UCLA film school. Worked in nudie films and as assistant to Roger Corman who backed his first feature film, *Dementia 13* (Brit.: *The Haunted and the Hunted*). Served Seven Arts as house writer (*Is Paris Burning?*, *This Property Is Condemned*) until company absorbed by Warner Brothers. Coppola then made *You're a Big Boy Now*, *Finian's Rainbow*, and *The Rain People* before attempting his own studio in San Francisco. After studio collapsed, Coppola was hired to make *The Godfather*; also made *The Conversation* and *The Godfather Part II*. While operating as studio head, backed George Lucas to make *THX-1138* and later acted as producer on *American Graffiti*.

"I have spent my life," Francis Coppola said, "just trying to have a career." He was the first of the true movie brats, a man who absorbed cinematic tradition and learned how to use it. He was impulsive, volatile, sometimes absurd, and sometimes pompous. But he had a strategy. More than anything, he wanted independence from the studio machines and the bureaucratic limits of the film business. He became the patron on whom the other movie brats learned to depend, part tycoon and part creator. "Francis Coppola," said his own onetime patron Roger Corman, "likes to think of himself as a filmmaker."

Coppola was himself the first graduate of the school of

Corman. He served his time as soundman, dialogue coach, assistant, and second unit director, all while he was still working on his master's degree at UCLA. He graduated to the patronage of Seven Arts and Warners, as those two companies married and changed; and his first feature film for that major studio served as his master's thesis, *You're a Big Boy Now*. He bid for freedom and a studio of his own, but the experience turned sour. Broke, he found himself short of friends in a business that hates losers. He recovered by luck, and the project by which he saved himself was *The Godfather*. It proved a spectacular recovery that restored his power. This time, he had the power to be a sponsor, friend, counselor, and sometimes financier to the others who followed him. He is the architect of a generation of filmmakers, however much they later diverged from him in style, subject, and feelings. From the start, he was the glittering symbol to men like George Lucas and John Milius, while they were still at film school. "Francis was the great white knight," Lucas says. "He was the one who had made it. He was the one who made us hope. . . ."

Francis Coppola was christened Francis Ford Coppola. He dropped the middle name in 1977 on a sudden whim; he knew a man who never trusted anyone with three names. He was raised in New York, a child of a solidly middle-class family; his father played flute for Toscanini in the NBC radio symphony orchestra and, more usually, conducted the band for touring stage shows. Coppola's parents were hungry for success in their children. They pinned their greatest hopes on Francis's elder brother, who seemed more likely to succeed. Francis Ford was sickly, confined to bed with polio. He played with movie cameras, cutting together home movies at the age of eight in which he was always the hero. On 212th Street in Queens, he charged his friends admission.

Coppola was seduced by film. But instead of going straight to film school, he first studied theater arts at

Hofstra University in New York state. It was a deliberate delay. He played at director with student companies. He staged a grandiose musical with a thirty-piece professional orchestra. "I did the wheeling and dealing to pay them," Coppola said. "When the overture started, it looked like it was going to be a Broadway show, but then it went progressively downhill."

In 1960, he enrolled at UCLA in its graduate film course. Film school had not yet become fashionable nor oversubscribed. Coppola found it altogether too close to a vocational training course. He had put off studying film because he wanted to learn about drama and performances, the substance of movies rather than the cold technique. Now, he found his fellow students were all too keen to learn a job and know how to win a union card. Coppola wanted technical knowledge, but his first interest was always writing and performance. Of his teachers, only the Hollywood veteran Dorothy Arzner, the woman whose clever direction of hack studio projects subverted many vacuous men's fantasies into real films during the 1930s and 1940s, seemed interested in the same things. She had suffered the system, but she kept respect for the power of actors and the eloquence of the camera. Among technicians, she was the humanist.

Coppola learned the most outside of school. His ambition was to make film. He shot footage whenever camera, stock, and subject were offered. He began with sex films, in the innocent days when sex meant a glimpse of breast rather than a surgical exploration of sex mechanics. He made *The Peeper*, a short gag about an overeager voyeur who hears that pinup pictures are being shot in his neighborhood. The would-be peeper tries every imaginable device to spy on the camera sessions, but all of them backfire. A twelve-foot telescope, painfully hauled to his apartment, proves so precise that it will focus on only the navels of the girls below. The premise was witty, but the commercial prospects would have been dim except for the fact that an exploitation company had bought, and wept over, a nudie Western. The plot line involves a cowboy who, kicked in the head by a horse, sees all his herd of cows as naked women. It was a film in need, desperate need, of grooming. Coppola provided it, knitted together his film and the Western, and the result was released as *The Wide Open Spaces*. Later, Coppola provided color three-dimensional sequences for a tedious, flat German film in black and white; it was released as *The Belt Girls and the Playboy*.

It was the high point of Roger Corman's career in exploitation films. His alliance with AIP was at its strongest, and he had not yet abandoned directing for a distribution corporation of his own. He scoured film schools for likely talent. "He would tell his secretary," Coppola recalled, " 'Ring up UCLA. Get some film student who'll work cheap.' " Coppola wanted work and to get it he masqueraded as Thomas Colchart, turning a sentimental, philosophic Russian science fiction movie into a monster picture. While working, he was careful to stay under Corman's feet. Late at night, when Corman left, he would still be cutting. Early next morning, when Corman arrived, he would be slumped, exhausted, over the editing table. This ostentatious enthusiasm worked. For the film, *Battle Beyond the Sun*, he was paid only $200. But he had become a protégé of Corman. He was used for odd jobs. Corman needed a dialogue director for *Tower of London*; Coppola did it. When Corman went to Ireland in 1962 to make *The Young Racers*, Coppola was on the crew. He acted as soundman and shot the racing sequences. Corman encouraged and tested him, as he did all his associates. The reward for the competent assistants was a film of their own.

"Roger can't resist making a second picture," Coppola said. "Not when he's already paid the crew's expenses." Crew, cast, and specialists were already assembled at Ardmore studios in Eire. Corman stalwarts like Luana Andrews and the sinister British character actor Patrick Magee still had days on their contracts when Corman could ask them to work. Coppola used the opportunity and calculated an idea for Corman. "I described the scene of

70

some lady who goes into a pond and sees the corpse of a little child and gets axed to death," he said. "Everything I knew Roger would like." Corman agreed to put up $20,000 on the condition that the film bear a title he considered commercial, *Dementia*. The budget was tight even by Corman's standards, and Coppola bought himself leeway by raising another $20,000 from the British-based producer Raymond Stross. All Coppola needed now was a story line that would link cash, title, actors, and the ax murder. He devised it in three and a half days.

Coppola maintained *Dementia* was more fun than any other film he ever made. But the result is no lost masterpiece. The film is shabby, harshly lit, and wordy—Irish Gothick with an air of grand indulgence.

It opens on a pitch-black lake, where a rich man and his money-grubbing wife are talking cynically against a background of romantic pop music. The man dies; the widow has to hide the death to make sure she will get her share of the money. Back in the house, the widow is confronted with the mystery of the constantly reappearing corpse of a girl drowned six years before. The family's mother mourns this child obsessively, tossing a flower on the grave each year in a solemn, family ritual. Eldest brother wanders about the house with an oxyacetylene torch, because he is a sculptor; a younger brother plays with lighted candles, because he is dotty. A blankly mad doctor stalks stone corridors with the corpse in his arms. There is an ax murder, with the overcurious widow done to death after she has found a mysterious underwater shrine; and the blonde corpse is dragged, bloodily, along the lakeside. The final revelation of the ax killer—the younger brother, for the record, who had also drowned his young sister years before—is actually more confusing than the mystery. The plot twists, turns, and knots itself together.

In Britain a bothered censor excised the bloody corpse. This is ironic, since those shots decorate the wall of a discotheque in Coppola's next film, *You're a Big Boy Now*. In America the Corman title was changed to *Dementia 13*. There has never been an adequate explanation of the *13*, but there exists an anonymous 1940s melodrama about a severed hand called, simply, *Dementia*. Coppola suggested, cynically, that AIP calculated they just might take in money with the film on the thirteenth of every month. The film's most notable appearance (its title, that is) is in George Lucas's *American Graffiti*; it is on top of the bill at the State Cinema on Main Street.

Coppola had constructed the model exploitation film—a loose plot that stumbles between scenes which would each make a billboard. *Dementia 13* (Brit.: *The Haunted and the Hunted*) has a child's corpse reappearing among the cobwebs of a sculptor's disused studio; the mother on a pilgrimage to the body, as though to some holy shrine; the underwater grave marked "Catherine, forgive me." The murder of the wicked, widowed blonde is viciously effective; and the corpse of the child is laid out, again, on a fountain in the grounds to await the last eruption of the crazed killer. Each scene works. But to connect them, Coppola needs words. Subplots appear with the marmalade at breakfast time. Conspiracies are hatched in prolonged voiceovers and in the typing of letters and the writing of diaries. The pacing goes awry. The climactic attack of the ax killer has less power than the moment when the new widow breaks into what had been the dead daughter's nursery; and, as she looks along the shelves of unused toys, a clockwork circus monkey begins to clash its cymbals. It is a simple, juddering shock that Steven Spielberg was to replay later in *Close Encounters of the Third Kind*. And although the nighttime shooting—night for night instead of faked daytime footage—could be compared with the films noirs of the 1940s, such as *Double Indemnity*, the comparison would be thin. Coppola's schedule left no time for complex camera tracks, subtle lighting, or much refinement of editing; and the visual quality, with harsh light picking out relevant objects in a rich, black night, is more a product of circumstance than design. Inevitably, some absurdities survive. The film thanks Aer Lingus; and there is a lengthy, irrelevant sequence in which an Aer Lingus plane lands by an Aer Lingus gangway, and an

Aer Lingus announcer gives an Aer Lingus welcome to passengers waiting by an Aer Lingus baggage belt. Worse yet, the child's corpse, occasionally but perceptibly, blinks.

Some Coppola trademarks are already apparent. The family in their Gothick mansion are clearly a set of pathological specimens. This family psychopathy, an obsession with inherited character, recurs in most of Coppola's other films. Dynasty and heritage appear again in *The Godfather*; family relationships lead to murder in *The Conversation*, to repression in *You're a Big Boy Now*. The wicked widow is a sketch for the sadistic blonde bitch in *You're a Big Boy Now*. And for a film that works by shock, the cutting is surprisingly legato. While the doctor walks the length of some castle catacomb with the daughter's body in his arms, the camera holds steady and unblinking, with no cutaways or tricks. The shot disconcerts through its sheer steadiness. Even on a budget and a schedule that allowed him no chance for the constant retakes and the loose dramatic structure he later used, the style begins to emerge.

In the year of *Dementia*, 1962, Coppola won the Samuel Goldwyn writing award for a project called *Pilma, Pilma*, which was never made. He spent a week shooting spare footage on *The Terror*, one future star among the many who assembled for that film; he married, the next week, an artist he had met in Dublin; and the week after that, he was hired as a writer by Seven Arts. It offered him $375 a week to do the impossible. Its business was packaging films—preparing scripts, enticing stars, and handing financial responsibility over to some major studio. Seven Arts had bought an option on Carson McCullers's elusive novella, *Reflections in a Golden Eye*, a Southern story of repressed homosexual passion, ruined women, and decadent fantasies, set in an army camp. Nobody had been able to quarry a script from this exotic material, and time was running out. The $50,000 investment in the right to film the story was now at risk. Coppola seemed as likely a prospect as anyone. On the strength of his prize, rather than his film, it interviewed him and bought him. He repaid them with a script that was changed beyond recognition, he says, when John Huston finally filmed the story in 1967. But Seven Arts was pleased with its new acquisition. They gave Coppola a raise, to $500 a week, and made him, in effect, house writer, the man who would polish, create, or salvage an average of three scripts a year.

It was the start of a long association between Seven Arts and Coppola. In time, Seven Arts swallowed Warner Brothers; and the amalgam was taken over by Kinney Service Corporation. But between 1962 and 1970 Coppola stayed with the company, its new partner, and its eventual parent. The rules of this marriage were radically different from the relationship between an old Hollywood writer and his studio. Coppola was not a hack who was assigned a desk in a thin-walled office where he could hear another team of writers working on his own project. He was working for independence. Out of his links with Warner–Seven Arts, he made his first major feature film; was allowed to try a radically new approach to making a commercial film with *The Rain People*; and even, briefly, acquired the financial muscle to act as patron with his own studio. The new, hollow Hollywood needed ideas; and in the land of the thoughtless, the man with even one project is king.

Inside a more orthodox studio, conservative Universal, or rich Twentieth Century-Fox, Coppola might have lost his way. At Seven Arts, the very nature of the company gave him his chance. Originally Seven Arts had been a tannery called Donnell, Carman and Mudge (Canada) Ltd. In March 1955 it abandoned its business; and by November of that year it had sold off all its plant and goods and equipment. All that remained was a shell, packed with money and securities that were looking for a home. In December 1957 it found a new business, buying television rights to movies and hawking them to stations in Canada, the United States, and a handful of territories in other parts of the world. This tentative step into show business led to ambition. If Seven Arts could sell film, it **could also** make it. But the choicest profits did not seem to lie with the studios. The real profit was in taking the first risks, assembling story, stars, and director, and allowing some other corporation to take over the financial burden of actually producing the film. Naturally, Seven Arts required a fee for its services from the major company that bought its package; and it usually negotiated for itself a generous cut of every dollar of distributors' gross income. In the first phase of its American operations, from 1957 to 1965, Seven Arts assembled twenty-four packages. It bought books, plays, and screenplays; and Francis Coppola was the writer who made them acceptable to a major studio. On the writers' work depended a large part of Seven Arts's credibility.

In 1965 it had become successful enough to be tempted into distributing film for itself. Seven Arts's profits looked healthy; and new money, associated with the ubiquitous Wall Street house of Allen and Company, was available. The sources of new capital were deep and rich enough to allow private conversations between the Seven Arts board and Jack L. Warner, the largest private stockholder in Warner Brothers, and the last survivor of the bicycle-salesman brothers. On November 23, 1966, Seven Arts Associated Corporation, the American end of the Canadian company, paid $31,477,200 for 32.26 percent of Warners. Jack L. Warner remained on the company's payroll as a producer; but power passed to Kenny and Elliott Hyman of Seven Arts. In 1967 they cleaned up the outstanding stock, dealing with such details as Frank Sinatra's sizeable holding in Warners's recording operation. A new company was born: Warner–Seven Arts. The merger naturally meant uncertainty; but it also meant the Hymans had the resources and the scale to back films, especially when the ideas came from their house writer. Coppola took his chance.

Those scripts that Coppola prepared for Seven Arts had rarely reached the screen in a form he approved. Now he found himself collaborating on *Is Paris Burning?* with

Gore Vidal. In his spare time he worked on a screen adaptation of an obscure British comic novel about the pangs of adolescence, *You're a Big Boy Now*. He had bought the rights to David Benedictus's novel himself, and the adaptation was a labor of love, a mixture of absurdist sight gags and sudden transitions and wickedly accurate parody of solemn successes like *The Group*.

He went into alliance with Phil Feldman, the onetime lawyer for the gigantic Famous Artists agency, who had served as vice-president in charge of motion pictures at Seven Arts for four years. Now that the company had merged with Warners, Feldman had decided that he wanted to be independent. Whether he sensed the Warners deal would leave him stranded in a vast, corporate pool or whether he simply wanted to cash in his credibility with the Hymans is quite unclear. But with Coppola's script, he announced a program of six movies.

On their own account, Feldman and Coppola started *You're a Big Boy Now* on hope and credit. "We were shelling out our own money," Coppola said, "and using credit cards and what have you." The newly merged Warner–Seven Arts gave the film a grudging blessing. It was to be completed, on New York locations, in twenty-nine days. Coppola reacted by preparing a rehearsal version of the script, which played briefly in a theater without scenery or costumes; and by videotaping the shows with a live audience to check what moves and lines worked best. (His fascination with tape as an aid to rehearsal and improvisation continued ten years later on *Apocalypse Now*; and it was a taped improvisation which persuaded a skeptical Paramount board to cast Marlon Brando in *The Godfather*.) Once he had characters and gags, he could shoot fast, in a style which was deliberately designed to allow him to ground the film in its cutting rather than the action and composition of individual shots. The result was a style that, as Coppola said, "became the biggest cliché in the world"—visual absurdities like a girl glimpsed reading in a fountain, free-wheeling treks across Central Park as decoration for conversations, captions to label sections of the story, jumpcuts and abrupt transitions, and cutting to match a pseudorock score from the Lovin' Spoonful. "It was actually," Coppola claimed, "the first film of its kind that used one of those so-called hard rock scores. But all the others were out by the time *Big Boy* was released."

The influence of Richard Lester (*A Hard Day's Night*) and the French New Wave is obvious enough. The story reflects some of Coppola's filmic misogyny. A growing boy is beset by monstrous women—a sadistic bitch of an actress; a clinging, hysterical mother; a plain, passive girl friend; a landlady who keeps a cockerel on the stairs to prevent stray women from reaching the bedrooms. In the hysteria, it is hard not to side with the bitch-goddess Barbara Darling and her icy assurance to the impotent boy that there is nothing wrong with him that "a firing squad won't fix." When Coppola attempts parody, the indulgence takes away his edge. The childhood of the bitch actress is sketched in while the film runs with the speeded motion associated with revivals of silent films; Barbara Darling faces ravishment by a lecherous, bald, albino hypnotherapist with a wooden leg. Barbara's problem neatly echoes the sexual confusions of the girls in *The Group,* a link reinforced by Elizabeth Hartman's presence in both films. But the fast motion introduces a different, disruptive joke, and the parody is blunted. Moreover, Coppola adds theatrical jokes—the awful off-off-off-Broadway show, riddled with static symbols—to the often painfully funny tensions inside the central family. Indulgence spoils the sharpness of his observation.

There is evidence that Warners took *Finian's Rainbow* seriously. It was a 1940s Broadway show, left on the shelf for two decades because it was thought to be controversial. In 1947 it boasted the first racially integrated chorus line that Broadway had seen, all happily dancing the carefree life of sharecroppers in fictional Missitucky. It was filmed the year that Martin Luther King was murdered.

E. Y. Harburg, the man who wrote the lyrics for *The*

Wizard of Oz, began with two tentative ideas for nonmusical plays. One involved a leprechaun with a crock of gold that grants wishes; and the other, a Southern bigot who finds himself turned black. Neither worked. "But then it came to me," Harburg said. "Why not combine the two stories by having one of the leprechaun's wishes used to turn some senator black? Then I knew I had something." His instructions to his collaborator, Burton Lane, were simple: "All it needs," he said, "is something like *Porgy and Bess.*"

What reached the screen was a classic studio assignment. Warners had Petula Clark on a recording contract; her style was sharp-voiced like Julie Andrews, and she had the same perky, angular beauty. Since musicals like *The Sound of Music* had been immensely successful, it was clearly time to put Ms. Clark into the same sort of vehicle that had made a superstar of Ms. Andrews. Warners wanted all the proper attitudes in the film; the sharecroppers' savior and romantic lead was to be a folksinger from Haight-Ashbury. It wanted to help Harburg make his points that "riches come through trusting one another, not burying gold" and that there is a certain "inanity" in racial intolerance. Even Coppola seemed briefly infected by respect for the property. "It was," he said, "a hot potato because of the racial issue in it. . . ."

At first, Coppola wanted to shoot the film on location in Kentucky, with the muscular choreography that a Michael Kidd (*Seven Brides for Seven Brothers*) might have prepared. Instead, Warners insisted that the film be confined to the backlot at Burbank; and Fred Astaire brought in Hermes Pan, the formal perfectionist who had created the dance for *Top Hat, Swing Time,* and *Silk Stockings.* The conflicts over both story and style became apparent early. Astaire and Pan had, between them, invented the ground rules for the classic film musical. They had established that the camera should never leave a production number once it had started and that the dancers should always be seen full-length. Coppola showed scant respect for either rule. He was even prepared to improvise dance numbers to fit the camera tracks already laid. During shooting his lead dancer burned her feet on a metal stage, and she was out of commission for a week. Sets for the next sequences had not been built. To keep the film on time, Coppola simply instructed his cast to move to the music of two major production numbers, and he led them from the camera. He almost justified the device by very exact cutting on musical cues so that the editing helped disguise the paucity of dance ideas. Hermes Pan quit the film. When *Finian's Rainbow* finally appeared, the studio was so enthusiastic about its chances that it blew the print up from 35mm to 70mm, to give it the air of a grand musical event. That proved nearly fatal. The shape of the image changed and the film lost its one asset, Astaire's feet.

Coppola took the film as a journeyman assignment, something a trustworthy young director around the studio would do despite the absurdly low $3.5 million budget he was offered. "It is not," he said, "a personal film." He claims credit for salvaging the script and preventing the crass changes that would have put its patronizing story in the real world. "I had the idea you shouldn't rewrite it and update it. I guess I was wrong," he said, "because *Finian's Rainbow* was a terrible book originally."

It is the kind of story in which a fey Irishman capers into a rustic valley with his beautiful daughter, hotly pursued by the mortgage men who want to repossess the valley and a leprechaun who wants to repossess his crock of gold. Will fey Finian use the crock of gold for social change in the valley, a dreamworld where well-fed, happy sharecroppers dance and sing, black alongside white, in perfect harmony? Will he save the life of Og the leprechaun, whose survival depends on the wishes in the crock of gold? Will the racist senator be changed in heart when he finds that he himself has turned black? It is that sort of show. Coppola misfires from the first shots. He puts Astaire and Clark before a series of grand American panoramas—the Statue of Liberty, the Golden Gate, Monument Valley, Mount Rushmore; the sound track oozes a sentimental song, "Look, Look, Look to the Rainbow." Coppola wanted an effect of spatial dislocation, a sense of never-never land. Instead, he locates the film firmly in the American dream.

His Missitucky sharecroppers are put in a world of real aspirations; and the gap between this sentimental vision, where dance is enough to hold off the bailiffs, and the brute, appalling reality of sharecropping life is all too obvious. Rainbow Valley is full of dreams of the day when the "idle poor" [sic] will become the idle rich. The valley people welcome the arrival of the Sears, Roebuck catalog, and consumer credit, with ecstasy much like a lovers' greeting in other musicals. Riches, we are told, bring privilege; but credit makes it possible to make money. It is as blatant a hymn to consumerism as any put on screen, an affirmation of the 1940s faith that Americans would soon grow so rich that class differences would become irrelevant and everybody would be content. Material goods would heal all social wounds. Even the lynch mob that plans to slaughter Ms. Clark as a witch is finally converted, singing a last reverential version of "Look, Look, Look to the Rainbow" in the smoldering ruins of an old barn. Reality, however cruel, can be dissolved with gentle, liberal dreams. The idea is patronizing and wet. It also misread the times. It was gentle, liberal, and vaguely humanistic in the year that Richard M. Nixon, talking of law and order, was elected president of the United States.

All Coppola's clever games at the editing table could not disguise the dated nature of his material; the film appeared to be half-hearted, and it failed at the box office. It illustrates a fatal flaw that eats at Coppola's filmmaking. He makes appropriate noises to hearten his liberal constituency—"Francis," John Milius says, "makes films that say 'War is Hell' "—and then concentrates on performance, style, and rhythm. His skills do not present the message he says he intends. In the two *Godfather* films, he claimed to expose American capitalism and actually crafted a fine dynastic epic. In *Apocalypse Now*, he created wild, psychedelic effects in a story of a war whose

80

real scars were still all too apparent. Coppola grew up comfortable, sure that a person's will can change anything, that "all you have to do is go out and shoot a movie." Only with privilege is it possible to be so sure.

Finian's Rainbow impressed Warners mightily. Coppola remembered the studio virtually counting the millions before the film was released. He was offered $400,000 to make *Mame,* and he turned it down. He understood that the power that came from making a big musical could be turned to his own ends. He might appear a maverick, but that would not matter, for Hollywood had become a hollow place. In 1968 he said: "I don't think there'll be a Hollywood as we know it when this generation of film students gets out of college." Coppola was beginning to formulate his own schemes to change the way things worked.

It was on the set of *Finian's Rainbow* that Francis Coppola first met George Lucas. Lucas had arrived on a Warner Brothers scholarship to observe the making of a feature film. He had already been out in the desert with Carl Foreman on *Mackenna's Gold,* and "watching them make movies got pretty boring after a while," Lucas says. "Warners had just been taken over by Seven Arts and the place was desolate. They were making one film—and that was *Finian's Rainbow."*

Lucas spent his first few days determined to escape the set and work in Warners's legendary, but empty, animation department. Coppola found out and was constructive. "Look, kid," he told Lucas, "help me. You come up with one good idea a day and you can actually do stuff for me." The two proved natural allies. "We were the only people on the production under forty or fifty," Lucas estimates, ungenerously. "We had both been to film school, and we both had beards."

Lucas started as the Polaroid cameraman, checking shots. He soon became one of the trusted advisors in the editing room, a role he was still playing a decade later when Coppola was cutting *Apocalypse Now.* "We became very close friends," Lucas says, "because in every single way we're opposite, two halves of a whole. Coppola's very impulsive and Italian and flamboyant and sort of extravagant. I'm extremely conservative and plodding. He was constantly jumping off cliffs and I was always shouting: 'Don't do it, you'll get yourself killed!' He would jump anyway, and for a while nothing too bad would happen. I used to be called the seventy-year-old kid."

The cautious kid was, ironically, the man who helped Coppola's desire for autonomy find its place and its form. Lucas was still bright with the shine of USC and innocent of big studio politics. Coppola responded. Lucas stayed around to work on the crew of Coppola's *The Rain People,* and brought in the brilliant Walter Murch to work on the sound. Out of *Rain People* grew the friendships and the organization that gave Coppola his own studio, which was set the vital few hundred miles north of the Hollywood shark pool; it was the model for Shangri-Coppola, Steven Spielberg's phrase for the ideal independence that all of the movie brats tried to build.

The Rain People, like *You're a Big Boy Now,* was started on Coppola's cash and courage. He had the tatters of a script that he had written for a creative writing class in 1960; it showed the lives of three housewives—one newly married, one older, and one the mother of several children. The original form was swiftly abandoned, but what remained was the story of a woman unsure if she was ready to be either wife or mother. Coppola shot a few hundred feet of film at a Long Island football game, drafted a rough script that changed daily during shooting, and persuaded Shirley Knight to join the project. That was enough of a package. Warner–Seven Arts barely understood why their journeyman writer and director should want to make this eccentric, personal film; but since he needed only $750,000 to make the film, which was less than twice the director's fee they were prepared to offer him on *Mame,* they wrote the check. Coppola packed cast, crew, and even editing table into vans, and he set out on a four-month pilgrimage across eighteen of the United States. He won independence because he had been so solid and useful as a company man, because *Finian's Rainbow* had cost only $3.5 million when $18 million was quite thinkable for the extremely expensive and complex business of assembling a musical, and because the full extent of the *Finian* disaster was not yet clear. Coppola was working out in practice his most deliberately extreme claim—to "pattern his career after Hitler." "The way to come to power," he once said, "is not always to merely challenge the Establishment, but first make a place in it and then challenge and double-cross the Establishment." Coppola made a workable film out of *Finian's Rainbow*, paid his dues, and now left Hollywood, physically and spiritually. His crew for *Rain People* had only seventeen members. His cast was led by James Caan, a friend from Hofstra, and Shirley Knight, with whom he had always wanted to work. Most were friends, recruited informally by Coppola and Lucas. "I just got a phone call from George in the fall of 1968," Walter Murch remembers. "He asked—did I want to come along? I think for Francis and George that film was the prototype. If they could operate making a film out of a storefront in Ogallala, Nebraska—and do it successfully—then there was no reason why they should live in Hollywood."

Working away from a studio had curious results. The end product had a less rigid design; it could contain more improvisation. When the crew found a grand parade in Chattanooga, it was incorporated into the film. Coppola had been able to pick his associates, and on *Rain People* he learned to trust them, to discuss things with them. On location he made take after take of single scenes, waiting to see what would emerge from the final shaping on the editing table; and the sound, although less central to the film's concerns than the track of *The Conversation*, was almost as complex and sophisticated. Coppola learned to put himself more at risk, to allow a team to develop his ideas. His habit of retaking was to recur most dramatically on *The Godfather*, when baffled observers on the set claimed he could not possibly have an exact idea of the effect he wanted. His equipment was, as it was later to be at American Zoetrope, far ahead of the industry as a whole; the editing table, for example, was a Steenbeck when the Los Angeles studios were still using Movieolas. (European and American fashions in editing equipment were exact opposites in the 1960s and early 1970s.) Coppola was building his team and creating the base from which he could later defend himself against anything the Hollywood bureaucrats might do. "It may be a bad movie when it's finished," he said of *The Rain People,* "but it starts from sincere beginnings."

If *Rain People* suffers, it is largely because of what Coppola later claimed for it—that it was a feminist movie ahead of its time. All it was—and this is remarkable—is a film about a woman. Its central figure is a Long Island housewife, newly pregnant, who tries to define herself by a long escape across America. She is unsure how much responsibility she wants or can take; and she is forced to face the problem when she picks up a hitchhiking college football player who has been left mindless by an accident. He, "Killer," becomes the surrogate for the child she is carrying. From the start, we know that she loves her husband; and that her husband, in turn, owns her. When she has driven away he tells her, chillingly: "Don't let anyone feel you—or our baby." She talks with her parents who cannot understand her troubled consciousness. Her escape across the country defines her in terms of the men she meets—the husband she leaves; Killer, whom she tries to seduce in an erotic game of "Simon Says" before she realizes how dumbly he will obey her; the policeman, first glimpsed as a black-shaded figure out of *Psycho* and for whom she leaves Killer, who must then fend for himself. In leaving Killer and asserting her own sexual needs, she is also seen as betraying her responsibility; and the result is a bloody shoot-out in a trailer park, with Killer near to death and the woman crying over his body that she will care for him. In the end, she is forced to take responsibility for a man, and answer a man's needs, a betrayal of any feminist intention. But Coppola captures her confusion, her doubts; she signals each new role, with careful make-up to meet the policeman-lover, with maternal feeling when she deals with Killer. She often refers to herself in the third person—"She's pregnant," or "She-me-your wife." As a description of a woman whose own identity has been mostly obliterated by suburban marriage, the film is startlingly good. Its troubles start only when it is seen as something more, and when it ends in melodrama. Coppola's story-telling skills often seem to dissolve at the very end. Robert Evans and Paramount Pictures imposed the ending of *The Godfather*; a committee of associates was debating almost until the release date what the proper structure and ending of *The Godfather Part II* should be; and Walter Murch, left to edit *The Conversation*, had to choose between several possible resolutions. *The Rain People* looks uncommonly like another example of a committee ending.

The long cross-country journey gave George Lucas a chance to press the prospect of San Francisco on Coppola; it was close to Modesto where Lucas was raised. "Francis wanted independence even more than I did," Lucas says. "We wanted a little studio where we could mix and edit our films." Both wanted a fixed base where they could remake the mobile operation that produced *Rain People*. "We stopped off in San Francisco," Lucas explains, "and Francis, who is not one to ponder things much, said: 'This is great—let's move.' We got back in the fall of 1968 and moved up in April 1969." On November 14, 1969, a San Francisco attorney filed the papers for a new corporation to be called American Zoetrope. Its sole shareholder was Coppola, its vice-president was George Lucas, and its treasurer and secretary was another friend, Mona Skager. The movie brats had their first studio.

The three-story warehouse at 827 Folsom was a cherry-vanilla dream of a place, with a pool table and an ancient espresso machine in its central lounge—and seven editing rooms, screening and editing rooms, and a Keller three-screen editing table as well. It became an obligatory stop for any film journalist on the West Coast, an outpost for young filmmakers, a solid symbol of their dream of freedom. "Francis," as George Lucas says, "was the great white knight who had made it" and who now found the money from Warners to start a production program based at Zoetrope. Within a year of the studio's opening Coppola backed George Lucas's first feature, *THX-1138*, supported John Milius while he wrote the first draft of *Apocalypse Now*, and sponsored a generation of other young filmmakers. He reveled in Zoetrope. "Finally, after ten years," he said, "I've recaptured the energy of working on a college play."

His operation was modeled, consciously, on Roger Corman's. "The real concept," according to Lucas, "was that it would be an independent, free production company that would make seven or eight films a year in varying degrees of safeness. We might do a couple of films that seemed fairly safe and reasonable, and then do some really off-the-wall productions. The theory was that it would all eventually balance itself out and the operation would make money. It was a way to give first-time directors a break and do what studios ordinarily would not do."

The fact that his operation was based in San Francisco had two sizeable advantages. Unlike studios with millions of dollars already invested, or producers who used their facilities in Los Angeles, Zoetrope could buy whatever equipment it wanted. It had no reason not to be revolutionary, by the standards of a technically conservative business. And the union barriers to flexibility in Hollywood were missing in San Francisco. The local of IATSE, the technicians' union, was mainly theatrical; it had so few members involved in film post-production work that it allowed them to switch jobs as they wanted in order to keep in work. Walter Murch, for example, was on IATSE's books simply as a post-production worker, which meant he could be credited as editor, sound editor, or even writer. That lack of rigidity was a key to the excitement of Zoetrope for film school graduates who had learned the whole range of film technique. "Someone who's been to film school has a kind of inverted pyramid of experience," Murch says. "Because of the curriculum, you are forced to do every-thing; and only gradually do you focus on one thing. Whereas, in the industry, it's the exact opposite. If you enter as an assistant soundman, you become a soundman, and then, perhaps, a sound editor. Technological change comes very, very slowly. If we had set up in Los Angeles, everything would have been very different."

The only trouble with Zoetrope was its need for capital. The logical source of cash was the Hollywood that the bright new filmmakers most despised. It was the era of *Easy Rider*, when Dennis Hopper's drug odyssey across America had made untried talent and unfamiliar subjects acceptable. Any production program that offered new talent was attractive. Francis Coppola, an extraordinary salesman when he wants to play that role, went south to find the cash. Warners was, again, in metamorphosis. This time, it was adjusting to new owners—a conglomer-ate called Kinney, whose various businesses rented cars and found them parking spaces, cleaned offices, published *Mad* magazine, and buried the dead. The new Warners management was led by Ted Ashley, whose talent agency had been part of the Kinney empire; and the Warners deal with Coppola staked rather little money for a generous return. Warners would put up $3.5 million, but it would go no further until the first film arrived for screening. On each film either Coppola had to be personally involved or else the budget must be less than $500,000. Warners also kept, in effect, final cut, script approval, and the power to reject Coppola's schemes and make him buy them all back. That last flaw must have seemed very theoretical; but the impulsive Coppola and the cautious Lucas should have spotted it. It almost ruined them.

Gary Kurtz visited George Lucas while he was cutting *THX-1138*. Their conversation was the indirect product of the meeting between Kurtz and Coppola during their Corman days; and the meeting was the germ of *American*

Graffiti. Kurtz remembers the exhilaration that surrounded Zoetrope. "Coppola got involved in these rather complicated projects, using a lot of energy," he says. "He alternates between liking the idea of shepherding these other projects and getting frustrated with them when they don't necessarily work out the way he saw them." But in those days, Coppola was the happy patron. Lucas's first feature film was almost ready. It was time for Zoetrope to show Warners what it could do.

It became known as Black Thursday. Francis Coppola went down to Los Angeles with a rough cut of *THX-1138*. The studio had seen nothing since the script; now it was confronted with a bleak, bleached film, full of whited-out visions of the future. The film had no compromises, and Warners's reaction was just as direct. They loathed it. Gary Kurtz believes: "I think Francis sold *THX* on the basis of the screenplay, but Warners didn't buy it on that basis. They didn't see what was written on the page. They saw another movie. It happens all the time."

On Black Thursday Coppola returned from the shark pool in Hollywood with desperate news. Warners's men might dislike *THX-1138*, but they had at least paid for it; and, later, they released a slightly altered version whose commercial fate was not helped by their minor tampering. That, relatively, was the good news, for the Warners men also declared that they disliked everything that American Zoetrope was doing. They disliked the story of *Apocalypse Now*, a script by John Milius about a Green Beret squad operating on the borders of Cambodia that George Lucas was to direct; and they hated the work of Gloria Katz and Willard Huyck, who were later to be coauthors of *American Graffiti;* and they rejected projects from Matt Robbins and Hal Barwood, who had to wait seven years for the chance to make their own first film, *Stingray*. Warners, as Coppola put it, "unnaturally and unwisely jettisoned American Zoetrope, and all the talent which is in the so-called youth movement."

Worse still, they demanded repayment of all the money spent on preparing seven other projects and the entire cost of Zoetrope's equipment and "everything else," according to George Lucas. "Usually, a studio would never make a producer pay money back or buy his scripts back. But that's what they did with Zoetrope. We were broke, and close to half a million dollars in debt. We were blackballed from the industry. Francis was trying to get pictures off the ground, but there was constant talk behind the scenes —'Don't hire this guy, he's crazy!' They talked about me too; that was one of the problems in getting *American Graffiti* off the ground."

Warners's reaction was understandable, given the lemming instinct of Hollywood's rulers. Warners's commitment to a brash young maverick like Coppola followed the success of *Easy Rider;* the failure of some other young directors, with their unmemorable statements about adolescent angst and campus politics, reflected badly on all young directors. Gary Kurtz also suggests that Warners, as conservative in politics as any other studio, looked askance at the obvious fact that in Hollywood terms "the people Francis had associated with him were extremely radical from a political point of view."

When Warners dropped Zoetrope, they divorced themselves from Coppola. At thirty, he had an admirable record as a writer; his script for *Patton* was on its way to an Academy Award. But as a director of his own projects, he seemed washed up. He had a handful of journeyman pictures behind him, and a single personal statement that had not set the box office cash registers ringing. He was broke; and, to listen to the Hollywood gossips, he was finished.

"We want one big picture a year," Frank Yablans was fond of telling his colleagues at Paramount. "The rest are budgeted to minimize risk, and hopefully, they will make money too." The idea of the "event" movie was elevated almost to a theology by Paramount. But instead of the vastly expensive epic, they wanted their big picture to cost less than $6 million. Once they had the right subject—"emotion, a structured story, jeopardy, romance, and action," Yablans said—they were prepared to spend heavily on advertising, fix high seat prices and thus risk intervention by the federal authorities and then send the film out across the country in the kind of saturation booking that was once reserved for films about which the moguls had severe doubts. That was the way *The Godfather* was manufactured. It opened across the nation with seat prices fixed at $4, when $3 was regarded as normal for a downtown cinema showing a first-run movie. Federal lawyers tried to prevent the price-fixing, in a test case in Washington, D.C., but they failed. With adroit publicity, the film had a release pattern that was almost certain to return its $6 million negative cost within days; the $12 to $15 million needed for Paramount to see a profit was earned within weeks.

At the beginning, Paramount had backed the author of the book, Mario Puzo, by paying him $80,000 to finish his book. The deal was struck on the basis of the first hundred pages of the manuscript. Paramount gave him an office, a secretary, a bank of telephones, and a refrigerator stocked with soda pop. He represented only a minor investment, but he delivered a best-seller. Before the film opened, the novel had sold one million hardback and twelve million paperback copies. Even so, the studio was unhappy about the idea of a Mafia film; because of an earlier exercise, *The Brotherhood,* they doubted if anyone would come to see the inner workings of organized crime exposed. The first screen treatment for the book would have set its action in modern St. Louis, to save the cost of recreating the past; and its budget would have been $2.5 million. It was to be a quickly made thriller that would exploit the success of the book. The main problem for Frank Yablans in New York and Robert Evans in Los Angeles, the uneasily paired executives who ran Paramount under the watchful eye of their conglomerate parent Gulf + Western, was to find a team that was prepared to make the film.

They hired Al Ruddy, a small-time producer whose four theatrical films had all come in under budget and ahead of schedule and whose television series "Hogan's Heroes" had been a steady success. Ruddy never hid his motives for signing on. "This film," he said, "will make us top of the heap." He was the first who argued that the modern setting would not work; "The Mob," he said, "just do not shoot each other any more." But setting the film in the past, even the close past of the 1940s, would mean expensive set-dressing, complex work on locations, sixteen period-taxis on the payroll, and an additional $1 million on the budget. Paramount was skeptical until the book's success was reinforced by protests from the Italian-American Anti-Defamation League. The league aimed to enforce a simple crime control strategy: the Mafia, the Cosa Nostra, and other organized groups of criminals within the Italian community would be eliminated at a stroke by simply not mentioning them. Controversy and a best-seller made *The Godfather* seem a candidate for the event movie of the year. Paramount consciously decided it would be a hit.

Now it had to find a director. After Coppola had been chosen, and completed his quite extraordinary dynastic romance, Robert Evans justified the choice on ethnic grounds: "He knew the way these men in *The Godfather* ate their food, kissed each other, talked. He knew the grit." But before Coppola was even a candidate, the film was offered to Peter Yates, the Englishman who made *Bullitt,* and to Costa-Gavras, the Greek who made Z. The studio was looking for a director prepared to work on an assignment where control would basically lie with the executives in the Paramount suites on Columbus Circle in New York. They wanted a thriller that would exploit the apparent *roman-à-clef* element in Puzo's book, that would have an air of lifting the lid from a fascinating social phenomenon without unduly disturbing the audience. Coppola had the skills to accomplish this. In the end, he did far more than Paramount could have expected.

Who found Coppola is a question that can only be finally resolved when Paramount's files are open to public inspection; if, that is, they ever are. Because he succeeded, everyone claims credit: Evans for seeing the cultural links, Yablans for spotting a talent in eclipse, and Ruddy for listening to the advice of a friend at MGM and putting Coppola on the short list when it was proving difficult to find a director of real talent. Ruddy's earlier films had been idiosyncratic and intelligent; he had no interest in a purely cynical exercise. Once Coppola was hired, Ruddy and he were natural allies on script, period setting, and an increased budget. Coppola's massive debts from American Zoetrope made him willing to take a studio assignment; and Ruddy's ambition to break into the real big time made him determined to produce a monstrous success. Both knew precisely why *The Godfather* mattered to them. If it worked, they would have the money, the power, and the names. They could be independent again, but with resources that had previously been just a dream.

When the filming began, in the streets of New York, both Coppola and Ruddy had their troubles. The crew members were uneasy with their young director. Gordon Willis, the cinematographer, quit the set at one point because he did not believe Coppola knew what he was doing. Constant retakes upset both actors and crew. Rumors suggested that Coppola would be replaced within days or weeks by some senior Hollywood hand like Elia Kazan. Even after Coppola's experience and his UCLA training, an orthodox editor kept complaining that scenes had not been "covered"—that is, that there would not be enough material shot from different angles to assemble coherent sequences in the editing room. Robert Evans, based on the West Coast as production chief, tried constantly to impose budget restrictions. The motive was simple: studios had come close to bankruptcy by fantasies of the gross return that took no account of a film's cost. But the effects could be absurd. When Ruddy and Coppola argued for shooting the scenes of Michael Corleone's exile in Sicily, Evans thought upstate New York would do. Paramount believed Marlon Brando was an impossible choice as Vito Corleone, the godfather of the film's title. He was alleged to be irascible, unpredictable, and unprofessional; to the studio, he was over the hill, a onetime star who had done little in the 1960s that suggested he could still draw an audience. Coppola won over the studio skeptics with a videotaped test. Brando, with no makeup and no script, collapsed suddenly into the old, still powerful shark, Corleone. The rough test proved convincing. But casting minor roles proved almost as troublesome. Auditions were prolonged and painful; Coppola's friends, such as James Caan, and Coppola's family, such as his sister Talia Shire, who plays Don Vito's daughter, were viewed with grave suspicion. Ms. Shire's performance on set did not impress the crew. There was cynical talk that Coppola, like the Corleones, evidently believed in family. All this, unjustified in the event, made a disturbing context for work. Coppola was broke and ruined; and he needed a success. To get it, he had to compromise.

More overtly than usual, the studio had final cut on the film and exercised that right. Coppola was visibly happier when he could retreat to the Zoetrope facilities at San Francisco and work on the film; there, he had buffers against studio pressure. But it did not help the final film. Coppola ended his first version, after the bloodbath in which Michael Corleone wipes out his rivals during the christening of his godson, with Kay Corleone lighting candles in a church, a symbol of the power of the idea of family that gives a choice between the world of gangsters or the priesthood to those deprived members of the Italian-American community who have no other escape from their economic prison. Evans wanted something different. He demanded that the film end as the door closes in Kay's face, shutting her and the audience out from the workings of the Mafia family. The curtain has lifted for a moment, and we, as voyeurs, have the vicarious thrill of seeing organized crime at work; and now the self-contained, exotic business of crime continues, hidden. Evans won the battle. At the end of shooting, Coppola, tired and sick, turned to an assistant director. He gave him three rules for making a film—to arrive with a completed script, to work only with people you trust, and to work in such a

way that no studio can order or veto change. "I have failed,"
Coppola said, "on all three."

The Godfather came in $1 million over budget, an impressive achievement given that the original plans had
been set for ideal conditions, and New York streets in
wintry conditions are not the easiest of locations to control. More troubling to the studio were the long delays on
editing; they had apparently not realized how much of a
Coppola film is designed in the editing room. The film was
meant to open at Christmas, but it missed its dates. As
with any film that opens late, there were rumors that the
project had proved impossible to salvage. The film was
incoherent, the insiders said, and Brando could not be
heard or understood. It was all a dreadful fiasco.

Ruddy had to do battle on another front, with the irate
members of the Italian-American Anti-Defamation League.
They believed that the very thought of filming Puzo's book
was a slur on the entire Italian-American community. At
rallies and in petitions, they tried to stop the film; or at
least to make it impossible for the crew to work on the essential New York locations. With a great deal of public fuss,
the producers agreed to cut all references to the Mafia or to
the Cosa Nostra from the script; there had, originally, been
only one. The world premiere was offered to the league as a
benefit for the Italian-American community. One member
of Paramount's board resigned over that concession. Once
friendly relations had been established, problems in filming street scenes suddenly melted away. Only Joseph Colombo, president of the league, was in no position to be
convinced. While the film was being made, he was shot in
the streets a few blocks from the locations. The shooting
was apparently the work of his business associates.

The Godfather was a company product. When it was
launched, it proved a staggering success; indeed, its profits
overbalanced the profit and loss accounts of Gulf + Western and made the film division embarrassingly and disproportionately profitable. Brando was not only not
inaudible, he was extraordinarily effective. Coppola's ap

parent incompetence had produced a rich-textured film. But he had finished with studio hacking. He had 6 percent of the profits of *The Godfather*, Ruddy had 7.5 percent, and Puzo had 2.5 percent. Moreover, he was suddenly a desirable name. His interest was enough to persuade Universal to go ahead with George Lucas's *American Graffiti*. And Paramount, flush with its impressive record as a studio, wanted to capitalize on that success by tying the top directors to itself. When Coppola signed for *The Godfather Part II* on June 22, 1972, he did so for a generous deal. On the first $10 million of distributors' gross he took nothing; but on the next $10 million he took 15 percent. After that his average stake was 10 percent. In the first four months of 1975 alone, *Godfather II* grossed $22.8 million. After Paramount's $1.2 million deduction for various expenses, the Coppola Company was guaranteed at least $1,728,000; and the Coppola Company was, of course, Coppola himself. Even when he had set aside money for a pension plan and for taxation, he could expect $1,152,000 from a four-month release of the complex sequel to his first major commercial success. More significant than the rich cash rewards was Coppola's new status. Paramount needed him and his films more than he needed Paramount. It was a complete reversal from the broke director scratching for a studio assignment. It began with Frank Yablans's plans to build studio power.

After *Love Story* and *The Godfather*, Paramount decided to create its own family. Yablans wanted a scheme that involved "turning back toward studio control," as he put it, "but not where we have dictatorial power." He proposed to three top Hollywood directors an ingenious scheme for turning their fees into capital. The three were William Friedkin, a director whom Robert Evans had once dismissed as "that bum," but who had now won an Oscar for *The French Connection*; Peter Bogdanovich, the scholarly filmmaker who had made *The Last Picture Show* and *What's Up, Doc?*; and Francis Coppola. Together the three would own half of a new company, first called Premier Directors Company, and then rechristened, with more apparent modesty, The Directors Company. Paramount would keep only half the equity in this Delaware corporation, but it would provide all the cash. Each director was to make three films for the studio in six years and serve as executive producer on a fourth. The total budget would be $31.5 million, and no single film would cost more than $3 million. Paramount's interest was obvious—a constant flow of product from directors who were then the hottest properties in town. The directors would have a haven: "I think," Yablans said, "what appeals to them is not having to auction their talents all over town." They would have virtual autonomy, since the Directors Company was to be a unit separate from Paramount itself. They could make small, personal films; Coppola was to lament, two years later when disaster films were most fashionable, that studios were simply not interested in directors whose projects did not demand gigantic budgets for burning skyscrapers or exploding airships or sinking ocean liners. And, in due course, the company would go public, and the directors could capitalize directly and legitimately on their names.

The trouble with the deal was its high nonsense content. The financing itself made clear how much the studios needed the creators of film. Even First Artists, the consortium of superstars like Barbra Streisand, Steve McQueen, Paul Newman, and Sidney Poitier, had been launched with considerable support from merchant banks in Europe and the United States, including the ill-fated British minor bank Keyser Ullmann and the fashionable failure Slater, Walker; and the superstars had to find one-third of the budget of each film they made. Directors did not need banks or money of their own. Other major studios tried to match Paramount's deal while it was still a matter of gossip in Beverly Hills, for the deal offered an enticing prospect of escaping the fixers—the agents, lawyers, packagers, independent producers, and dealers in tax shelters. But just as stars could prove fickle in the 1950s and 1960s, so directors could change their minds now. Bogdanovich delivered for the Directors Company: he made *Paper Moon*. But he already had a three-picture deal with Warners. It is arguable that overproduction to meet his contracts actually damaged his career; in 1978 he had returned to work for Roger Corman, his first patron, on a film shot in Singapore. William Friedkin had still not completed *The Exorcist* when he joined the consortium; in the week before Paramount announced its new project, he signed a quite separate two-picture deal with Universal. He never made a film for the Directors Company, but he did take a share of the profits from *Paper Moon*. Francis Coppola was heavily involved with *The Godfather Part II,* a film on which Paramount had no intention of surrendering any more of the equity than it needed. It was difficult to see how the three directors could possibly keep up the schedule that the new company demanded, even granted the fact that all Hollywood directors who have made more than one film are likely to have a flurry of paper contracts that commit them to offering their next projects to more than one studio. "This is," Yablans said, "a familial relationship. What made this deal possible was the degree of simpatico between the directors and the studios; we're all in our early thirties and we don't have a great hierarchy." Moreover, Yablans had great hopes for the money-making potential of the trio. "They've gone through their growth period," he said, "indulging their esoteric tastes. Coppola isn't interested any more in filming a pomegranate growing in the desert. They're all very commercial now."

Yablans was wrong on two counts. The desert film was actually made by George Lucas, a short that was confected while he was bored on location with *Mackenna's Gold.* And the family relationship, however warm, did not produce the films. Cynical studio executives who had no links with Paramount had been among the most warmly generous admirers of the scheme: "as long as it means the boys can still make films with us." It did. They did. And the Directors Company was allowed a decent, private death.

The only film that Coppola made for the company was *The Conversation.* It is an intricate film that laces together the sounds and images from a conversation overheard by a professional eavesdropper and then concentrates on the eavesdropper as he tries to decipher the conversation. There is murder and greed; but, more central to the film, the obsessive privacy of the eavesdropper is smashed. Nobody knows his phone number, but his phone rings. His private words are overheard. Once his professional skills led to a killing; this time, he tries to intervene. The result is disaster. At the start of the film, he is orchestrating an intrusion into the lives of a young couple; rifle-sight microphones and sudden zooms establish his violation of others' privacy. At the end, he is left in an apartment that he has stripped of everything, in a last, paranoid attempt to find out what machine betrayed him. Because he became involved, because he felt guilt, he is himself destroyed.

It always seemed a project very personal to Coppola, a product of his fascination with technology—the rifle-sight microphone—and the idea of building the film around a character who would be peripheral in an orthodox thriller. He first developed the story in 1967, finished drafting it in 1969, and rewrote it just before shooting started. It finally appeared as the American press was wakening to the full, awful implications of the Watergate break-in. "I never meant it to be so relevant," Coppola said. "I almost think the picture would have been better received had Watergate not happened." It owes a clear debt to Antonioni's *Blow-Up,* in which a photographer develops, prints, and then struggles to interpret an image that turns out to fix a murder; Harry Caul in *The Conversation* does much the same thing with sound. Coppola looked again at Hitchcock films before shooting; but he owed more to Henri-Georges Clouzot, whose *Les Diaboliques* contains the same sledgehammer reversals in which victim and attacker suddenly change their apparent roles. The film was made by Coppola's company, from Coppola's script, under Coppola's direction and production, and at Coppola's base in San Francisco. It would seem, clearly, Coppola's film. But there is a clue, left trailing in a published interview, that makes the film's authorship less clear. Coppola talked of writing many of the scenes for sound and for the sound-editing technique of Walter Murch. "Since I was working on *The Godfather Part II*," he said, "I asked Walter to edit the film."

"Essentially," Walter Murch says, "Francis left me on my own." The result is that many of the effects in *The Conversation*, some central and some incidental, are not the work of Coppola at all; and even the construction of key sequences like Caul's discovery of the murder and his desolate end in his stripped apartment owe more to Murch and the Coppola associates in San Francisco than they do to Coppola, the film's apparent author. The film is a perfect test of the *auteurist* theory that tries to establish the director as a film's prime creator. It won the Grand Prix for the best film at the Cannes Film Festival in 1974, and it established Coppola's critical respectability. Yet it was not the work of one man. Its central device involves a repeated sequence of film in which vital words of the conversation occur. As the sound becomes clearer, the camera seems to move in tighter and tighter on the couple, as though we were focusing more exactly on their talk. That device is an optical blow-up of the orthodox footage Coppola shot. It is central to the film's meaning and development; and, clearly, it reinforces the links with *Blow-Up*. It was invented by Walter Murch "because it seemed right."

Murch is modest about his contribution. "Pacing of a film," he says, "is something you can gauge by the way actors play a scene, the way the camera moves, the way lines are written and delivered. You get your cues on pacing from the shots. The editor's contribution is to interpret that pacing." That is true for more naturalistic films on which Murch has worked, such as Fred Zinnemann's *Julia*; but it is less than the truth when a film is as intricate as *The Conversation*. As Murch says: "In the whole last half of the film there are only about five lines of actual dialogue, other than the conversation itself. It's a matter of exclamation rather than dialogue. All the content of the film is being carried by the sound. The material wasn't paced out, it wasn't itemized in the script. Shots were shot, and I structured them."

Coppola meant his story to be a modern horror story, "with a construction based on repetition rather than exposition, like a piece of music." It began as a film about privacy, but it ended as a film about responsibility. Harry Caul is haunted by memories of a good job of bugging he once did that ended in death. Now, he misunderstands one key line in a conversation he is paid to overhear. A corporate boss wants his wife and her lover shadowed. The couple seem to say: "He'd *kill* us if he could." Actually, as Caul realizes too late, they say: "He'd kill *us* if he could." They are the killers, pursuing power and money. But to save them from the fate he thinks he has overheard, Caul is prepared to desert his long-suffering, dim woman, expose his privacy to invasion, and even allow talk of the earlier killing to upset him enough to give a scheming woman a chance to steal the vital tapes. He steps outside the cozy, professional world of eavesdroppers into moral responsibility. It is a fatal mistake. He has all the technology to know what people say and none of the instincts that would tell him what they really mean.

There is little exposition. Coppola always intended that Murch should cut the final film and take responsibility for its structure. Only a supervising editor would, for example, know how to handle the repeated shots in which Caul wanders out of frame while taking a phone call; and the camera rests on the information we can glean from his apartment rather than on his face. On Murch's own account, he inverted entire sequences. Caul has to enter a hotel room after a murderous struggle. "What I wanted him to do," Murch says, "was to check the toilet first, then the bathtub, then leave the room, think for a minute, and flush the toilet; the bathtub carries all those memories of *Psycho*, it's much more intense than the toilet. You think somebody is going to be in the bathtub just because of film history." In fact, it is the toilet, flooding blood, which proves the clue that the killing has happened. Murch also ended the film for Coppola. "It was a very hard film to end, and there were so many ways that we tried while editing," he says. "We ended with Caul going back to the confessional, we ended with the scene of him and the girl in the park."

The Conversation becomes an important film for critics and historians. Editor and director demonstrably have a comparable share of responsibility for the finished product. Film is a collaboration. Everyone around Zoetrope was fascinated by *Blow-Up* and discussed it constantly. It is not surprising that Coppola opens his film with a mime in Union Square, just as Antonioni ends his with a mimed tennis match; nor that Murch should use a visual quote by having the remembered conversation "blown up" to the point of comprehensibility. Murch did much of the basic, structural work on the film, but its central device was Coppola's: "focus," as Murch says, "on someone who is a peripheral character in most senses." Coppola screened Hitchcock before shooting; but it was Murch who played off expectations of bathtubs and shower curtains from *Psycho* in assembling the film's climax. By ending with Caul in his desolate apartment, his ruin is seen as the main focus of the film, a shift in theme. Murch's brilliant sound work provides much of the text, as well as the under-pinning of the film. But only a handful of directors, Coppola and Lucas among them, really understand the use of sound as a modulator in dramatic action. "Orthodox movie-makers," Murch says, "think of assembling the sound like getting a negative back from the lab; it's something mechanical that is farmed out. They would be impatient with any subtleties." And even when the editor's role is of such clear importance, it still remains impossible to assign proper responsibility to individuals for their exact contribution to the end effect. Murch says: "To draw a line between something that is an editing room concept and something that is a script concept, that is a very shaky exercise."

As a matter of record, the credits for *The Conversation* are less generous than Coppola has been elsewhere. Francis Ford Coppola appears first and second on the list. Walter Murch appears at number eight, buried between the production designer and the property master.

At Paramount, the time of miracles seemed to have come to an abrupt end. Coppola has screen credit on the major disaster *The Great Gatsby*, a reverential version directed by Jack Clayton and written by Francis Coppola. He had written the script in three weeks, in the year of the first *Godfather*; and according to the producer of *The Great Gatsby*, David Merrick, "he got a lot of help. Clayton should get coauthor credit, but the Screen Writers Guild counts the number of words and determines who gets credit on the screen. They don't give credit for construction, polishing, or creative work that is actually seen on the screen." Coppola should be duly thankful to Merrick for putting such generous limits on his responsibility for the plodding, literal, dreary film that appeared. At times, it seemed that the scenario was being read aloud and illustrated rather than filmed. When the movie floundered into New York, a doomed vessel despite its colossal build-up, it was nicknamed "The Great Ghastly." Its star, Robert Redford, was absent. His press agent announced that he would not be attending the premiere, "not after he'd seen the film."

The *Gatsby* disaster exposed the power politics of Paramount to public scrutiny. On the West Coast, Robert Evans had been the strongest supporter of the project. He had even offered Merrick *Paper Moon* and *The Godfather Part II* in exchange for *The Great Gatsby*. But despite such eccentric judgement, Evans had the Bel-Air circuit—the upper echelons of studio bureaucrats and their natural, party-going allies—sewn up. In New York, Frank Yablans was watching the wild success of *Love Story* and *The Godfather* diminish into memory. The profits on those films had distorted Gulf + Western's balance sheet to the point where the conglomerate could not hope to make so much money from so little capital at risk without making more winning films; in all the other businesses that Gulf + Western owned, the return on capital remained within reasonable limits. But Yablans was not delivering the gigantic successes without which the share-rating of his parent company would decline, and without which his parent company would find it more difficult to acquire new businesses by offering its own shares. Yablans and Evans were paying the price for having done much too well, much too soon.

Coppola celebrated his birthday in April 1974 by watching the release of *The Conversation*. As patron, he had put his name to *American Graffiti*, and that film was now among the contenders for the Oscars. From that film he had more than healthy profits. "Francis," George Lucas says, "has made millions off me, and at the same time I'm happy about it." Coppola's tax bill in 1973 had been more than $570,000; in 1974 it would be more than $401,000. Coppola had left behind his status as hired-hand director and was well on the way to becoming a tycoon in his own right. He was also involved with an act of reparation—a sequel to *The Godfather* that would be more than a romantic, indulgent story of the highest levels of the politics of crime. He was adding the second panel to his picture of the Mafia.

Coppola intended his second Godfather film to correct the first, to destroy any lingering illusions that he wanted to romanticize the young Mafia chieftain Michael Corleone. Later, he would cut the two films together for television— the Coppola Company took $2 million from NBC for the new version—and show clearly that he intended them to represent one narrative. We plan to deal with both films together.

In *The Godfather* we meet a dynasty, a powerful patriarch and his various children—his impulsive son, his weak and vacillating son, his war-hero son. They form a Mafia family, the trigger fingers for a gang war in the New York of the 1940s. It is the classic formula for a bestselling novel—an unfamiliar, exotic world with identifiable family relationships at its core. We are constantly confronted with intimations of the corruption that surrounds the centrally corrupt family. At the opening wedding party senators and judges send their apologies; and, later, part of a deal to start narcotics trading is that Don Vito Corleone, head of the family, should deliver the politicians and judges that he owns. Michael Corleone, the war-hero son of the family and the man of honor, is literally blooded by the act of avenging an attack on his father; he has to kill a police chief who has sold out to the other side. He becomes his father's shadow and starts to dominate the frame. Through intimidation the family moves into Las Vegas and the big time; they already have the film unions, so a threat of labor trouble can be used to help a studio head decide to find a part for a failing, Family actor. They constantly talk of "business"; if a man betrays another it is only "business." Women are rigorously excluded from "business." Michael Corleone, wooing his future wife Kay as a black limousine shadows them, assures her that his father is "no different from any other powerful man." Coppola himself was vocal in identifying Michael Corleone, the hero turned gangster turned power broker, with America. "The Mafia," he said, "is no different from any other big, greedy, profit-making corporation in America. It has been tolerated because the FBI was always more interested in chasing suspected Communists than dealing with the Mafia, which was a form of private enterprise."

He is right in part of his diagnosis; in 1959 the New York office of the FBI had four agents pursuing known Cosa Nostra figures the length of its filing system. More than four hundred agents in the same office were battling to hold off the leftist menace. But, as in so many details of *The Godfather*, the Mafia is not just like any other American business. It is a special case of business, where issues of employment, profit, marketing, and exploitation are secondary to the romantic aura of family battles, gunfights to resolve issues, epic conflict, and unsubtle corruption. As an analysis of American capitalism and its infinitely complex ways, *The Godfather* is no more than a fine melodrama. When Coppola talks of the real Mafia, he invites the objection that his version is singularly unhistorical. Joe Valachi claimed with an insider's authority that the Cosa Nostra had become almost an alternative government; the Mafia, or Cosa Nostra, always had ready cash that they used to bail out and to control businesses from the garment industry to Wall Street security houses. Organized crime was based in the 1940s on the drugs trade, not just illegal narcotics imported into America for addicts, but also ethical drugs smuggled into postwar Italy for anyone who could pay. The power and the relationship to legitimate business are not in either of the films. The Corleone family's olive oil–importing trade is seen, literally, as a shop front; and their main activities are gambling and prostitution with a suggestion of jukebox franchises and protection and talk of labor business. They are identified, carefully, with crime and its romantic aura. Only if the audience knows in advance the scenes in which Coppola is pointing at truth, or disguising it, can the film be seriously read as an attempt to expose the workings of American money. The films themselves contain only a set of occasional slogans to suggest the wider context of their action; and they contain nothing to suggest that the exotic Corleones could have some relationship with our own economic life. Indeed, the Corleones do have one "virtue" no real "family" ever achieved. Unlike any recorded Mafia don, Vito Corleone opposed the narcotics trade, and lived.

At the end of *The Godfather*, Don Vito dies his natural, timely death; and Michael Corleone takes his chair. The chair is like a papal throne and the process of accepting homage from the family members is like the papal *bacciamano*. Before, the climactic slaughter of his rivals is intercut with the christening of Michael's godson—the gold and pomp of the Church against the brutish, bloody machinations of the family. Coppola constantly uses this metaphoric identification of two strands in Italian-American culture. At the start of *The Godfather*, shadows on the wall of Don Vito's study echo the confessional as a poor undertaker asks for the justice he believes he cannot win from the authorities. In *The Godfather Part II* the young Vito slays the Black Hand with casual brutality during the procession of San Gennaro. We see the killing alongside the bands, the Madonna stuck with dollar bills, the apparatus of faith. Early in both parts of *The Godfather* religious ceremonies take place that are paralleled by the conspiracies in which the family members have to engage. In Part I, it is a wedding, full of ethnic jollity; and at the same time, Don Vito does business. In Part II, it is the most sacred moment of a first communion, followed by a vulgar party that shows how far the family has come from its origins; and, after the first communion, Michael Corleone browbeats the senator into cooperation on a gaming license for Las Vegas. Church, family, and "business" become indissoluble elements of the Corleones' life; they allow Coppola a marvelously operatic use of pomp and violence that operates at an irrational level.

This device is a key to Coppola's romantic methods in the first Godfather film; and it is ironic that they contribute so much of the real power of his apparently more analytic *The Godfather Part II*. Here, Coppola attempts a diagnosis of what Kay Corleone calls "that Sicilian thing," with its life of "almost two thousand years." He attempts to isolate a virus and shows its progression. A child comes to America as the carrier of a sickness—vendetta. It is 1901 and the child is escaping the man who killed his father, mother, and brother. He comes through Ellis Island, where he is named for his hometown of Corleone. He is diagnosed as a smallpox carrier and put into isolation. The medical examination and the gray isolation wards carry enormous emotional power because we already know that this child will carry his vendetta disease to the point of emerging as a Mafia don.

Coppola builds *The Godfather Part II* on a series of transitions, from the warm, russet-gold, overlit world of Vito Corleone in early New York, finding his feet, battling the Black Hand, emerging as a power in the neighborhood, to Vito's favorite son Michael, betrayed by his immediate family, answering charges at a congressional inquiry, losing his wife and child, left desolate with infinite power and a barren future. At the end Coppola shows us, ironically, the other moment when Michael Corleone was isolated— when he was the only son to go to war, the one on whom the old Don Vito pinned hopes of respectability, perhaps even the presidency. The sympathy we might have felt for Michael in the first part of the film is now turned to horror. In *The Godfather* he promised Kay he would make the family legitimate; in *The Godfather Part II* his criminal success has closed that option. The radiance of the young Vito's love for his family—watching his wife and son with tender attention—gives way to snowy landscapes, toys abandoned, a door that Michael slams in the face of Kay, and the knowledge that Kay has aborted the child she cannot tolerate bringing into this vicious world. It is the breakup of this family nexus that Coppola presents as the most tragic and appalling part of crime, not the corruption of a senator or the lies Michael tells to a congressional inquiry. Coppola said of the first film that it was the "classic epic about the head guys"; and of the second that it showed "the succession of power and the fact that the Mafia have ceased to be just thugs, but have become part of the Great American belief that anything goes as long as it makes a profit." The second film cuts back and forth in time, usually on a reference to heritage or a son; it does show succession, or, rather more clearly, the inheritance and the development of some disease like syphilis that can be transmitted through generations. But the ways in which the Mafia become more than thugs are romantic. Pignatelli, the would-be informer on the Corleones' activities, kills himself when reminded of the duty of a Roman senator who has done wrong. The Corleones, even with their client senator, can be put down as men with "oily hair in a clean country," and Michael is dismissed as "trying to pass yourself off as a decent American, you and your whole fucking family." Their integration is not yet complete. Their major businesses remain prostitution, which helps them frame the senator, and gambling, which they discuss in Cuba as the revolutionaries arrive. There is still no suggestion of the scale or the use of Mafia power in America.

For what *The Godfather Part II* analyzes is something different and far more interesting. Vito Corleone, as he rights wrongs in the streets of New York, steals from the rich and gives to the poor, destroys the white-suited Don Fanucci who has preyed on those least able to afford it, is a social bandit with some honor. The romantic presentation of his world up to the moment of the cold murder of the don, suggests that we might have a certain sympathy; that sympathy erodes as we witness the vendetta killing of the man who killed Vito's father and brother. Still, the system of values is intact; Vito remains a figure tinged with heroism, recognizable as the don who will help a poor man at the start of *The Godfather*. This man is not "just a thug." But he is following the course that others like him followed in Sicily for generations. "They may look after themselves," as E. J. Hobsbawm wrote, "and become a strong-arm rural bourgeoisie, like the Mafiosi of Sicily." Hobsbawm distinguishes between the social banditry that can be politically constructive, and the robber barons whose end is power and money for its own sake. *The Godfather Part II* shows that transition, from peasant bandit protecting his own to powerful, bourgeois businessman protecting his wealth, position, and life. The reasons—family, neighborhood, duty—that partly justify the actions of Vito are missing in Michael. Pignatelli knows that, at the first communion celebrations when he drunkenly bellows at Michael for abandoning his roots; brother Fredo, with a drunk blonde and a traitorous plan, epitomizes the change; and Michael himself has a hint of what Vito's rebellion might have meant when he sees the courage of a Cuban revolutionary arrested by Batista's guards. But it is no more than a hint. The revolution in Cuba is only a sideshow in the film, a dash of refugees to the American Embassy and a few vandals smashing parking meters. It lacks significance. For the transition is not seen by Coppola in any political sense. It is the end of family, of tradition; and it is the working out of a disease that might once have been called a curse. Coppola, again, is diagnosing the psychopathy of a family; and the apparently real background of his two Mafia films is actually a dangerous distraction from the powerful matter that is central to them.

After the second part of *The Godfather* Coppola's position in Hollywood was assured. He had the courage to make an idiosyncratic film on a large budget, $13 million, for a film that did not pursue a simple narrative line. The fact that the film's structure was in doubt until the last minute, and friends and associates crowded the editing rooms to help sort out its fundamental problems, was unimportant. Coppola had delivered a powerful sequel, that was enough for Paramount; and, critically, he had a great success. He had shown again that, as director or entrepreneur, he never lacks courage, even when he lacks judgement.

His plans to capitalize on his success changed from month to month. When *The Conversation* opened, he said he wanted to make only small-scale projects, little theater-film affairs that would have no great pretensions to international fame. He cared more, so he said, about the help he had given young talent than about being a "force in either the politics or the power structure or even the business end of filmmaking." He soon found the two activities were not so easily separated. Four months after talking of retirement, he bought 8.66 percent of Cinema Five, a New York–based film distribution company. The man who had renounced power now seemed set for the ultimate power play. He talked of the vital importance of ownership, final cut and control of how and where a film played. Like the American Zoetrope years, this was a time when Coppola wanted a revolution.

He wanted directors to "escape from the kindergarten usually reserved for them. We're still regarded as children the companies have to contend with." He resented the fact that a talent as considerable as Carroll Ballard—"I regard him," Coppola said, "as the most gifted director I have ever become involved with"—should have to "wait five years, hat in hand, for someone to decide to let him direct." It was fighting talk. Zoetrope had been an attempt to build a separate studio, but one that would ally with a major corporation for distribution. Cinema Five looked like an even more radical departure, challenging the "majors" at all their games. Many of the old Zoetrope associates were enthusiastic. They were tired of the faded prints, the dud sound, and the cheapjack restrictions that theatrical release often involves. Coppola seemed to be finding a new way out.

But Coppola was still the volatile, impulsive man that Gary Kurtz remembers. He was building a small empire around San Francisco. He mortgaged his earnings from *The Godfather Part II* to bid for FMPX, a loss-making radio station whose earnings were barely enough to cover its payroll. He bought 82.5 percent of *City*, a news weekly that appeared on Sundays in the Bay Area. He lost $500,000 on its first appearance, according to reports at the time; staked $1 million on revamping it in the summer of 1975 as a square-shaped, stapled substitute for Sunday supplements; and finally chose to fold the company in disillusion. Its most useful result was a story, *The Brotherhood of the Grape*, which Coppola planned to film. He had a theater called the Little Fox; under and around it grew the technical side of American Zoetrope. He had property: an eight-story office building painted pistachio green, from whose top-floor studio he could choose to look out on the Golden Gate or the Condor topless theater. He had 50 percent of a Beverly Hills real estate company called Albuquerque Meadows. He and George Lucas had separated their production companies, but he still had an extraordinarily sophisticated film studio for post-production work. What he really wanted was the support systems that his money could buy for film production and nothing else.

He allowed his bid for FMPX to lapse. His link with Cinema Five produced no revolution. When he was seeking a distributor for *Apocalypse Now*, he sent the film's marketing director Lee Beaupré to New York to check the machinery of distributors and their expertise. Beaupré recommended United Artists and Coppola agreed. He folded the City Publishing Company, and dropped all but a handful of production plans. He still backed Carroll Ballard to make *The Black Stallion*, a project that had been discussed in the earliest days of Zoetrope; and he recruited Wim Wenders, one of the brightest young European directors, to make *Hammett*. Beyond that, he returned to what he most wanted to do, making film.

There would not be small films, nor would earlier talk of the "fun and fantasy" in the Coppola Company distract him from the massive Vietnam horrors of *Apocalypse Now*. He had the money to buy independence on most projects, but he chose one so catastrophically expensive that banks and United Artists were needed to float it. "The films cost so much," he said, "that to really veer from that orthodox way of telling a story, you have to be independently wealthy and subsidize it." *Apocalypse Now* was to be a vision, something phantasmagorical; to back it, Coppola is said to have mortgaged everything. His various companies were now, he told his staff, to be dedicated to one thing, "me and my work." In a memorandum that reached *Esquire* magazine, he warned of the dangers of loose talk about the business and the disregard for money that so many of the staff had had in the past, which "has come close to crippling me on several occasions." He set standards of dress to dispel the "seven-year ambience of a hippy hangout around the old American Zoetrope that attracted a certain group of young people anxious to work in the film business." He spelt out that "the era of American Zoetrope being a haven for young filmmakers or other directors and creative people to find a home is really not in the cards."

The ponderous memo probably confirmed Hollywood's worst suspicions; John Milius had once called Coppola the "Bay Area Mussolini." But it means only that Coppola has changed direction, again. He may veer back. For his role as entrepreneur was demanding; it could not continue without interruption. Coppola could look back on years in which he was the main support of many of the children of Hollywood. In some cases, they owe their survival to him. "He subsidized us all," John Milius says. "George Lucas and me, Willard Huyck and Gloria Katz, who wrote *American Graffiti*, Hal Barwood, Matt Robbins. Nobody can underplay the debt they owe Francis for that. He is responsible for a whole generation; indirectly, he is responsible for Scorsese and DePalma. You cannot overemphasize the importance he has had. If this generation is to change American cinema, he is to be given the credit, or the discredit. Whichever it may be. . . ."

George Lucas

Born 1944 in Modesto, California, son of small businessman who owned a walnut ranch. After dim high school career, served two years as social science major at Modesto Junior College before attending film school at the University of Southern California. Taught photography to Navy personnel; won scholarships to watch Carl Foreman and Francis Coppola at work; and formed lasting alliance with Coppola, who hired him as assistant on *Finian's Rainbow*, *Rain People* and as vice-president of American Zoetrope. Coppola backed Lucas's first theatrical film, *THX-1138*, produced *American Graffiti*. In 1977 Lucas completed *Star Wars*.

Modesto is a small country town that lives off its wine and its farms. Beyond its few streets lies the walnut ranch where George Lucas was raised. It has one little cinema on its main street. "Films by Jean-Luc Godard," George Lucas says, "do not play Modesto."

It follows that Lucas grew up away from the sophisticated influences that a major city would have offered. His adolescent passion was drag racing, the fine tuning of surreal cars until they roared into fast flight. He was one of the "Superkids," a member of the separate adolescent subculture that grew away from its community to form a mobile, affluent group on its own. He cruised the strip at night, chasing girls and listening to the blaring of the car radio. He was determined to be an auto mechanic and a racing driver, someone who had access to the marvelous, sleek machines that speeded, legally, on tracks instead of perilously on country roads. The dream left little time for schoolwork. He dropped out of high school with average grades of D+. He barely made junior college. There he took photographs for racers and thought of becoming a painter; his father was not enthusiastic. He also studied the sociology that was later to help him build his most spectacular success.

His interest in film came accidentally. He helped build a racing car for Haskell Wexler, the cinematographer; and he narrowly escaped death in a car crash. The meeting, and the accident, convinced him that he should use his visual talents rather than his mechanical ones. Painting seemed a gamble, and photography was problematic. The simplest and easiest solution seemed to be film school. It was a period when nobody thought of building a career on film school, but Wexler helped Lucas to get into USC. "I got there on a fluke," Lucas says, "and coming from a small town with one little theater I didn't really have that much of a background. Producer and director were for me the same general category—the person who made the movies."

His background in painting drew Lucas to the animation department of USC, and the benevolent influence of Herb Kossower. From there, he moved to cinematography; and, by the end of his film school days, he had become, on his own admission, "an editing freak." The progression is logical. It left him with a fascination for what he calls "visual film, the sort of thing the French unit of the National Film Board of Canada was producing." It was film as tone poem, film as metaphor, film divorced from narrative form; he still feels uneasy with theatrical film and its need to push a story along. That weakness often shows in *Star Wars*; Lucas makes a marvelous fireworks display, but finds it difficult to link the explosions and stars and rockets together.

In school he quickly made up for the cinematic dearth he had experienced in Modesto. He found Truffaut and Godard; he learned to love the sensuality of Fellini. He discovered the underground filmmakers of San Francisco, the avant-garde directors like Jordan Belson. That was what an "art film" meant to him. "Up there around San Francisco," he says, "it was a whole different world."

Through friends like John Milius and Walter Murch, he

began to explore facets of cinema that otherwise might never have occurred to him. "At USC we were a rare generation because we were open-minded. We had guys there who did nothing but Republic serials and comic books. I was being exposed to a whole lot of movies you don't see every day. I don't know how else I could have learned so much in the time."

Lucas was a star, but not exactly a model, pupil. He dominated student film festivals with movies more sophisticated and accomplished than his peers. But he constantly broke rules. He bought extra footage to make films longer than class projects allowed. He used his first one minute allocation of film to produce the animated short that won his first student film festival prize. In all, he made eight films while an undergraduate. It was a starry career, and his problems started only when he left school. "Everybody banded together to try to crack the industry," Lucas remembers. "But the door was still closed tight."

Lucas rushed through his undergraduate work because he expected to be drafted for the war in Vietnam. When his turn came he was classified 4F and given a medical exemption. He was unemployed and uncertain. For a time he worked as a cameraman for Saul Bass, the designer of movie titles and director of animated films. He made a living cutting documentaries for the United States Information Agency. "That," he says, "was when I decided that I really wanted to be a director." He went back to USC graduate school for a single semester, January to June in 1968. He was a teaching assistant; he trained navy photographers; and he assembled a formidable crew to make a science fiction short called *Electronic Labyrinth: THX 1138:4EB*. It was a simple, stark picture of some future, authoritarian society. Computers and electronic codes are set against a man running the length of a blind, white corridor. Every move is watched; reality is monitored by cameras and screens. It is powerful but simplistic, a metaphor rather than a narrative. When it was expanded later, its effect was blunted by greater length. What he had already created was a strong poem.

In this short Walter Murch played the voice of God; it

was partly his script. But George Lucas was the director. The pair made "a blood pact like Tom Sawyer and Huck Finn," according to Murch. Both were up for a Warners scholarship to watch films being made in a studio. They had been collaborators throughout their college days and "we agreed," Murch says, "that whoever got the scholarship would turn around and help the other guy."

The winner was Lucas. He went to observe the making of *Finian's Rainbow*; and from that grew his partnership with Francis Coppola. The new alliance gave him a chance to bring Murch into the crew of *The Rain People*, while he himself served as "general assistant, assistant art director, production aide, general do-everything." On the side Lucas worked on a documentary about the making of Coppola's film, "more as therapy than anything else," he says. "I hadn't shot film for a long time." But his main occupation, between five and nine-thirty every morning, was work on a new version of the *THX-1138* script, a project originally devised with Murch and Hal Barwood. It was Lucas's first feature script; he thought it was "terrible." Coppola, when shown it, said simply: "It is. You're absolutely right."

"I wanted to hire a writer," Lucas says, "but Francis said: 'No, if you're going to make it in this business you have to learn how to write.' So he really took me out of my strong points." With Walter Murch, he prepared a new script; it became the first, and only, project of American Zoetrope as a studio.

The making of *THX-1138* was like a film student's dream. There was money enough to work properly, but the studio chiefs in Los Angeles never saw rushes or dailies. Warner Brothers saw no material at all until the rough cut was taken down from San Francisco for their inspection. Only Coppola, their friend and patron, had immediate influence on the operation; and he was, in effect, one of its architects. Working with friends allowed unorthodox methods. Murch allowed the intricate sound track to grow along with the images that Lucas himself was photographing, directing, and editing. The sound montage was an organic part of the film, not a decoration imposed afterward. The tiny crew, with the actors shaven-headed, could travel to locations in a single minibus. George Lucas was out on his own.

His THX-1138 is an individual man who lives in a drug-soothed, bleached-out, nightmare future where sexuality is banned, where all heads are shaven, where ruthless and literally heartless robot police keep order in a subterranean world. Passion, will, love, and lust have all been abolished. As in Truffaut's *Fahrenheit 451*, television has become a surrogate for sex. Only THX-1138 and his roommate called LUH have, for a moment, failed to take their tranquilizers. They find love together and decide to risk the almost inevitable charges of drug evasion. But SEN, a middle-aged man, has lost his roommate and he has decided to rig the computer to allow him to live with THX. Between the discovery of love and sexuality, the wiles of SEN and the risk of certain exposure as a drug evader, THX-1138 goes on the run. He breaks from his prison, a white void, with a hologram who always wanted to be real; and he makes for the surface of the world, past the stinking, dwarfish shell-dwellers and up a final chimney to the surface of the Earth. Below, bathetically, the chase after him is suspended because it has gone over the predetermined budget. THX stands against a giant, desert sun. A bird flies by. That is the substance of the story.

The film works at a near-abstract level. Its premise is classic in science fiction: an individual asserting himself against the social machine. Its first sequence is a quote from a Buck Rogers serial, with Our Hero "exploring the wonderful world of the twenty-fifth century." Its theme encompasses the same crushing of identity that is central to William Cameron Menzies's *Things to Come*. But Lucas works by different methods. The camera is often literally distanced from the action, to establish the weirdness and aridity of the underground world. Only for lovemaking does the camera close in on individuals; and then, it is in soft focus. The paraphernalia of the future world is voyeuristic, full of cameras that pry, screens that show, observers heard casually asking for tighter close-ups on THX as he is stunned into passivity. Its technology is as closely observed as the machines in *Star Wars*. Brisk, brash jet cars escape down endless tunnels, just as in the later film Luke Skywalker takes his jet car across the deserts of Tatooine. Electronic gauges show the robot police closing in on THX-1138 as he speeds for freedom; they resemble electronic games boards or the computer displays used in the attack on the Death Star. The delicate, spun probes that examine the body of THX are like the robot probe that threatens the Princess Leia in her cell. Parts of *THX-1138* have the same guts, panache, and vigor as the later film; they resemble a dress rehearsal. "But it's just not that entertaining," Lucas says. "It's not that commercial a movie." One central trouble common to both films is the lack of character development; but at least in *THX-1138* the premise of the plot is that individuality has been suppressed, that the workers conform in shuffling herds like the geometric processions in Lang's *Metropolis*. Only two individuals are presented, because anonymity is the essence of the underground world.

THX-1138 plays off language in a way that is highly curious. Murch and Lucas evidently wanted to warn their audience of every possible route to nightmare, since the bland voices which control this bleak society are given a set of apparently conflicting clichés to recite. The constant, unfinished question of the authorities is: "Are you now, or have you ever been . . ." It echoes, obviously, the House Un-American Activities Committee at work. Yet an omnipresent voice also offers "the blessing of the State, the blessing of the Masses"; and the eye of God follows monklike figures who have power through faint suggestions of Catholic orthodoxy; there are confessionals where stand pictures of a face like Christ's, and there is a system of repentance and absolution. There is even a constant reminder—"Buy, Be Happy!"—that an affluent, consumer society has dangers too.

Under this wordgame, *THX-1138* is about a particular form of individualism. Lucas calls it the Horatio Alger myth "that if you want something bad enough, you can do it. We are living in cages with the doors open." He finds the same theme in *American Graffiti*; there the cage is

118

life in the small California town, which anyone with initiative can escape. He is sufficiently committed to the idea to see its roots in his own film school days. "Most students sat around and grumbled 'I can't make movies. They won't let me make movies.' I managed to make eight or nine films while I was at school. And I still find the same attitude. I have a friend who works in commercials, and I found him sitting with a hundred thousand feet of film and a full crew and he was saying that what he really wanted to do was to make a feature. And I said: 'What's to stop you?'" Lucas firmly believes that "if you're good, you'll make it."

That facile attitude explains why the full-scale *THX-1138* fails. It is not enough of an idea, a theme, to carry a full-length film. And it is not quite so obvious a proposition as George Lucas likes to think. If he had not been the white, middle-class son of a California businessman, he might well have found it hard to escape his "cage." Many others are not as fortunate. Brute economics keep them trapped. *THX-1138* is committed, paradoxically, to the ideology of plenty—the idea that the constant supply of material goods makes class irrelevant, that will is enough for success. Lucas himself is not a brash man; he is determined rather than arrogant, shy rather than over-assertive. But this self-confident ethic allows him to paint only a shallow, tepid picture of his future society.

The day Warners saw *THX-1138* the American Zoetrope dream was dead. Worse yet Warners recut *THX-1138*. "I don't feel they had the right to do it," Lucas says, "not after I had worked on that thing for three years for no money. When a studio hires you, that's different. But when a filmmaker develops a project himself, he has rights. The ludicrous thing is that they only cut out five minutes, and it really didn't make that much difference. I think it's just a reflex action they have."

The film was not a commercial success, although it found a steady audience in universities around the campus circuit. When, seven years later, it was rereleased in the form George Lucas had originally intended, it still did not take off. Even the fact that it came "from the makers of *Star Wars*" could not make its cold vision into something popular.

It was while Lucas was cutting *THX-1138* that Gary Kurtz came to visit him. Kurtz wanted to discuss the problems and virtues of the Techniscope process, but the talk ranged wider. Together they speculated about the idea of a rock 'n' roll film set in the late 1950s or the early 1960s, in the days before the Beatles and the killing of President Kennedy and the war in Vietnam. Over the next years Lucas distilled his own adolescence in Modesto into a script. He worked with Willard Huyck and Gloria Katz, USC graduates who had married after a suitably romantic meeting at a lecture by Roger Corman. The project was constantly stalled and shelved. Huyck and Katz were offered a chance to make a film of their own, a horror project called *Messiah of Evil,* later advertised as from "the makers of *American Graffiti.*" George Lucas and Marcia Lucas, exhausted by the horrors of the Zoetrope collapse, set off for a long vacation in Europe with packs on their backs. *THX-1138* was showing at the Cannes Film Festival, uninvited, in a back street cinema, but the trip to Europe was mainly an escape.

When they returned, Lucas found that United Artists was prepared to put up a little development money for the *American Graffiti* idea. With his other collaborators out of commission he decided to hire a writer. He found, quickly, that he should have stuck to Coppola's advice. The script was professional but disastrous. It was not authentic. With distaste Lucas says: "The man had put in playing chicken on the road instead of drag racing."

"That was my life," Lucas explains. "I spent four years driving around the main street of Modesto, chasing girls. It was the mating ritual of my times, before it disappeared and everybody got into psychedelia and drugs." He had no intention of allowing the film to be inexact. He wanted to recreate the years when there was, apparently, innocence; the years of transition, before Vietnam, corruption, drugs, and time changed everything. The time he lived was a vital part of our fantasies. It is in the lyrics of the great rock 'n' roll numbers. Europeans who knew nothing of cruising, surfers, or going away for the summer and crying until September; who did not have cars or high school rings; who never wore Chantilly lace; we, too, shared the world of rock 'n' roll.

The tension between our dreams and Lucas's life is what makes the film work for so large an audience. The low light filming, with its curious, golden radiance, becomes a dream. Time is collapsed. All the central characters are confronted with a turning point in the course of a single night. Yet that night could be placed anywhere within a decade. Cars and music span ten years, an era rather than a date. The slogan for the film—"Where were you in '62?" —makes the setting seem fixed in time, but it is not. The reality, the underpinning, is the music; and that goes from the start of Eisenhower's second term to the end of Kennedy's more golden years. "George wrote the script," Walter Murch says, "with his old forty-fives playing in the background." From the beginning, the group—Kurtz, Huyck, Katz, and Murch, as well as Lucas—discussed which tune best went where. They open the film on a giant amber light; as the camera pulls back we realize it is the marking on a radio dial. The structure of the film comes from the radio program, the songs that disc jockey Wolfman Jack plays. Characters take cues from the music. And Wolfman Jack is the unseen center of it all, father figure as much as circus master.

The Wolfman's howl, his wild rock and his wilder phone calls, are part of California mythology; this is long before the time when the Wolfman was found in television commercials. In reality, the Wolfman broadcast from Mexico. "His voice would drift all over the West," Gary Kurtz says. "He would come and go over California on the whim of the weather. While you were listening, he would suddenly fade away; it was a strange, ethereal feeling. And he got the most outrageous phone calls." There were always rumors about him: that he broadcast from an ever circling plane, that his taste for rhythm and blues proved he must be black.

But within the film the Wolfman has another dimension. Like a father, he resolves problems, calms fears, and arranges for meetings that would otherwise be only longings. The one character who ever comes close to him is Curt; after confronting him, it is Curt who can escape the town, while the others stay fixed in their past. Curt is the would-be cynic with a romantic spirit, frightened of catching the plane to go away to college. He spends the night of the film's action, against his will, with a gang of punks. He catches a glimpse of a wonderful blonde girl in a white T-bird, sailing past him on Third Street. The Wolfman is his only means of contact with his golden vision. He finds the courage to drive out to the radio station, enter the corridors, and face the station manager through a maze of reflecting glass; the sound track, in precise counterpoint, plays "Crying in the Chapel." The manager assures him the Wolfman is not there, the Wolfman is only on tape; but as Curt leaves, the manager puts back his head and lets out a Wolfman howl. In that moment of realization, Curt finds the power to face an outside world. On the surface we are watching a meticulous reproduction of the real teenage culture of California in the early 1960s. Beneath the surface is, in terms of Freudian psychology as developed by Jacques Lacan, something as strong and basic as the resolution of an Oedipal complex—that is, Curt learns to repair his sense of loss at separation from mother's earliest warmth. The force of *American Graffiti* comes from the fact that its dreamlike quality also contains reference to the real force of dreams.

American Graffiti is also funny; and it backtracks to the situations and shots of movies in the late 1950s. There are echoes of *High School Confidential*, of *Rock Around the Clock*, of Nicholas Ray's template for the high school film, *Rebel Without a Cause*. The film's climax, a drag race in which the sympathetic John Milner is forced to realize that he has been beaten by yet another generation that overtakes him, is visually close to the chicken run in *Rebel*. The difference is the quality of nostalgia, the knowledge of time passing.

Milner is a child of twenty-two, with a memory that goes back five years; he is getting old, and he feels that "the strip is shrinking all the time." Yet he is still played in the image of James Dean, kindly lit, allowed his dignity; his "piss-yellow deuce coupe," barely a foot off the ground, is allowed its splendor. Only when Milner knows he would have lost the drag race if his rival had not skidded off the road is there a sense of pathos and loss. The character is based on John Milius, an ardent surfer. "George told me about it while it was going on," Milius says. "I guess he saw me in that light because I was a surfer going past my time."

The values of the film come from its social background. The group of teenage characters all have cars; and those who do not are outsiders like Terry the Toad who must be loved despite their obvious material failings. That is the message of dim, blonde Debbie's final commitment to the Toad. Ranking is by possessions; college education is a chance for everybody; there is a sense of democracy among the kids. The love of neighborhood and the profound sexism—the only characters whose fates are described at the film's end are men—suggest the link with suburban values that the film's context would lead us to expect. This is Middletown, in its sunny, golden California version. Women are invisible because they have given up their hard-won independence in wartime for the more stolid values of homemaking. Material goods eliminate the problems of class and aspirations; John Milner, car mechanic, has a machine of his own like Curt Henderson, the would-be writer. The nostalgia in *American Graffiti* is as much for social values that had lost their power by 1973 as it is for the externals of the rock 'n' roll generation.

Ned Tannen was in trouble when the script of *American Graffiti* reached his desk at Universal. The screenplay had been rejected by United Artists, after its initial flush of interest; and it had been "turned down by every other company in town." But Tannen liked the idea. "God knows," he says, "I've made enough mistakes so I can say this wasn't one of them."

Tannen was at the end of a program of films made by directors who had not yet made money. Universal was voicing its corporate doubts about new talent programs. It worried about Dennis Hopper's project after *Easy Rider*, a film apparently lost in Peru on a diet of drugs, drink, and rumor; that project produced the extraordinary but unreleased *The Last Movie*, a fine film about filmmaking. Milos Forman had made his first American film, *Taking Off*, for Tannen; Douglas Trumbull, the creator of soaring space stations and visions of infinity for Kubrick's *2001*, had made a modest, marginally successful science fiction film called *Silent Running*. John Cassavetes made *Minnie and Moskowitz*, the film that helped Martin Scorsese stay alive in Hollywood by providing him with a job and cash. Frank Perry had contributed two films. The program contained quality and imagination. All it lacked was profit. "Really," George Lucas says, "Tannen's program had been cancelled."

"I was having a very difficult time," Tannen says, "persuading the company to let me make *American Graffiti*." Partly, it was a project that came to Universal at the wrong time. "Universal was a very conservative company," Gary Kurtz says. "It was making most of its money in TV, and gearing most of its theatrical film to an eventual sale to TV." The unconventional would not, Universal feared, attract a free-spending network. Moreover, the project arrived just as all the studios were preparing to clear away the debris left by the young directors so eagerly hired after the success of *Easy Rider*. "This community goes through a series of hot flushes when it believes some new messiah is on the horizon," Tannen says. "Those programs could be called the *Easy Rider* syndrome, and they produced some pretty staggering movies."

Then there was the problem of explaining *American Graffiti* to a board of directors. Samuel Arkoff later hit the perfect description: "It is," he said, "a beach picture *x* years later. Well done." But for Tannen, "it was just an idea. Nobody knew what it was. It wasn't based on some book that was a huge best-seller. It wasn't a special effects movie where you have all sorts of gyrations and people could say, 'Oh, boy! That's terrific!' It was a terribly personal, small story." There was no single line on which it could be promoted. "Pictures like *American Graffiti* have to be discovered. There's no way you can hype that kind of movie. What are you going to sell it on?" Even when the film was complete, Tannen says, "nobody in the company had any concept of what that film was. It's funny thinking of it now. It didn't seem funny then."

Universal made a condition for allowing the project to go ahead: find a big name. Lucas did not want stars. The only possible figure who could convince the all-powerful head of the studio, Lew Wasserman, was a producer —Francis Coppola. He was finishing *The Godfather*; he was established and known; he would do very well. Gary Kurtz remembers: "George and I went to Francis and asked him if he'd come into the project with us." (Ned Tannen remembers approaching Coppola himself.) The name proved enough for Universal to put $750,000 into making the film.

Evidently, the "name" they demanded was not enough to make Universal believe the project stood a chance of success. Lucas asked for $10,000 to buy the album rights to the songs he was planning to use on the sound track; Universal refused. When the film had been released, and its success was obvious, they had to pay $50,000 for the rights to the same material. While Coppola and Lucas were exiled from the lot by a strike of the Writers Guild, the studio altered the film. They refused to release the film in stereophonic sound although it had specifically been designed for stereo. And when they first saw a print, there were angry studio executives who believed the entire film was unfit to be released. It took a stormy outburst by Francis Coppola to save the film. Universal owes its gigantic earnings to Coppola's temper.

George Lucas intended the film to be his personal vision; and because he was an experienced cinematographer, he wanted to control precisely how it looked.

When shooting began he pushed himself to the edge of his endurance, working twelve to sixteen hours a day. "I had shot my first picture myself," he says, "and I tried the same on *American Graffiti*. It was just extremely difficult." He had chosen to film on location, in two towns close to San Francisco, San Rafael and Petaluma, that had barely changed since the early 1960s. "We were using very low light levels and it was extremely hard for the operators to see what they were doing. We had two cameras going, and we were using lights of two foot-candles in some scenes when the usual low light level is about two hundred foot-candles. It just looked mushy." By the end of the second week of shooting, half-way through the schedule, it was obvious that Lucas was close to exhaustion. Coppola intervened and told him to ease up; it was simply not possible to be both cinematographer and director on a film that would have been hard to finish on time even with the help of a full crew. But Lucas was determined not to lose the elusive, radiant quality he wanted. "I was leery of bringing in some big Hollywood cameraman," he says, "because a cameraman is what I am, essentially. Francis told me to bring in a friend; and since I had worked with Haskell Wexler, and he had helped on *THX-1138*, I asked him for help." Wexler, one of the best cinematographers of his generation, had a generous habit of answering such appeals. "He was shooting commercials during the day, but he came up almost every night. He did it for free, as a friend. In the end I gave him some points in the movie, and Francis chipped in and gave him some points and he made money. But he came to help just out of friendship." Together Wexler and Lucas kept the soft, warm tone of the film; they devised the gold that surrounds its images of cruising the main street, in search of a dream, a good time, a girl.

Walter Murch came in to shape the sound when the visuals had already been assembled. Universal's skepticism about the project meant money was tight. That changed the scope of the sound and its relationship to the image. In two sequences the change was probably constructive. One is the scene where Curt has to prove his fitness to joint the streetwise Pharaohs by sabotaging a police car. The officers lurk in a used-car lot; Curt fixes a cable to the back axle of their car, and, as a speeding car screeches past, the officers drive off into midair, their back wheels anchored in the used-car lot and the body of their car smashed on the road. In the other sequence Terry the Toad has taken to the fields with Debbie and lost his borrowed car. As the couple walk through the dark woods, Debbie tells flesh-crawling stories of the Goat Killer, a homicidal maniac who leaves a severed goat's head beside his victims. "Both sequences would have had a score," Walter Murch says, "if there had been a budget for it. Since there wasn't, we made a score in sound effects." For the story of the Goat Killer, the eerie, elusive night sounds are more disconcerting than music could be; and, since the radios are far away from the action, the sound does not break the logic of the constant rock 'n' roll music.

That logic was changed by Universal's refusal to make stereo prints of the film. "Originally, we designed the film in stereo," Walter Murch says. "The sound track was theoretically a radio show, with some tracks re-recorded to sound as though they were coming from the cars. As a car drove by, you would have the sound of music driving by. All through the film, people would be swimming in a soup of sound." In the film as it was originally released, that effect does not quite work; even the giant radio dial in the first shot is not quite enough to make the point. Numbers sometimes echo action or character very patly. In the stereo version that Lucas insisted was his condition for allowing a sequel to be made, there is complex crosscutting between speakers at the front and back of the cinema as well as from side to side. The effect is stronger. If you remember, we lived with the radio on; music frames and counterpoints the action.

The pain of Black Thursday came back on the night that Universal first saw the film. Lucas had put his life on the screen, in a film made by his company and largely at his risk. For three years' work he had taken $20,000, rather less than an average schoolteacher could hope to make. And now, in a crowded San Francisco preview, the studio pronounced its verdict. "This film," said one executive, "is a disgrace."

Ned Tannen saw the last of his films failing before it had a chance to start its life. "There was one man who worked in this company," he says, "who shall be nameless. But he was probably the senior editor in Hollywood and he has been in every film book on American cinema. He thought *American Graffiti* was totally unreleasable, and he wasn't unique." The studio's shock was compounded because they had not seen a foot of film before the preview. Like *THX-1138*, *American Graffiti* had been kept carefully away from Los Angeles, Hollywood, and the particular studio executives who had to decide its fate. Now they were assembled with an audience of a thousand to see the final form of their dubious project. "The audience loved it, and went crazy," Lucas says. "Then the lights came up, and the people were walking out, and this one studio man walked back to tell us what he thought of the film. He said it was an embarrassment."

That was when Francis Coppola lost his temper. "He just blew his top," Lucas says, "he was so mad." He bellowed at the studio man: "This poor kid has worked his ass off for you, making a really terrific movie the audience loved, and for no money at all. And you can't even say thank you to this kid, at least for bringing the picture in on schedule." In full flight Coppola reached for his checkbook. "I'll buy the picture back right now," he said. "I'll write a check now. I think it's a great film and I want it back." The check won the point. Faced with this degree of passion, certainty, and cash, the studio executives backed down.

Still, they recut the movie; and still, Lucas resents the fact. "It didn't make the film shorter in a way the audience can feel or understand," he says. It's more a moral issue than anything else." *American Graffiti* lost one sequence because Universal could not buy the rights to a song; "and they had told us," Lucas says, "that they were so friendly with the copyright owners." Another went for reasons of length; Universal, in a fit of unusual punctiliousness, insisted the film should run precisely the 110 minutes required by the contract. "That scene was one of the best in the film," Lucas says. It put Steve, the central character of the film, against his math teacher. "It really strengthened that character," Lucas says. "In the film they put out, Steve is a nothing. The odd thing is, it was the second most popular scene in the movie at the preview, according to the cards we got back." Ned Tannen says that George Lucas agreed to the cuts, such as they were; but Lucas, barred from the studio by the writers' strike, talks of Gary Kurtz "trying to keep them from destroying the film. You spend three years of your life on a movie, and someone comes along and puts a great crayon mark along one side of it and it just drives you crazy."

When the final version was prepared, the studio still quavered and dithered over its release. It might, someone suggested, be a suitable movie for television. "There was a lot of last minute jockeying," Ned Tannen says, "about where it was going to play and how it was going to be advertised." Almost nobody in the studio could understand the title. Against this bland hostility, Lucas and Kurtz took to guerrilla warfare. They rigged the audience for screenings within the studio. "Normally fourteen stodgy old men sit in a room and that's it," Lucas says. "So, we said okay, we'll show them the movie. But we want to show it with an audience of at least a couple of hundred people—crazy kids, everybody's secretary. And after about seven or eight of those screenings, they began to admit that maybe they did have a movie after all."

What hurt most was the background of the men making this decision. "They're people who have never made a movie in their lives," Lucas says, "agents and lawyers with no idea of dramatic flow. But they can come in, see a movie twice, and in those few hours they can tell you to take this out or shorten that. The movie industry was built by independent entrepreneurs, dictators who had a very strong feeling about movies. They knew what they wanted and they made it happen. Now both *American Graffiti* and *Star Wars*, conventional as they were, also were totally off-the-wall projects. I believe a Jack Warner or a Darryl Zanuck would have said, 'Yes, it's a great idea, let's do that.' And it would have happened."

Star Wars began as fourteen pages of story. United Artists, entitled to see each Lucas project because of its interest in *American Graffiti*, refused it. "Universal never formally said no," Gary Kurtz says, "but I knew from talking to the people there that they were uneasy about the idea." As Kurtz and Lucas continued to build enthusiasm within the film world for their earlier movie, their new project for a space fantasy began to seem more plausible. It is a curious form of Hollywood logic: back winners, whatever they do. "If it hadn't been for that success," Kurtz says, "we would not have been able to get *Star Wars* made at any studio because they all had the same apprehensions."

This is how it worked. "We finished *Graffiti* at the end of January, and the answer print [the first full version of the movie] was ready in the first week of February," Lucas says. "That was when we had the arguments about the release dates. We made the deal on *Star Wars* on the first of May, and *Graffiti* came out in August. But the film was building before release. And it was really in Hollywood that it was beginning to build." All Twentieth Century-Fox promised in the May deal was the money to start developing a script. Like all Hollywood deals, this one moved step by cautious step. It did not guarantee the film would ever be written, let alone made. But by the second and third steps in the contract, *American Graffiti* was in release. "It did well in New York and Los Angeles, but it took a while to grow. It wasn't until well into October and November that we knew it was going to be an enormous hit," Gary Kurtz says. Neither he nor Lucas could control the marketing of the film or prevent Universal from selling off the rights in various states of the United States before exhibitors had a chance to see the film. Kurtz had planned to bide his time. "I thought we could go to theaters across the country and say, 'Look, the first week's take is good, the second week is good, book this picture.'" In fact, the second and third weeks of the release were what *Variety* calls "socko" and even "boffo." Mr. Wasserman, the head of Universal, intervened. He ordered his executives to scrap other bookings and made theaters bid again for the film. Mr. Wasserman is not lightly disobeyed.

Now, *Star Wars* was not some obscure science fiction project. It was the next film from the men who brought you the megahit, the superfilm, the most profitable film ever to cost less than $1 million to make. "Each week," George Lucas says, with a mock-rueful expression, "the figures would get worse and worse and more and more ridiculous." The absurdity struck him most painfully because he was still broke. "I was so far in debt to everyone that I made even less money on *Graffiti* than I had on *THX-1138*," he said later. He was living on $9,000 a year. The main prop of his and his wife's lives was Marcia Lucas's work as an editorial assistant. He had borrowed from almost everybody he knew, from his parents, from Coppola, and from his lawyers. He had also spent years working on the prospect of making *Apocalypse Now*, without studio backing or even the chance of it. Now, he decided to have a success.

Star Wars was manufactured. When a competent corporation prepares a new product, it does market research. George Lucas did precisely that. When he says that the film was written for toys—"I love them, I'm really into that"—he also means he had merchandising in mind, all the sideshow goods that go with a really successful film. From the start he thought of T-shirts and transfers, records, models, kits, and dolls. His enthusiasm for the comic strips was real and unforced; he owned a gallery selling comic book art in New York. His first film, *THX-1138*, begins with a suitable text from an old Universal serial. It presents Buck Rogers, and reminds the audience there is "nothing supernatural or mystic: take Buck, he's just an ordinary human being who keeps his wits about him." Star-struck audiences could take their cue from that line. The success of *Star Wars* was neither mystic nor supernatural; neither quality informs its brilliant, empty shell. George Lucas simply kept his wits about him.

From the start he was determined to control the selling of the film and its by-products. "Normally you just sign a standard contract with a studio," he says, "but we wanted merchandising, sequels, all those things. I didn't ask for another $1 million, just the merchandising rights. And Fox thought that was a fair trade." Lucasfilm Ltd., the production company George Lucas set up in July 1971, "already had a merchandising department as big as Twentieth Century-Fox has. And it was better. When I was doing the film deal, I had already hired a guy to handle that stuff."

Lucas could argue, with reason, that he was protecting his own investment of two years' research and writing; and he was also protecting his share of the $300,000 from *Graffiti*, which he and Kurtz used as seed money for developing *Star Wars*. "We found Fox was giving away merchandising rights, just for the publicity," he says. "They gave away tie-in promotions with a big fast food chain. They were actually paying these people to do this big campaign for them. We told them that was insane. We pushed and we pushed and we got a lot of good deals made." When the film appeared, the numbers become other worldly: $100,000 worth of T-shirts sold in a month, $260,000 worth of intergalactic bubble gum, a $3 million advertising budget for ready-sweetened *Star Wars* breakfast cereals. That was before the sales of black digital watches and Citizens Band radio sets and personal jet sets.

The idea of *Star Wars* was simply to make a "real, gee-whiz movie." It would be a high adventure film for children, a pleasure film that would be a logical end to the road down which Coppola had directed his appar-

132

ently cold, remote associate. As *American Graffiti* went out around the country, Lucas refined his ideas. He toyed with remaking the great Flash Gordon serials, with Dale Arden in peril and the evil Emperor Ming; but the owners of the rights wanted a high price and overstringent controls on how their characters were used. Instead, Lucas began to research. "I researched kids' movies," he says, "and how they work and how myths work; and I looked very carefully at the elements of films within that fairy tale genre which made them successful." Some of his conclusions were almost fanciful. "I found that myth always took place over the hill, in some exotic far-off land. For the Greeks it was Ulysses going off into the unknown. For Victorian England it was India or North Africa or treasure islands. For America it was out West. There had to be strange savages and bizarre things in an exotic land. Now the last of that mythology died out in the mid-1950s, with the last of the men who knew the old West. The last place left 'over the hill' is space."

Other conclusions were more practical. "The title *Star Wars* was an insurance policy. The studio didn't see it that way; they thought science fiction was a very bad genre, that women didn't like it, although they did no market research on that until after the film was finished. But we calculated that there are something like $8 million worth of science fiction freaks in the U.S.A. and they will go to see absolutely anything with a title like *Star Wars*." Beyond that audience, Lucas was firm that the general public should not be encouraged to see the film as esoteric science fiction. "We sent them constant memos," he says. " 'Do not call this film "science fiction," it's a space fantasy.' "

The final plot line was concocted after four drafts in which different heroes in different ages had soared through space to worlds even wilder than those that finally appeared. It was a calculated blend. "I put in all the elements that said this was going to be a hit," Lucas says. He even put a value on them. "With *Star Wars* I reckoned we should do sixteen million domestic"—that is, the distributors' share in the United States and Canada would amount to $16 million—"and, if the film catches right, maybe twenty-five million. The chances were a zillion to one of it going further." Wall Street investment analysts, even after the film had opened, shared his low estimates. They felt it could never match *Jaws*. "It's my feeling," said one, "that the fear element draws a few more people."

Both makers and analysts were wrong. *Star Wars* was a "sleeper," a film whose vast success was in doubt until after it had opened for a while. Those doubts affected studio attitudes toward its budget. Only for a great "event," such as *The Godfather* or *Jaws*, will the studios be tolerant and relax their purse strings a little. Lucas and Kurtz had to do battle over budgets. The original sums were so tight that Kurtz told the board of Fox: "This will only work if everything goes perfectly. And it very rarely does." During shooting the designer of the monsters fell sick and he left his work for the sequence in a space tavern incomplete. The sequence did not work in its original form, but the studio would allow only $20,000 more to restage and reshoot the entire scene.

Compared with *2001*—Lucas calls Kubrick's film "the ultimate science fiction movie"—the special effects in *Star Wars* were cheap. Where Kubrick could allow his space stations to circle elegantly for a minute, Lucas always has to cut swiftly between individual effects. But that became part of the film's design. Where Kubrick's camera was static, Lucas and Kurtz encouraged their special effects team to develop ways to present a dogfight in space with the same realism as any documentary about World War II. As is usual in animation, they prepared storyboards, precise drawings of how each frame was to look; but, unlike most animation, they based the drawings on meticulous study of real war footage. They looked for the elements that made an audience believe what they were seeing. For Lucas it was a return to his original interests at USC—the basics of film, recreated with models, superimposition, paintings, and animation. "We used a lot of documentary footage," Kurtz says, "and some feature film footage. We looked at every war movie ever made that had air-to-air combat, from *The Blue Max* to *The Battle of Britain*. We even looked at film from Vietnam. We were looking for the reason each shot worked, the slight roll of the wings that made it look real."

John Dykstra, assistant to Douglas Trumbull on *2001*, retreated to a warehouse in Van Nuys, California. There he developed a camera that could move through any axis, to match real-life movement of wingtips or fuselage, and he linked it with a computer which could remember the movements and duplicate them exactly when a different model was before the camera. That way two separate models, photographed separately, could seem to do precise battle. The surrounding planets were on a painted background; the laser fire was added by animation. Superimposition brought all the elements together. Developing the technique took most of the year and the budget allocated to special effects. "The fact is that we didn't have the money," Lucas said later, "and the key to special effects is time and money. I had to cut corners like crazy. I cut scenes left and right. And I cut out over one hundred special effects shots. The film is about 25 percent of what I wanted it to be."

Arguably, the effects work to better dramatic effect than the spectacle of *2001*. Lucas was invading the territory of Edgar Rice Burroughs, not a laboratory. He was making a series of Tolkien episodes, with dragons, hobbits, wizards like Gandalf, and dark forces with storm troopers like Nazgûl for support. There is no respect for science, no residue of the onetime staple of film—the menace of the atomic age. In this patch of deep space, giant craft can thunder like jet airplanes, and the London Symphony Orchestra can blast its romantic horns and violins. Mere physics says that space is silent. And Lucas contrives his battles well enough to spare us any desire to concentrate on the precise specifications of the craft involved.

But he does not tell a story. It is the basic failing of the film. It lacks true narrative drive and force. It is a void, into which any mystic idea can be projected; an entertainment, brilliantly confected, which is quite hollow. Its only idea is individualism: that a man must take responsibility for others, even at great personal cost and peril. Its idea is, in classic form: "A man's gotta do what a man's gotta do."

The iconography is bizarre. Darth Vader, the dastardly villain, is black. That is common in science fiction. Even in the supposedly liberal *Planet of the Apes* series, the wicked and stupid gorillas are the military, and they are black. The honey-colored chimpanzees are the wise, good scientists. The closer to the color of a California WASP, the better the character; it is a fair rule of thumb. But Darth Vader's forces are storm troopers, armored in white. The wicked Grand Moff Tarkin lives in a gray green world, with gray green uniforms; he is clearly a wicked Nazi. Yet when our heroes take their just reward at the very end, there are images that parallel the finest documentary of Nazism, Leni Riefenstahl's *Triumph of the Will*. "I can see," Kurtz says, "why people think that. I suppose it is like the moment when Hitler crosses the podium to lay the wreath." Critical confusion is not surprising when there are allusions to Nazism as both good and bad. French leftist critics thought the film was Fascist-oriented; Italian rightists thought it was clearly Communist-oriented.

Nor is the vague pantheism of the film coherent. *Star Wars* talks much of the Force, a field of energy that permeates the universe and can be used for both good and evil. It is passed on, with a sword, just as the sword Excalibur is passed on in Arthurian romance; the influence of chivalric stories is strong. But when the Force is used by Luke Skywalker to help him destroy the monstrous Death Star, he is urged only to relax, to obey instincts, to close his eyes and fight by feeling. The Force amounts to building a theology out of staying cool.

Star Wars has been taken with ominous seriousness. It should not be. The single strongest impression it leaves is of another great American tradition that involves lights, bells, obstacles, menace, action, technology, and thrills. It is pinball, on a cosmic scale.

The true curiosity of *Star Wars*, beyond its clever artifice, is the ways in which public response was molded and stimulated. Publicity discussed the sources on which Lucas drew to construct his story. Indirectly that is a key point about the film. It does use film language that derives from the strengths of certain genres—the films about the Knights of the Round Table, the old moralistic Westerns, and the cheap serials that poured from Poverty Row, in which Buster Crabbe was always a hero whether he appeared as Buck Rogers, Flash Gordon, or Tarzan. The story advances, not by any orthodox storytelling, but by telling the audience what to expect. It depends on their cine-literacy. "The real problem was exposition," as Gary Kurtz says. "We always saw the first movie as a kind of introduction to the environment of the characters."

It does not draw on the film grammar, strictly defined, of the films that share its conventions. "If you showed this film to an audience in the 1930s," Kurtz says, "they would not be able to follow what is going on, just because of how filmic language has evolved. The use of fades, dissolves, how things have to be organized was all a little primitive in those serials. We have the advantage of being able to jump over all that now."

But it does use cliché. Luke Skywalker pleads with his homesteading relatives to be allowed to be released from the harvest to join the space academy; it is the repeated theme of films by John Ford, the divide between the settlers and the wanderers. The only direct quotation from Ford in the film, and that a tenuous one, is the fact that the relatives die and their ranch is burned, as in Ford's *The Searchers*. But our experience of Ford's films, and others that use the convention, allows us to read the scene between Luke and his aunt and uncle in more depth than the scene itself would permit. The same mechanism works for the character of Han Solo, a cowboy braggart who blends cynicism with a potential heroism; it works for the duel between Darth Vader and Ben Kenobi, when the story requires Ben's sacrificial death; and it works when a monster tells Luke that it does not like his face. We can immediately read the start of a saloon brawl. Duly, that is what happens.

The cheap serials that poured from Gower Gulch used similar devices. There were conventions for how a proper villain and a proper hero would look. In Ben Kenobi, the hermit knight, we have a perfect equivalent of a Merlin. Lucas even filmed in Death Valley, a basic location for the filmmakers of Poverty Row. But what he takes from the serials is their morality. They always pitted good against evil, without equivocation. They used romantic dress, predictable stories; and "most of the stories," according to Gene Fernett, a historian of Poverty Row, "were glorified morality plays, much more acceptable to audiences as Westerns than were the old morality plays." Now that serials are dead, and Westerns have absorbed ethical relativism, *Star Wars* is left to inherit that tradition of moral certainty. It is no accident that it should also have the romantic dress and the distant setting that absolute moral values now require: "a long time ago in a galaxy far, far away." It offers the ultimate escape, withdrawal from complex questions of morality, and a display of magnificent fireworks as a bonus. It is a holiday from thought.

On May 25, 1977, *Star Wars* went out on test release to twenty-five theaters. In nine days it had grossed $3.5 million. Within two months it had recouped its $9 million costs and its prints and advertising bill, and it was in profit before its general release. Some cynics settled at Ma Maison and the other Hollywood haunts, and they remembered the fate of other films that had gone well on test release: *Young Winston, Hello, Dolly!,* and *Darling Lili.* All had sunk without trace. But *Star Wars* was different, and the industry did not need to fall in love with amiable droids or cheer the heroic Luke Skywalker to see why. The cost of the film was controlled, unlike the run-away juggernauts that broke Hollywood in the 1960s; indeed, in real money terms, *Star Wars* was made on a budget that would not have bought a modest drama in the early 1960s if it involved overseas filming. Its marketing was directed, cleverly, at an audience that was known to exist—the young in summer. It was released carefully, at ordinary ticket prices. Its prospects had been properly researched. Most cynics, even at Ma Maison, read the signs and bought stock in Twentieth Century-Fox as fast as they could. As the share price soared, student groups justified the rise. Again and again they returned to their favorite fantasy. And *Star Wars* received the ultimate accolade which proved its appeal to the young of California; the queues were joined by those dealing in loose marijuana cigarettes.

Twentieth Century-Fox waxed fat on the profits. It kept 60 percent of the film's earnings. Neither Kurtz nor Lucas would talk of how the rest was divided. Alec Guinness was said to be the richest actor in the world because the producers had given him an extra half point in the profits. British tax rates made that claim seem unlikely. But the real point of interest was the attitude of Kurtz and Lucas to giving away profit in order to thank their associates. "Some of the profit was obligated by contract to certain people. Some of it wasn't," Kurtz says. "We used the uncommitted points to say 'thank you' to people for doing a good job. People tell me that's unheard of in the movie business, but I really don't think so. It's a private contract. People just don't talk about it."

George Lucas kept a sizeable interest in any sequels that followed *Star Wars*. That was written into his original contract with Twentieth Century-Fox, at his insistence. The money will be the seed of his other projects. He still dreams of making personal films, concentrating on the poetry of cinema. Ned Tannen says: "The fact that *Star Wars* is the biggest hit ever made and that he doesn't think it is very good, that's what fascinates me about George. It's what I really admire about him, and I certainly think he is wrong."

Brian DePalma

Born 1940 in Philadelphia, son of orthopedic surgeon; raised in Newark, New Jersey. Majored in physics at Columbia University, where he worked in theater and film with Columbia Players and won student film festival prizes for movies such as *Wotan's Wake*. Won writing fellowship to Sarah Lawrence College, where he directed first feature *The Wedding Party* in 1964. First commercial success was *Greetings*; went to Hollywood on disastrous *Get to Know Your Rabbit*; stayed to make *Sisters, Phantom of the Paradise, Obsession, Carrie, The Fury.*

B rian DePalma is a cold and calculating filmmaker, a cerebral man making films in a playground. Around his office stand the bones of one of his films: there are storyboards for every scene, photographs of all the actors pinned in neat rows, and heaps of scripts in different versions. He designs his films schematically, organizing his effects. Once he wanted to be the American Godard, the maker of films that challenged ideas of film. He dissected the documentaries that white, guilt-ridden liberals too often make. He allowed his audience a distance between the performance on screen and reactions to it, a chance for individuals in the cinema to choose what information they would take from the film. He made people aware, constantly, that film is something artificial and created. He showed screens within screens; he split the screen in two; he showed cameras at work; he parodied other filmmakers' styles. His was a cinema of ideas, not a simple window on the world.

He changed. His name now is on the board at the Twentieth Century-Fox executive block, a sign that he is one of the handful of important people in the studio. The other names are producers, directors, the studio executives who make the decisions, and the salesmen who market the product. He has joined them. His early ideas still have echoes in the form of his films, but the substance of radical thought has dissolved in bloody special effects and romantic melodrama and outrageous parody. Where once his films were designed to make people think, now they make people scream. He still loathes Hollywood and escapes to New York as soon as projects are finished. But he is uneasily aware that he needs the machine of the film industry, even if it contaminates and blights. He loves the studio for what it lets him do; he wants success like his friends George Lucas and Francis Coppola and Steven Spielberg. He wants a spectacular hit that will fix his power and keep his name on the executive board. But much as he loves the machine, he cannot live with it. His is the classic dilemma of the one-time independent filmmaker who finds that it takes time for him to find again that degree of independence within the labyrinth of the studios.

A film by DePalma is never accidental in any detail. He can offer a financier a precise prospectus: "Those are the actors, there's every shot in the picture, there's the script. You get exactly what you see there. I'm not a director like Francis Coppola or Marty Scorsese, who shoot so much material and work variations on a theme, trying to discover something as they are shooting. That's fine, but that's a whole different way of working. For Francis and Marty, their movies are almost created in the editing. For me, it's just finishing the design."

DePalma's exactness is like Hitchcock; so, often, are his themes. He plays with his audience, sometimes teasing them so that they involve themselves completely in the action, sometimes distancing them by abruptly introducing a device that makes them recognize the artifice in what they are watching. He uses humor in the middle of horror. In using split-screen devices, his characters may move from side to side on the screen, breaking the logic of the divided image. In his early films the audience is expected to work: in *Dionysus in '69* he shows a Greek tragedy performed before a New York audience; in split-screen the cinema audience can choose whether they will follow audience reactions from the young theater-goers or watch the drama itself. But later, he seduces the audience into sharing a character's dilemma, or he offers them simple horror. His later films work, cleverly, by making the audience accept the reality of what they see. In *Obsession*, the audience has to be caught up in a romantic, tragic melodrama, like any classic Hollywood film that stays within the conventions of realism. In *Carrie* the split-screen device is not designed to make the audience choose what information they want; it is designed, and it fails, to involve them and horrify them. DePalma talks often of voyeurism, of the director as voyeur because he is peering through the fourth wall at the action he photographs; of characters as voyeurs, which they often, literally, are in his early movies; of the audience as voyeurs. It is a confusing metaphor because it contains quite separate strands. Its confusion is not surprising, because DePalma's work rests on a muddle—a muddle of admiration for Hitchcock's ability to design and contrive, with a more chilly view of the artifice of cinema.

As a student at Columbia University, DePalma discovered Hitchcock. "At first, I didn't know exactly why I was so impressed," he says. "It was like suddenly finding someone who is speaking your language and realizing that there is a vocabulary. You begin to be aware of a very grammatical use of the camera, something you only see in a very few directors. I began to realize why Hitchcock engages you so strongly; you were in the same position as the character. You saw the same information the character saw." The essence of cinema seemed to lie in point-of-view shots. But DePalma was fascinated by the idea of voyeurism. "When you're watching something voyeuristically, you can watch the most inane things. You can watch a woman ironing across the street and the key question is: will she go to the refrigerator and take out a sandwich?" He began to think about what cinema could do that theater could not, and he examined the "material of film, instead of just using the camera as an objective recording device for dramatic action. Voyeurism is a direct link with a point-of-view shot." It followed that if something was to be cinematic, it could not deal simply in character scenes, in ideas. "If you start photographing people talking about something, you're already losing the intimacy of the form. You can't hold the audience. They're looking at their watches."

His long hunt for what it is that film alone can do has resulted in movies that sometimes judder from effect to effect, moment to moment. He admits the fault: "My weakness is that character scenes tend to bore me, even though I can make them quite effectively. Essentially, I'm shooting two people talking to each other, and you can't really do too much more than that when you're trying to establish an emotional relationship between two people. You've got to let the audience settle down and make that connection." Unlike most directors, "my roughcuts are usually shorter than my final version. I throw all the character scenes out. The film runs like a crazy windup toy. Then, I start building them back in again."

The mind and the matter were easier to bring together in the early films. There was a political dimension to the games and shocks. There was time to explore ideas. De-Palma's earliest features often split into three sections, each adopting a different style or a different convention of film. As his career developed, he began to realize how much he needed the machine of the film business; and, as he learned that, he suffered a succession of blows. He was fired from his first Hollywood film. He was "dead" for a while in the town that is too superstitious to know failures. He worked in independent productions that were undersold; even when his *Phantom of the Paradise* went to Twentieth Century-Fox for $2 million, it was marketed disastrously and flopped. His friends have the superfilms that allow them to dictate their terms, and he is still waiting. The early, fascinated explorations of cinema grammar, with all its contradictions and paradoxes, has given way to ambition. Brian DePalma wants his freedom back.

"I decided to make a movie because it seemed like something very easy technically to do. I was in college and a member of the Columbia Players, and they wouldn't let freshmen direct plays. So I helped set up a film." For $150 he bought a second hand Bolex 16mm camera, and he used his allowance to finance a forty-minute short, *Icarus,* that he now admits was "pretentious and disastrous, but, nonetheless, a beginning." He had originally planned to be the cameraman because he had the scientific background; his subject was physics. "But I had a falling out with the director. That left me with the cast, and I had to start all over again. I became a director because I had the camera and the film."

DePalma's student films were partly financed from "some equipment I had won at science fairs. I sold that and had some capital to invest." On that and money from home, about $500 a year in all, he managed to complete a second short, *660124, the Story of an IBM Card.* "Pretentious," he says, "but a little better, technically."

His interest in movies grew slowly. "I never became a real movie junkie, like Marty Scorsese and some of my other friends. They have a terrific vocabulary; I sort of acquired it as I went along." As he became more interested in film, he switched course from science to fine arts. He learned film grammar, he says, by making film. "It is the only way you really learn." And he fell under influences that were specific to New York. "What is predominant in the city," he says, "is television. That's where all the networks are and Hollywood seems very far away. All the film schools are oriented toward documentary." He fell under the influence of cinema-verité, of the

Maysles Brothers, and of Leacock and Pennebaker; although those influences spread across the country, the experience of New York streets gave DePalma's ideas a political edge. In the city he learned about class differences, without suburban comfort or the insulation of Beverly Hills or Modesto, California. "I didn't even know there were communities like that in *American Graffiti* until I came out here," he says. And with the documentary makers, he also learned to revere the French New Wave, then reaching American screens for the first time through the New York Film Festival. Godard, above all, was then his idol, although now he tends to play down the influence. In the late 1960s he was certain that he wanted to be the American Godard.

DePalma's third student film proved a breakthrough. It was a simple exploration of silent cinema styles called *Wotan's Wake;* it was liked by Pauline Kael and it won prize after prize, including the Rosenthal Foundation Award for the best film by an American under the age of twenty-five. He hovered on the fringes of New York University film classes. "Jim McBride and Mike Wadleigh were somewhere wandering the corridors. Marty was editing in the class I was making a picture in. But I was very much an outsider." His student film success helped him win an MCA writing fellowship, in the up-river isolation of the mainly female Sarah Lawrence College. For two years there he labored on his first 35mm feature, *The Wedding Party.* DePalma was producer, director, editor, and writer; the film was made with Wilford Leach, a teacher, and an affluent classmate, Cynthia Moore, who put up $100,000 of her own money to get the project made. It is a display of film pyrotechnics: flashy jump-cuts between improvised scenes and frenetic experiments in camera movement and editing style. It owes something, perhaps not enough, to Jean-Luc Godard. Once made, it remained on the shelf despite constant screenings for possible distributors; and its only public showing was financed by DePalma himself in 1969, after the success of *Greetings.* Under all its fast motion and slow motion and sudden juxtapositions, there are some distinguished names: Jill Clayburgh is in the cast. And Robert DeNiro walked in for a casting call and found himself a part.

After *The Wedding Party* was made and the writing fellowship ended, DePalma was back to the hand-to-mouth existence of a would-be film director in New York. The praise that was heaped on *Wotan's Wake* helped him find documentary jobs; he shot *The Responsive Eye,* a record of the opening of the op art show at the Museum of Modern Art in New York, in four hours; and he made money from documentaries for the U.S. Treasury Department. That money allowed him to film *Murder à la Mod.* Its murder story is complicated by DePalma's exercise in styles—the style of soap opera for the first section, since the murder victim lives a soap opera life; in the style of Hitchcock, so DePalma claims, for the second; and in the manner of silent comedy, such as *Wotan's Wake,* for the third. The climax becomes logical since it is shot from the point of view of a deaf-mute. Again, no distributor would take an interest, and DePalma, after opening it himself at the Gate Theater in the East Village, quietly interred the remains.

He had managed to establish himself as promising, and as a promising director, he was entitled to the polite interest of at least one of the recurrent Hollywood new talent programs. In fact, he spent months sitting around the offices of Universal in New York with Charles Hirsch, the head of the studio's new talent programs. "Out of that frustration," he says, "smoking cigarettes and waiting for someone to return our calls, we came up with the idea for *Greetings*." Hirsch's title was grander than his power. He had been appointed because Universal thought he knew New York directors, and he might find some bright new filmmaker; but before *Easy Rider*'s success it was hard to persuade the studio to take any of his recommendations seriously. When *Greetings* was made Universal kept its distance; its basic conservatism had always led it to consider new talent programs much as it would consider charm schools for aspiring starlets: decorative, but not functional. The film was started on 16mm, with $10,000 that Hirsch raised from his parents and from a friend of his parents. "We started to shoot," DePalma remembers, "but there was something wrong with the camera and everything came out a little soft. That took up a whole week of shooting, half our schedule. We looked at the material, and I said to Hirsch: "The worst thing about this is the way it looks. Let's go to 35mm." Fortunately, the laboratory scratched the first material we sent them, all the way through. They felt so badly about it, they gave us the rest of the film and the processing free."

The film was made for $43,000; it took in more than $1 million. It brought DePalma general recognition for the first time. With his crew of eight, who were friends and students from New York University, he managed to make a virtue out of the limitations under which he was working. Purely for economy, he used very long takes. These tend to allow improvising actors to maunder on, but they also give the film a loose, episodic character that develops an exhilarating picture of the generation of 1968 and their particular problems and obsessions. Just because it was shot while the worries were real, it has a raw edge that later reconstruction cannot bring. The film's heart is the plan of three friends to help one of them evade the draft, the most immediate problem facing most of the people working on the film at the height of the Vietnam war in 1968. In its three episodes one man has to be kept awake all night so that he can be exhausted in mind and body when he goes before the draft board. The treatment is picaresque, a series of near hallucinatory encounters. In the second section DePalma returns to his constant obsession with the killing of President Kennedy; in a prolonged take he shows a would-be expert on the assassination tracing the path of the bullets across the naked body of his girl friend. It is a repellent image which captures the weird erotic charge that talk of the Kennedy killing carries in necrophilic radio shows and publications. In the last section DePalma nods to the changes in sexual attitudes: one of his central characters is fascinated by pornography and is inventing a new form of art—peep-art. With all three components put together, sex, assassination, and the draft show a group of young Americans at a point of cultural transition. And they are shown in a context that is real, for *Greetings* is a street film, where the locations are exact and the extras are actually men who are to be drafted. *Greetings* becomes a report on the past.

This time the finished film did find a distributor. Frank Yablans saw it. He had not yet climbed his way to Paramount and *The Godfather*, and he was years away from his role as an independent producer at Twentieth Century-Fox, where he produced DePalma's *The Fury*. He was working with a small-time New York distributor called Sigma 3, which specialized in the sort of films that played art houses across the country. Yablans was excited by the film. He bellowed at his bosses: "If you don't pick up this film, I'm quitting." And, by himself, he stomped round the country to sell the film. DePalma still remembers his campaign with awe. "Literally," he said, "Yablans went from theater to theater with the print under his arm."

The film made money but DePalma saw little of it. It also won the Silver Bear award at the Berlin Film Festival. It was a critical success that was also marketable, largely on the peep-art sequences. DePalma followed it with a film that proved of more intellectual than commercial interest. It is called *Dionysus in '69*, and it records a version of *The Bacchae* of Euripides that was invented by a theater company called the Performance Group. Their form of theater involved interaction with the audience, a relationship as well as a performance. DePalma shot the play with two cameras, recording both the text of the play and the way in which the all-American audience—hip, aware, stoned, and liberated—reacted to the ancient Apollonian and Dionysian ideas. DePalma's film was a documentary that questioned what documentary actually means, and an exercise in the complex grammar of using split-screen. For DePalma used the nature of the performance to work on ideas of editing. Usually, director and editor decide what the audience shall see. They direct our eyes and predict how we will react. DePalma opens options. "Instead of always getting right to the core, sometimes it's better to let things evolve very slowly; you see, cutting itself cuts the human movement and also cuts the sense." By putting the action against the audience on the screen, the film's own audience had a greater freedom to decide what they most wanted to watch. They had to work and establish a relationship with the material presented on the screen.

But although he spent a year constructing *Dionysus in '69*, he had a more pressing commitment: *Greetings* had proved enough of a success for the distributors' parent company, Filmways, to want a sequel. A deal was struck for $120,000. By DePalma's standards it was positively generous budgeting. Again, he used the chance to make his audience work for its pleasures. His film is full of reminders that what a filmmaker puts on film is created for film; and that what is called documentary involves a high proportion of faking, at a moral if not literal level. The sequel *Hi, Mom!* ended unbalanced, on DePalma's own admission. It was split into three sections. One again showed the voyeur character, working in his peep-art; but if he is a voyeur, making art for voyeurs, then where in the infinite regression does that leave us, the audience? The third section, abandoned when the film was completed, showed a housewife filming her own life in a housing cooperative. Between the two came the section that toppled the film's structure. It was simply too powerful to be contained.

In the second part we see the cinema-verité footage shot by a camera crew from NIT, "National Intellectual Television." They have visited a theater event performed by a black group in an empty tenement, and they have recorded the "reality" of what happened. The black cast, painted in whiteface, turn on the liberal, genteel white audience and they harass, rob, beat, and batter them. As

the whites stumble out, ruined physically and emotion-
ally, they cling to the shreds of their liberal posing. "Clive
Barnes," says one, "was right." The absurdity of the liberals, grotesque figures in their full-fledged radical chic,
is the least interesting part of the sequence. For what
DePalma does is to explode the idea of documentary. The
"real" becomes something performed for the cameras, a
sort of lie. "I was trying to show how you lie with documentaries," DePalma says, by way of confirmation. "Those
ridiculous documentaries you see on educational television
all the time about oppressed blacks made by white middle-
class filmmakers. The fact is that the blacks are being oppressed by the economics of that class, yet these people are
running around saying: 'Don't worry. It's all going to be
okay. Here are your food stamps.'"

Then the call came to Hollywood. The town itself is anathema to DePalma. But, as he says, "it is a tremendous playground, and a lot of people want to get in and play." He
took his chance after making *Hi, Mom!* "Warners were
making a lot of young pictures with young directors, and
they wanted some crazy, lunatic New York director to
make this crazy, lunatic comedy. That was the end of the
'give-the-kids-a-break' era when everybody had a picture
to do. George Lucas and I are the only people who came
in on that wave, and survived that wave."
  Warners offered a project called *Get to Know Your
Rabbit*. It was a starring vehicle for Tom Smothers, then a
television star with a faintly radical image. It told the story
of a market analyst who deserts his giant corporation to
become a tap-dancing magician, only to find that he becomes a business in his own right, the center of a corporation run by his former boss. "The idea," DePalma says,
"is that what America did with the revolution was make it
rich, and then completely castrate it. Any time there's a
revolutionary move in America, they find a way to mer-
chandise it so that it no longer affects the system. In fact,
it becomes part of the system." The making of the film was
not a happy experience for anyone; its sole virtue is the

casting of Orson Welles, the master magician and teacher of cinema, as the master and teacher of the magician in the film. "It was," DePalma says, "a situation I could not control. Environment really affects your work, for a start. What you can do has a lot to do with the space you're in. It was very difficult to create any kind of reality for a political comedy on a solid, Hollywood soundstage."

It did, however, teach DePalma the side of film he did not know: the power game. "Tom Smothers got the movie made, so Tom Smothers was the ultimate power. Your control always has to do with why a picture is being made. Is it because you're directing it? Because if it is, and you're the one making all the phone calls and getting people involved and talking it up, then you have most of the control. In theory you could always be fired, or you could be recut; but usually nobody wants to take that sort of responsibility.

"When you go in, everybody seems so helpful. And when you're working, a director does have a lot of power. In that era, especially, they gave you a lot of freedom. Only as you get older do you begin to realize what controls they had, how you were outmaneuvered." At times, the control showed in something as blatant as reinstating a shot that DePalma had refused to do. "I remember that the producers wanted to set up an exterior shot, a drive-up, which I hate. Drive-ups are always a waste of time. I refused, but when I came back from lunch, the camera was being put in place, to shoot the drive-up shot. I'd never had anything like that happen to me in my entire life. As it happens, that was while I was getting on with Tom Smothers. He came over to me and he knew I was unhappy and I explained; and he told the producers he wouldn't do the shot. My power, you see, basically came from his power. As long as we got on, it was fine." Toward the end of the film, however, Smothers and DePalma fell out; Smothers became disenchanted with the film; and the studio, acting like their own allegory, decided to change the ending and emasculate what political statement the film had originally contained. DePalma was fired.

"I was offered another picture," he says, "but I left that because I didn't go along with the casting." The film was *Fuzz*, made with Raquel Welch and Burt Reynolds. "Then I was really dead. Not only did I have one picture on the shelf, I'd walked away from another major picture for reasons nobody in this industry could figure out." It was a cold time. "Everybody is very pleasant. Everybody smiles. But nobody wants to have anything to do with you. They don't give you money, maybe $500 for a project if you're lucky. Because this is a town of winners. They don't want any losers. And they are very superstitious. They don't even want to be around a loser."

It was a time of self-realization. Dark ideas about the film machine began to settle together in DePalma's mind. His situation was desperate, not serious. "But if Ed Pressman had not been able to get the money together for *Sisters*, I'd have been like ninety percent of the other directors around town, looking for a job. As it was, I'd developed *Sisters* while I was working on *Get to Know Your Rabbit*." DePalma knew that he needed the machine of the film business; and he knew that he disliked that need. "I think I first saw the irony when I was out on a publicity tour for *Greetings*," he says. "I am in the midst of a society that is very capitalist, and whose values I completely reject. But I, too, become a capitalist. The problem is that by even dealing with the devil, you become devilish to a certain extent. You need the machine. And once you use it, you are a tainted human being."

Later, DePalma would build a film around that theme, *The Phantom of the Paradise*, in which a rock composer depends on a monstrous machine for his voice, and he sells his soul in blood to keep his voice. It is a constant theme with DePalma. "I try," he says, "to avoid the horrible realities of the life I have to lead in order to accomplish what I'm accomplishing." But he knows that "whenever you deal with money, there's no clean money. You can make message pictures, you can lead a Simon-pure life, but the very fact that you are in that world at all makes you a compromised individual. People who think they're going to sanitize this business, make it straight and honorable, are absolutely crazy."

In 1969 DePalma said that he wanted to be the American Godard. "That would be great." After his experience with Warners, he began to realize that he would have to find a middle way between his commercial and aesthetic needs. He had the awful example of Orson Welles before him, the wunderkind of *Citizen Kane*, unable to raise the money for his later projects and playing small roles in films like *Rabbit*. "When he lost the machine," DePalma says, "he lost so much of what he was." DePalma knew he did not want to be simply a director—a studio hack "who gets in a package with a couple of stars, they throw a script at him, he goes out and does it. He comes into the studio in the morning and he has to ask the guard which stage he's working on." But he wanted to make his own movies, and that meant money and crews and the studio machine. It is a dilemma he resolved brilliantly, once.

Sisters began with an image. "I had this split-screen idea: somebody crawling toward a window and writing their name on it in blood, and somebody watching from another window. You would be seeing it from two directions simultaneously. That was the whole thing, to get those two characters together. That to me is the essence of cinema. God knows, it should be other things as well. But it's that Eisenstein idea, putting those little pieces of film together to give some sort of emotional effect."

What developed from the image was DePalma's masterpiece: the film in which he integrated his taste for complex devices like split-screen, his understanding of Hitchcock's methods, and his ideas and his ambition to make a commercially successful film. *Sisters* (Brit.: *Blood Sisters*) went out through AIP as an exploitation film, sold on a bloody, sensational line; but, like the best of exploitation films, it has a clear intelligence which allows the film to be at once a shocker and an exploration of voyeurism in the cinema, the fundamentals of the medium. "It's very much the story of the voyeur getting it," DePalma says. "The reporter sees the man crawl to the window; she watches and spies, she wants to know what's really going on; and when she finally finds out, she's totally altered by it. It's like an ice pick in the voyeur's eye."

The debt to Hitchcock is immense; and, while the Hitchcock influence on other DePalma films is tenuous and flashy, it is fundamental in *Sisters*. It is a literary link. In the story a reporter is witness to a murder (like James Stewart in *Rear Window*) and can persuade nobody to believe it has happened. The killer is a girl who was one of a pair of Siamese twins. Like the mother figure in *Psycho*, the dead twin possesses her surviving sister; and like Norman Bates in *Psycho*, the sister is driven to kill when her sexuality is aroused because the dead sister, her other personality, takes over. The blackness of DePalma's humor often seems like Hitchcock. After the first killing the psychiatrist husband of the surviving twin conceals the corpse in a sofa; its unseen presence comes to dominate the scene, like the body in the chest in *Rope*. And the score is the work of Bernard Herrmann. When Paul Hirsch began cutting *Sisters* he laid violin shrieks from *Psycho* over the murder, music from *Marnie* over the love scene, and part of the score of *Vertigo* over the dream in which the reporter, Grace Collier, seems to experience the horror of the twins' existence before their separation, outcasts in a surreal world of hysterical nuns and Tod Browning freaks. All those scores are Herrmann's; they are the underpinning, and sometimes the emotional substance, of Hitchcock's films. DePalma tracked Herrmann down in London, where he was living in exile from a Hollywood that wanted big tunes and rock numbers. Herrmann's score for *Sisters* links the film firmly to Hitchcock.

The idea reworks the *Psycho* theme: the film opens on a sympathetic character who will be slaughtered early, just as the woman in *Psycho* dies the moment she engages our sympathy. The split personality—the homicidal dead and the apparently rational living together in one body—is a direct reference to the Hitchcock movie. But in DePalma's film it is not a mother suppressing her son's sexuality; it is a woman repressing her sister. Moreover, when the solution arrives—one twin died during the operation to separate the pair, and the survivor is racked with guilt for living on—it resolves nothing. The crazed twin who first killed her would-be lover now kills her psychiatrist-protector, Emil. The reporter, unable to persuade the police that she really saw a death, is driven into such shock that she herself begins to deny that she ever saw anything. Like the end of *Psycho*, simply knowing what happened does not remove the chill. And, like Hitchcock, DePalma allows himself black humor along the way. When the protector Emil is clearing up the apartment after the first murder, he slips on the blood in a semislapstick routine; and Grace, the reporter, succeeds in dropping the vital clue, a birthday cake, on a detective's foot. At the end, long after there is a solution, the private detective is still disguised as a telephone lineman, keeping watch on the sofa as it rests in a Canadian railway station, waiting for someone to collect the body.

Split-screen is the most striking of DePalma's technical devices in *Sisters*. The sequence from which the plot line grows is brilliantly executed. So, too, is the moment when reporter and police approach the twin's apartment as Emil is frantically clearing up the carnage. Here DePalma allows Emil to cross from frame to frame, breaking the sense of space. But there are other devices, apparently distancing, that punctuate the film and actually help the suspense. DePalma constantly places frames within the frame. He starts with a grotesque television program in which our apparent hero is watching a blind girl undress in the Peeping Tom Hour, and he is debating whether to stay, cough, or leave. DePalma refers constantly to forms of voyeurism—the reporter watching the apartment, the detective with the binoculars at the end. And, aside from DePalma's own ideas of the grammar and counterpoint of split-screen, he also adopts a classic Hitchcock device, that is, cross-tracking. He shows the reporter approaching Emil's hospital, cutting between shots following her from behind and shots tracking in front of her. The homage to Hitchcock helps tell the story. It is neither gratuitous nor flashy. It is the essence of the film.

"I think it is a culture looking for bigger and better highs," DePalma says of the rock world, "whether it is nostalgia or reminiscing or Armageddon." After the success of *Sisters*, Ed Pressman appeared with the money for a DePalma fantasy—the reworking of *The Phantom of the Opera* within the rock culture that fascinates him. It was his subject in *Greetings* in 1968, when rock was almost innocent; now, in 1974, rock had acquired glitter and sadism and gross, fascistic overtones. The demands of the audience had become monstrous. There had never been, for them, anything on television to match the impact of the Kennedy assassination, the endless replays and analyses. "That's what I think the rock world is about," DePalma says, "a world of people consuming themselves in front of you, and you're sitting there applauding and shouting 'Jesus! Do it better! Do it bigger!'"

DePalma's film about rock culture would contain its own assassination, cynically staged and shown on network television at peak hours. When a rock star is killed on stage, the people in the audience crowd around demanding an encore for the one act no man can repeat. The bloodbath that ends the film is greeted by an audience that boogies on as the monsters die before them. Even death becomes a performance, something unreal to be judged and appreciated. Rock horror existed before DePalma invented his *Phantom of the Paradise;* it had produced Vincent Price and Dr. Goldfarb and his bikini machines, a very minor subdivision of drive-in cinema movies. But it had never had so black an edge, nor so self-consciously clever a framework, for the technical devices of *Sisters* recur in *Phantom*. Split-screen allows the audience two views of action, although the effect is to diffuse attention rather than create suspense. At times the voyeuristic motif becomes absurdly complex. The Phantom watches the villain and mogul, Swan, make love to Phoenix, the girl of the Phantom's dreams; as he watches, Swan watches him on closed-circuit television; and the Phantom can watch Swan watching. The screen is, at one point, divided into a battery of four videoscreens, each framing different action. The ultimate joke is that Swan is immortal, unless a videotape of his contract with the devil can be destroyed. The real man is less real than his recorded image. DePalma's contempt for television culture is barbed and cruel. It is also intensely personal. If *Phantom* has any message beyond its pop art gaudiness, it is that the devil runs show business, and that all artists, like the rock composer Phantom, need the machine in order to function.

Before the film could be started legal trouble began. At first the film was to be called "Phantom of the Fillmore," in tribute to Bill Graham's rock Xanadu. Graham sued. The record label owned by the vicious Swan was to have been called Swan Song, but Atlantic Records had a Swan label. The name was quickly changed to Death Records. Rights to the *Phantom of the Opera* title and theme were in dispute. Producer Ray Stark at Columbia had bought the title from Universal and was planning a remake. He consulted his lawyers. The original name of Swan was to have been Spector; understandably, that was too close to Phil Spector, the record producer, and it was thought wise to change it.

Phantom tells how the wicked Swan stole the music of a young composer, and how the composer was framed on a dope charge, shipped to Sing Sing, had his teeth pulled by the Swan Foundation, heard his music stolen by Swan's record company, broke out of jail and into the factory of Death Records only to have his face crushed in a record press. Disfigured and monstrous, he becomes the Phantom of the Paradise, Swan's new rock theater. He wants a girl called Phoenix to sing his music. He blows up a surfing group who attempt his masterpiece, and he confronts Swan. He is given the machine that allows him speech and creation, and he writes his cantata on Faust. But instead of Phoenix, it is an unsubtly stereotyped glitter queen called Beef who sings on opening night, preceded by a sado-rock group called the Undead who, in the fashion of Alice Cooper, assemble a superman from the limbs of stray members of the audience. The Phantom kills Beef. Phoenix becomes the star and makes love to Swan as the Phantom watches. Now come the revelations. The Phantom is not a Faust figure. He has been dealing with a Faust figure in Swan. Both mogul and composer are signed to the devil. The Phantom discovers Swan's plan for a coast-to-coast networked assassination and foils it by destroying Swan's tapes. On stage Swan crumples into age, like Dorian Gray when the portrait was stabbed. The Phantom loses his mask and his deformity is revealed. Phoenix screams. The audience dances on.

The film is full of cinematic references, but, unlike *Sisters,* they obtrude as gags rather than telling the story. Beef is cornered in his shower by the Phantom; we see a shadowy figure, a knife cutting the shower curtain, an echo of Hitchcock's *Psycho.* Beyond the cheap joke there is nothing. The Undead bring their superman to life just as Baron Frankenstein gave breath to his monster in the early James Whale version of the story. The programmed assassination echoes *The Manchurian Candidate.* The Phantom's makeup, his lair, many of his actions, and his great music machine all echo earlier versions of *The Phantom of the Opera*; DePalma's Phantom kills the surrogate singer with a neon flash, while earlier Phantoms used a chandelier. The most fundamental reversal is the ending. In earlier versions the Phantom is pursued through the streets with flaming torches, a night creature to be destroyed. In DePalma's film he is another act to be enjoyed.

In Cincinnati a group of lawyers debated how to shelter their considerable incomes from the Internal Revenue Service and its demands. It was still possible to defer paying tax by investing in a film; because of that, Brian DePalma was able to make *Obsession.* It was a truly independent production, independent to the edge of despair.

Eight months after it was completed, a distributor finally signed to release it; the film's producer, George Litto, had carried a crippling bill for interest on bank loans for all that time. The film's release and distribution serve as a paradigm of the troubles and advantages of the now dead system of tax shelters, which made possible a film in which no distributor was interested. But the film also put severe financial strain on its producer because it was an honest use of the production services concept in American tax law.

"We really didn't have much to sell," DePalma says. "First, there was Paul Schrader's script, called 'Déjà Vu'. All I'd done was *Sisters* and that was considered an AIP picture. There was nothing really financeable. They liked the script, but they liked a lot of other scripts." It took two years to assemble the money—half from the would-be tax shelterers, a quarter from a midwest businessman, and a quarter from Litto himself, an ex-agent who had newly moved into production. "He's like most producers," De-Palma says, "which is like brokers watching the stock market. He's very aware of where certain capital is to be found."

The film was sold eventually to Columbia who, DePalma says, "tiptoed out with it. They were amazed by how well it did." The studio's problems in understanding what it had bought were an uncomfortable echo of Twentieth Century-Fox's problem when they bid $2 million for *The Phantom of the Paradise*. Even that investment, the largest advance a studio had ever given a wholly independent production, did not guarantee a workable strategy for marketing. *Phantom* appeared and evaporated. Now Columbia had given a smaller advance and taken longer to decide that they wanted *Obsession*. They had to contend with a film that had a kidnapping, a killing, and a devious plot line with echoes of the apparent reincarnation of the beloved in Hitchcock's *Vertigo*; but all this was wrapped in a romantic, soft-focused film, a love story that happened to be incestuous. Columbia was puzzled.

Paul Schrader wrote the script; he now believes that

Brian DePalma betrayed it. The story is set in the lush South of New Orleans, the South of romantic vision, all mansions, hibiscus, and Spanish moss. It plays Schrader's own legacy of Calvinism and terrible, crushing, mad-making guilt against the soft South, Italian splendor, and romantic ardor. There is a basic cultural division in *Obsession* that is never resolved. It is romantic and intense but it is also about guilt without the possibility of absolution.

It opens on a New Orleans party, a grand and romantic affair in a soft blue, gentle focus. Michael Courtland and his wife are celebrating their anniversary; they are "the cream of the new South," a romantically loving couple. At the foot of the stairs Courtland waltzes with his tiny daughter in his arms, a dance that will acquire ugly resonance at the end of the film. All is warm, and, abruptly, all is smashed. Courtland waits for his wife to join him in bed, but she never comes. He goes in search of her and finds a ransom note. He takes police advice and delivers only blank paper to the kidnappers. His wife and child die.

Years later, in Florence, Courtland haunts a church that his wife loved. There he meets a woman who is startlingly like his wife. They talk, they fall in love, they return to New Orleans and plan a grand cathedral wedding. Again, the warm world breaks apart. The kidnapping is repeated. This time, Courtland is determined to take real money; he believes that he can expiate his guilt by buying his lover's safety. But Courtland's conniving business partner plants paper, not money, in Courtland's case, just as he planted the apparently innocent girl in the church. The girl is actually Courtland's daughter, a survivor of the kidnapping long ago. The girl boards her plane back to Italy, feeling suicidal; Courtland kills his partner and dashes to the airport with the money, this time as tangible proof that he did love his wife and daughter. He also has a gun that he may use to kill the girl. She, meanwhile, has been taken from the plane after a suicide attempt. The final shot circles and circles the couple as they reunite, the girl whispering Daddy, Courtland registering blank shock. It echoes the waltz at the beginning; but it also serves as metaphor for Courtland's confusion. He has lost a lover and gained a daughter he thought was dead. He has loved but has broken the taboo of incest in doing so. The ending leaves no comfort; and the unsettling effect of that final shot is a trademark of DePalma.

At the end Courtland's act of atonement, the bringing of the money, only uncovers the sin of incest; no true atonement is possible. But the romantic gloss that covers this steely sense of moral helplessness is what throws the film off balance. DePalma lacks the Catholic complexities of a Hitchcock; and he is far removed from the brutal, Calvinist certainties with which Schrader was raised. "Although I had a very strong Catholic background," DePalma says, "I was brought up as a Presbyterian. I don't have any real feeling for Catholic vernacular, although it attracts me for some kind of strange reason." What remains in the film is a sense of psychological truth. *Obsession* spells out the Oedipal element in romantic, blinding love. It comes from past failure, from the moment of separation from mother-love; and this blind love, by comparison, is flawed, like Courtland's irresoluble love for the girl who is also his daughter.

As in *Sisters*, Bernard Herrmann played an extraordinarily important part in the development of *Obsession*. Although *Obsession* takes little from Hitchcock at a formal level, its story echoes the plot of *Vertigo*, in which a man believes he has found the reincarnation of a dead lover. Herrmann had been old and temperamental when DePalma asked him to score *Sisters*. "He had a very short fuse," DePalma says. "A lot of other people found him totally impossible." Still he was Hitchcock's composer. "*Psycho*," as DePalma says, "is not *Psycho* without Herrmann's music." Faced with impassive images, Herrmann could create emotional response that is not contained in the montage or the cinematography or the performances; he can suggest what is happening in the mind. By the late 1960s his credits were becoming scarce, although London agents offered his music to filmmakers by the yard, to assemble as they wanted. His music could appear in films he never saw, such as the Dutch production *Obsessions* with which Martin Scorsese was briefly associated. But DePalma, like George Lucas and Steven Spielberg in their work with John Williams, was interested in the possibilities of the full symphonic score. For that, the logical composer was Herrmann.

From the start Herrmann took an active part in the preparation as well as the final grooming of *Obsession*; he said, before his death, that he considered it his finest score. The film had originally been planned in three acts. The first would be the kidnapping, the second Courtland's unknowing love for his daughter, and a third would reveal the truth of all the relationships. Courtland would have gone to prison for killing his partner; his daughter, appalled, would finish in an insane asylum in Florence. Fifteen years later, father and daughter would meet, and the plot would be unraveled. Herrmann's reaction to that structure was direct. "Get rid of it," he told DePalma. "That'll never work."

As the film was developed Herrmann grumbled at sequences with too much exposition, criticized the pacing, and made perfectionist criticisms of the film's form. "I set up a lot of sequences just for him to play," DePalma says, and that is evident from the final film.

At least three important sequences depend on Herrmann's contribution for their force. When Courtland approaches the Florentine church where he met his wife, the camera movement is a classic device: we zoom forward with Courtland's anticipation but backtrack with his reluctance, both at once. The visual information is nebulous. We see steps and the green and white marble facade of the church. But the music, its two-note chords of omen and grief, its choral requiem, gives us all the emotional information we need. Behind the credit titles the combination of heavy sound track and visual richness looks pretentious; in context it is very powerful. So, too, is the device, at the ending, of keeping the camera swirling in full circles on the faces of Courtland and his daughter/lover as Herrmann's music provides the text of the emotions.

But the most striking of the film's bravura passages for the composer is the payment of the ransom in the second kidnapping. It is a leisurely montage: Courtland boards a paddle-steamer, takes his seat, and watches New Orleans pass. Paddles churn the water. Passing a quay, he must jettison the case that he thinks is stuffed with cash. He glimpses a car pulling up to collect the money as the boat pulls away. The sequence is repeated twice, almost shot for shot. It is part of the mirroring structure that makes wife and daughter identical in Courtland's mind. But its actual content is simple, limited, and slow. All the tension is in Herrmann's great chords. "It was his music," DePalma says, "which gave that sequence all its complexity. He was the master of giving a whole emotional subtext to the characters. That is what makes the film work."

What Brian DePalma needed now was a gigantic, superlative hit. His associates and friends had all managed to find themselves positions of power within Hollywood. But he still had to deal with tax shelter money in Cincinnati, skeptical studio heads, and salesmen who were uncertain what sort of product they had to offer. When he made *Carrie*, funded again on a production services deal by a consortium who called themselves "Carrie's Group," he thought he might finally break the barriers and become a power in his own right.

He had a fashionable story: a plain, frightened girl who has the power of telekinesis, a witch who can move objects at will. Carrie is the child of a repressive, puritanical mother who is obsessed by fear of her own sexuality and the imminent womanhood of her daughter. Carrie's first period, which takes place at high school, is something she has not been taught to expect or understand. She is jeered at for her fears, and she grows vengeful. Her mother forces her into a closet to do penance for "the sins of women," for the time when "Eve was weak, and God visited her with a curse until the end of her days." With menstruation Carrie becomes dangerous, fascinated by her own power to move the world. When the time of the high school prom comes, she is given the greatest privilege and the greatest humiliation that her schoolmates can devise. She is taken to the prom by a blond athlete, acting under orders from his girl friend; she is happy to be recognized by a boy and given the status that her teacher assures her comes from "getting a boy." But as she is crowned queen of the prom, on a rigged vote, a bucket of pig's blood spills over her. Drenched and maddened, Carrie becomes a demon. She turns tables over, unleashes hoses, hurtles bodies around the hall, and brings fire to consume her tormentors. Her white dress, a sign of her chance to play the prescribed role of a "proper" American girl, is drenched in blood. She walks from the burning hall, causes a car driven by her main tormentors to turn over and explode, and returns home to a house of candles and stillness, where her bizarre mother waits at the head of the stairs, knife in hand, muttering, "Thou shalt not suffer a witch to live." When the mother strikes, Carrie defends herself with knives, skewers, choppers, and peelers that move at Carrie's will and crucify her mother against the wall. She retreats to the closet, to the refuge of childlike repression of the threatening world; and her awful guilt brings the house down in flames around her. As a coda we see the only sympathetic girl in Carrie's school, the one who would not be associated with the trick of blood. The girl dreams. She goes, in softly framed images, to the place where Carrie died. The forward zoom and the backward track express her cautious walk. She lays flowers beneath a cross marked For Sale, which is scrawled over with a crude graffito, "Carrie White Burns in Hell." As she lays the flowers, a bloody hand shoots out of the earth to seize her.

Carrie is a repellent film. A woman's sexuality has often appeared ambiguous, even the mainspring of danger in DePalma's films; but here it is unequivocally seen as both menacing and disgusting. Menstruation brings ugly powers. The pig's blood that spatters Carrie at the prom is equated with menstrual blood. Carrie's destruction is halted only by her mad mother, whose early talk about the sin of Eve is almost justified by her knife blows that are designed to end her daughter's career of destruction. Woman's identity is seen, even by the kindly, ineffective schoolteacher, as something defined by "having a boy" or "having a man." DePalma uses his high school girls as erotic objects—nymphettes in the showers, girls doing push-ups on the playing fields, with the camera shuffling along, ogling. The film reeks of contempt for women.

This, DePalma fiercely denies. "I like to work with women," he says. "I like women characters. If I were interested in men, I'd make movies about men in similar situations. After all, in *Phantom of the Paradise* men represent both sides of the coin; the Phantom is tortured and manipulated and he strikes back. That is essentially what happens in *Carrie*." Besides, DePalma can argue with some box-office justification, "Women in peril are sometimes more interesting."

The catch is that Carrie does not engage our sympathies. At the moment when she is most humiliated, and when her revenge seems most reasonable, DePalma uses split-screen images. The effect is to distance us again from the misery of her position, and to make us see her only as the dangerous witch. She fits the stereotype of a woman who would be accused of witchcraft: she is plain, an outsider, excluded from the community and living in an old-fashioned home, isolated from real family relationships by the madness of her mother. She is the woman whom charity does not reach; and because of that, communities feel guilty about her and expect her revenge. When it comes, the audience is not allowed to identify with her. DePalma counterpoints the increasingly bloody and demonic figure of Carrie—eyes burning, will engaged—with the destruction she is wreaking. He admits the mistake: "Split-screen is one of the hardest forms to work with. Usually, it's twenty-seven shots of someone shifting a clutch or something dumb like that. The problem is that it basically demands a sense of counterpoint, and few people know how to tell things in straight, melodic line, without worrying about counterpoint."

In *Carrie*, he says, the device "was simply not effective. The audience wanted to go with her destruction. They want a basic Sam Peckinpah sort of sock, hit. But suddenly, you're distracting them. In *Sisters* the split-screen carries information, suspense, counterpoint. My mistake in *Carrie* was that you can't hit the heavy emotional things in split-screen." Even when Carrie's mother is crucified, the overclever camera follows the flying knives rather than illuminating motive or fear.

The film did well but it did not make DePalma the independent power he wanted to be. "It's frustrating," he says, "to have a success and not a blockbuster. I'm surrounded by associates who have monster hits." He knows how curious that argument seems from a man with radical pretensions, who talks at other times of his contempt for capitalism. "I worry about *Carrie* not doing forty million. That's how deranged your perspective gets. I find myself sitting with George Lucas and Steven Spielberg and talking about gross points or how the picture did in New Zealand. It's very easy to see that happening to other people, but when you find yourself doing it, you've got to pick yourself up and get the hell out of here."

Carrie could have changed his career. "When you make something that could set you up in a different position in the business and you lose it again, you have to start all over again. Part of it is money; the only time a director starts to see some money is when a picture takes an immense amount of money. That's when you see your share of the profit, for a change. After all, *Carrie* was my tenth picture, and for every dollar I make, the studio makes ten; it's not a matter of being greedy. But when you have a success, you want it to be as successful as possible. You don't want to be sold short."

The trouble lay, DePalma says, with the studio treatment of the film. "It could have been a very big picture indeed, but they thought of it basically as a horror picture. They didn't try to seek out a large mass audience like *The Omen* or *The Exorcist*. It had all the ingredients to hit that audience, but they merchandised it like a simple

167

horror picture. Then, they were astounded at how well it did. And then, of course, as the word of mouth got round and the audience began to build, they congratulated themselves on how successful their campaign had been."

He fought to get *Carrie* sold more aggressively. "My producer had left the producing business and become a television executive. I was by myself, up there with all those executives who liked me, took me out to lunch, thought I was wonderful, and did absolutely nothing I said. I kept saying to them at meetings: 'Look, guys, why are people going to see this movie? We do not have a bestseller. We do not have any major stars. So how are we going to cross the horror market? How are we going to get out to that big mass audience out there?' " He is envious of the muscle behind supernatural stories like *The Omen*. "They had a very big advertising push, plus, they had Gregory Peck which didn't hurt; plus, they were smart. They had big sneak previews. Everybody knew something was happening, something was coming. *Carrie* was opened in a multiple. We had just one sneak preview. That was very successful. But it wasn't enough."

He catches himself exposing too much bitterness. He explains: "I never was interested in money. That gives me an advantage. Money is just paper. The trouble is that it also represents power. You may not be interested in it, but you have to understand it. If you really know what it means to be a $500,000 director or a $50,000 director, that's power. It gives you influence. And that's the reason you try to get as much money as possible. When you're negotiating, you have to know what money means to them —the studio people, the executives, the agents." He talks of "them" as alien forces, the troublesome spirit in the machine. They have to be countered in an elaborate game. "A lot of my films deal with manipulation," he says, "because I am in a very manipulative business. And I am a very manipulative person. A director manipulates people all the time."

His example, still, is Orson Welles, the master he cast as a magician and teacher in *Get to Know Your Rabbit*.

"Just look at our gods," he says. "Look at Welles. He's the greatest director in the world, and he can't get a job and he's sold out. Totally. Orson Welles on the Johnny Carson show doesn't give us much to hope for. That is the story of this business.

"It's right there for you to see. Beware. Be aware of what you're getting into."

John Milius

Born in Malibu, California, 1944, son of retired St. Louis shoe manufacturer. Surfer, although sent to high school in Colorado, Los Angeles City College, and film school at the University of Southern California. Entered film industry as writer, credited on *Jeremiah Johnson, The Life and Times of Judge Roy Bean, Magnum Force*; uncredited on *Dirty Harry, Jaws.* Directed first feature in 1973, *Dillinger,* for AIP, where he had briefly been a script assistant. In 1974 made *The Wind and the Lion,* then entered production and in 1978 completed *Big Wednesday.*

The colonel of a cavalry regiment in India would have an office like the one John Milius maintains in a bungalow behind Burbank studios. There are decoy ducks, furniture made of cane, the head of a great beast "taken in Yukon, August 1975." Outside there is a stuffed bear, lying on its back; and, on the nameplate, the business is called A-Team. When John Milius wrote the first version of Francis Coppola's *Apocalypse Now* in 1969, the heroes were a crack squad of Green Berets operating on the borders of Cambodia and Vietnam, an "A-Team." The loyalties of John Milius are not difficult to place.

Once he was a surfer and a beach bum, waiting for the great waves in California and Hawaii. He prefers to forget that he was raised in West Los Angeles as the son of a prosperous retired shoe manufacturer from St. Louis. He takes his code of honor from Japanese culture, with its insistence on the vital role of a man's duty and self-will; even in making deals within Hollywood, he says, he has his own personal code of Bushido. He spends part of each day on the phone, dealing in guns. It is a trade which taught him how to handle negotiations with the studios. It reflects his taste for Purdey and Perazzi shotguns, for hunting to kill and eat, for codes of honor that have gone by. His is a world bounded by nostalgia. His heroes live on beyond their proper time, and their individualistic values emerge in a later society as the vicious side of anarchy. The contradiction in John Milius is this: he wants to be a samurai, and it is too late.

Both pose and feelings are important to understanding him. His ideas derive so clearly from cultures and classes to which he does not belong; they are values he has set out to learn. Because they are out of place in the suburbanite America he inhabits, they appear as an enticing, free, individualistic philosophy, glorifying robber barons, men who apply law as they see it, rogue cops, rough-rider presidents, and criminals and their would-be heroic opponents. His ideas are exciting because they allow a fantasy in which rules and regulations can be swept aside, in which bureaucracy dies, discipline comes from within, and individual will is glorified. The fact that all this is incompatible with the freedom of others makes it a socially dangerous line of thought; its language verges on the glorification of strength and will that go with fascism. Because Milius often invents the violent and brutal, and because he seems to despise the common currency of feminism, and because he is an elitist, he is anathema to liberals. He presents himself as a great, ursine figure who dreams of chivalric values and of a past where the duel and the tournament become the ultimate expression of individual heroism and conflict.

"The hunter does not exist without the prey," Milius says, "nor the prey without the hunter." In his films hunter and pursued mirror each other. They depend on each other to create the legend that alone will give them tenuous immortality. They wish to be seen as great men. They will become legends by exceptional acts. As the great men they will transcend the essential absurdity of the one act that can ensure their fame—dying. By becoming mythic figures, long remembered, they make their death worthwhile. What Milius shows is the process by which they build the myth.

The social consequences of this pursuit of legend are swept aside. The mountain man in Milius's script of *Jeremiah Johnson* could never suspend his war against the Sioux through conscience or through logical thought that he might destroy the innocent. "Johnson's revenge becomes legendary," Milius says. "The Sioux themselves say a tribe is measured by how great its enemies are." In *Dirty Harry*, a film that Milius rewrote substantially although he is not credited for it, a rogue cop goes out after a killer in defiance of the proper law; Milius's contribution was the idea of "the cop being the same as the killer, except he has a badge." In Milius's first film as a director, *Dillinger*, the criminal and the G-man both preen themselves for heroism, ensuring stories that can be told to the grandchildren of those who survive. "I deliberately chose Dillinger," Milius says, "because he was a pure criminal. Robbing banks to right social wrongs did not come into it. Dillinger and his opponent are building their legends, building an event. Dillinger actually says: 'You would do what I do, if you had the nerve.' " When Milius turned to epic in *The Wind and the Lion*, he again presented a moment of historical transition, tinged with a romantic regret for the honor code of the desert chieftain, the Raisuli, and a sympathy for the rough-riding President Theodore Roosevelt, a sympathy that exists despite Roosevelt's concern for public relations and his posing and game-playing. The games are a pale imitation of the desert duels and contests of the Raisuli's world; Roosevelt, in reality, is the leader of an imperialist nation that is sending Maxim guns to blast into the Arab world and stop the rival European powers from bringing the world to war. But he shares some of the values of the Raisuli, even though he knows them to be dead values.

Nostalgia for guns and "proper" war is a dangerous sentiment. Milius keeps a fine contempt for filmmakers who have no more to say than "war is hell" or "crime does not pay." But his position is equally simplistic because it never has to engage with present, social reality. The noble past becomes, like the noble savage of Romantic thought in the eighteenth century, an evasion of the immediate issues. It enables film to propose an alternative world into which audiences can, briefly, slip. The question is whether they retain the image of a hero when they leave the cinema. If they do, the impact is utterly destructive to social institutions, without the revolutionary perspective necessary to make such destruction work.

Some of Milius's system of values can be traced back to the moral certainties of early Westerns by John Ford. He has no sympathy with what he calls the "in-between generation" of filmmakers, the liberal television men who invaded Hollywood in the 1950s. His Dillinger never aspires to be a social bandit, righting wrongs, like Bonnie and Clyde in Arthur Penn's film. "I think our generation owes more to the time of Walsh, Ford, and Hawks," Milius says. "I don't particularly like the films of people like Penn and Frankenheimer. In fact, I think American film suffered a great deal because of them." Before he attended film school he rejected American film. "I couldn't afford to go to first-run movies," he says, "and being a surfer, I was kind of a slob. But I do remember the kind of films you took a girl to—*The Prize* or that thing that was called *The V.I.P.s* or *Where Eagles Dare*." He pauses. "That kind of filmmaking," Milius says, "did not interest me an awful lot."

But at the same time he was part of the generation that always watched the late movies on television. "Very early on," he says, "I identified the idea that the reason I liked certain movies was that the same names were attached to them. I figured out that a John Ford was like a William Faulkner or a Herman Melville or any writer that I liked. I wasn't really aware of what a director did; I even thought John Ford made *Red River*. But I learned that you could look at one man's work and follow it."

The key to Milius's values, if not to his style in movies, came in an accidental brush with Japanese cinema. It was in Hawaii in 1962, and Milius was chasing waves. "I stumbled into a theater and saw a week of Kurosawa's films. I thought, this is what I want to be—a filmmaker like this. I was a movie junkie, but for Japanese film. Not too many Japanese films played, but what there was I went to see."

He studied at USC because it was "an elitist school that trained people for Hollywood." Like Lucas, he had been a more than competent artist; his first interest at film school was animation. He won an International Student Film Festival Award for an animated short; but his interest did him little good when he graduated. "The only job I was offered was as an animator," he says. "I could not see myself sitting down and drawing the same figure two thousand times. So, with youthful arrogance, I reckoned I had enough money to live for a time, and I would be a writer. If that failed, I could always be a lifeguard. I knew that job."

Writing was part of a conscious design; Milius planned to become a director by becoming "an extremely expensive writer. That way, I could make deals which said the screenplay would cost nothing, provided I could make the film." The start was slow. In collaboration with Willard Huyck, he wrote *The Devil's Eight*, a low budget bikers' version of *The Dirty Dozen*. AIP bought the script and offered him a job as a story assistant, who sifts ideas for movies and helps to edit scripts. Al Ruddy, then working with relatively low budget films in the years before he became the producer of *The Godfather*, spotted Milius and asked him to work on the script of *Little Fauss and Big Halsy*.

"The big break," he says, "came a year later. Everything happened the wrong way round. I had already written *Jeremiah Johnson*, and now Francis Coppola gave me the opportunity to write *Apocalypse Now*." The project was intended to be another film for the ill-fated American Zoetrope. "On the strength of the first seventy pages of that, the studio decided it should buy *Jeremiah Johnson* and gave me *Dirty Harry* to rewrite." For *Apocalypse Now*

Coppola paid only $25,000. It proved a film that no studio would handle. Warners would not make it, but Warners would not let it go. "There was rioting in the streets about Vietnam," Milius says, "and I think they figured they could only make a movie which was definitely antiwar. Mine was not." But his ugly, surreal inventions about war and violence were clearly so strong that Warners was not prepared to risk another studio succeeding with the project; only with the collapse of Zoetrope was the way open for Coppola to reclaim and rework the script. The deal on *Jeremiah Johnson,* though, was considerably better because of the other script. The terms gave Milius $5,000 down and $50,000 if the film were ever to be made; it was made, it worked, and Milius finally pocketed $90,000. Studios began to think they might need this eccentric, atavistic figure; Milius rewrote *Dirty Harry* for Warners; and he began to cultivate his eccentricity. As a condition of work, he demanded that he be given a shotgun from Purdey of London and a day clear in which to admire it. A studio limousine delivered the gun to his door within two hours.

Milius was never attracted by the idea of being a filmmaker. "I am not fascinated by technology and technique like George Lucas or Steven Spielberg are," he says. His idea was to tell stories. If that meant becoming a monster in order to attract attention, he was prepared to do it. At Warners he converted his office into an imitation of a command post under siege, with guns and military equipment lying casually around. For the first time he posted the name A-Team on his door. He talked of his hunting exploits, of some mystical need to experience the reality of blood and death in hunting animals rather than driving to the supermarket to pick up a cellophane-wrapped package of meat. The talk of war and blood did not, however, give him a warrior past. John Milius, samurai, never passed the medical examinations for the U.S. armed forces.

"It is not good," Milius says, "when writers and directors have early success, and are not blooded, and do not have their work ruined, and do not have the critics attack them. That way, they begin to believe the stories of their success. Having so much of my work bowdlerized made me aware of its enormous fragility."

The trouble on writing assignments was sometimes amusing rather than devastating. The actor George Hamilton asked Milius to rewrite a few scenes for a film about Evel Knievel, the motorcycle stunt-rider. Hamilton complained that the script he had been given was appalling, and he was prepared to give Milius $1,000 a day for some surgery that would save the story's life. Milius took the script, settled in Hamilton's house, read the material, hurled it into a swimming pool, and beat it, ceremoniously, to death with a paddle. Then, in seven days, he rewrote the entire film out of professional pride. His fee was $7,000. When Hamilton returned, he smiled at Milius. "I knew," he said, "you'd do that."

But Milius suffered profoundly under John Huston, who directed Milius's script for *The Life and Times of Judge Roy Bean*. Milius had written a romance about a land where there were only "bad men and rattlesnakes," west of the Pecos in the last wilderness of the Wild West. "This is not the way it was," the first title says, "this is the way it should have been." It is the story of a man making himself into a legend, and apparently transcending death when he returns to save his daughter from the new generation of townspeople who have made Texas a land of oil rather than rough justice and cattle and raw whisky. "Bean was an archetypal American character," Milius says. "A man who comes in and builds something and then is discarded by what he built, a robber baron like Carnegie or Morgan rather than a frontiersman. I wrote a multifaceted character. There were dark, evil sides to that man as well as funny, charming sides. You saw that the evil was necessary at first, but that, as time progressed, it was no longer needed." Milius sighs. "I knew we were in trouble when they cast Paul Newman." Grandeur had become cute; the Judge became charming, the exact antithesis of the gross braggart that Walter Brennan played in Wyler's *The Westerner*. In that film Gary Cooper plays the Judge's opponent. In *Roy Bean* the casting of Newman proves as inappropriate as reversing the roles of Walter Brennan and Gary Cooper would have been. Stars have an awkward way of signifying particular values, however strongly they may act against them.

Roy Bean is a self-appointed judge, an outlaw who slaughters the social outcasts who try to rob him and who establishes himself as the law in a Texas town. "I know the law," he says. "I spend my entire life in its flagrant disregard." He is the head and center of the community until the future arrives: a prissy lawyer, armed with deeds and documents, who mobilizes the reformed ladies of pleasure into a moral army and rides the Judge out of town. The massive machines of oil production take the place of romantic emptiness and peasant life. But the Judge does not die. His daughter inherits his saloon and is preparing to defend it against the final onslaught of the modern world—the bailiffs. The Judge rides back out of the past, a figure long repressed by the community that he now haunts. The town burns in the gunfight that follows; and the Judge, as befits a figure of myth, rides into the flames to his own Valhalla. In a limp coda, Lily Langtry, the actress Bean idolized, visits the wreckage of the town and takes a polite interest. After fire, carnage, and the vivid disruption of present civility by a moral order riding out of the past, the coda is simply absurd.

Huston infuses this myth with self-indulgent charm. He even contributes a more than usually bizarre cameo performance as a mountain man who has long shared his life with a hard-drinking bear. "The whole thing," Milius says, "was horribly mangled." But despite Huston's indifference to his constant protests, Milius stayed on the set. "I fought every day," he says. "And I was blooded well. I was treated horribly. But I knew if I packed my bags and went home, I could never really face myself and say I gave the project my best."

With hindsight Milius developed a gratitude to Huston; he even cast him in the role of a worldlywise counselor to Roosevelt in *The Wind and the Lion*. "Huston really tortures you," he says, "but he was like a drill instructor at boot camp. Now I'm a real Marine and I can like my DI. And I really learned a tremendous amount about directing: how to run a set, how to deal with actors."

Milius had also moved one step further toward the goal of being a writer who was so expensive that it would be cheaper to allow him to direct. He had originally asked $150,000 for the script of *The Life and Times of Judge Roy Bean,* a bargain price that was conditional on Milius directing the film. John Foreman, the producer, refused the condition; but he did agree to pay $300,000 for the script alone. Higher prices have been paid in advance for original scripts, but rarely on a project which made so little money and had depended for its commercial chances on the star rather than the script. Milius had made himself so expensive that, in the year of *Roy Bean* and his collaborative sequel to *Dirty Harry, Magnum Force,* he at last became a director.

"I had a certain fondness for AIP," Milius says, "although they have lost their charm now. Then, they thought only of grosses." He made *Dillinger* for them, knowing he was lucky to have made it. "When I was a story assistant there, I didn't have much hope of directing," he says. "You had to be a cutter, an editor or something, or get to know somebody or perhaps work for Corman. You have to remember that even when *Dillinger* was made, many of the new directors had not yet had their main chance. Scorsese hadn't. DePalma hadn't, really. The people who are now the core of the industry hadn't made big films then."

Working within AIP meant limited budgets; but the company saw *Dillinger* as a picture more sophisticated than some of their other products, a film that might attract the generation that knew the legend of Dillinger as well as the more usual youth market. Milius kept his ambition low: "That film was a way of showing that I could make the actors run from one side of the screen to the other. And it proved I could stage a really terrific gunfight."

The final film was shorn of ten minutes, "the humor," Milius says. But it represents a clear development of his obsessive ideas: man as myth and society at a point of transition. Dillinger himself comes straight from the popular mythology of the 1930s, the bank robber who did not kill, the bandit who defied the economic constraints of a society that was collapsing under the burdens of unemployment, poverty, and misery. To the government he was Public Enemy Number One; to the people he was a hero. Dillinger was the man who did something about his economic suffering. Milius is careful to show the context of his legend; early on in the film he assembles a montage of classic 1930s photographs and newsreel footage.

Even Purvis, the cop who is determined to track Dillinger down, admits the potency of the myth. Purvis recognizes that anarchic individualism no longer fits the world, but he sees that it contributes to his own legend. When Machine Gun Kelly is trapped, he screams: "Don't shoot, G-Men!" And Purvis immediately grasps at the name. "He gave us a name," he says, "which became part of the legend." Hunter and hunted are interdependent. They mirror each other.

Milius shows the effort, the narcissism, that goes into making a legend. Dillinger and his girl, the half-Indian Billie Frechette, debate crossing the Mexican border to safety; but they stay in America, knowing that flight would break the legend. Before going out to rob, they ask each other anxiously: "How do I look?" They are obsessed with public image and newspaper response, but Dillinger wants more. In the bank robbery that opens the film, he announces to the camera that witnessing a Dillinger heist guarantees "stories to tell your grandchildren." And while the gangsters in *Thieves Like Us* and the accidental outlaws of *The Sugarland Express* and the robbers in *Bonnie and Clyde* all share this concern with image, none of them is part of a system as Dillinger is. Purvis is as much a mythomaniac as Dillinger himself; the two define each other and give each other stature. The cop clings to rituals that parallel the narcissism of Dillinger; he has a uniform, a formal dressing before each robbery in a bullet-proof vest, gloves, and an automatic pistol. He has a habit of smoking a cigar, ritually, after rubbing out some gangster. The circularity is completed by the end of the film. Dillinger has made a miraculous escape from a bloody onslaught that kills his gang. He visits the cinema to see *Manhattan Melodrama*, and Purvis finds him and guns him down. An end credit tells us that Melvin Purvis shot himself in 1961 with the gun he used to kill Dillinger.

The surprising quality of *Dillinger* is its warmth. In its rural scenes there are echoes of the humanistic feeling of John Ford, a favorite director of Milius. Dillinger is affectionate and loving with his family. Rural dance sequences underline a sense of community from which the Dillinger gang excludes itself by crime. Away from the gunsmoke Milius shows an ability to conjure lyrical images of America. This lyricism was to take him far away from urban crime or Western drama for his second film as a director.

Dillinger served to prove that Milius could direct. He had already produced scripts which contained almost too many good lines, too many good scenes; he barely allowed time for characters to develop between the rhetoric and the climaxes. Now he began to work on an idea that was deeply influenced by Alexander Mackendrick's film *High Wind in Jamaica*, an epic film told through children, in which the children would prove resilient, able to handle danger, torture, and death without the constant shielding that society provides for the young. Milius planned a film in which myth would be transformed through the perceptions of children; and the children would play an active part.

Willard Huyck had discovered an article in *American Heritage* while both he and Milius were at USC. It told how President Theodore Roosevelt had sent in the Marines to rescue an American man held captive by a desert chieftain in Morocco. It touched several chords in Milius. He reveres the rough-riding, quixotic Roosevelt, with his taste for guns and hunting; Milius has a portrait of the president on his desk. And this Roosevelt was not the careful diplomat of history whose most significant intervention in Morocco had been the Algeciras Convention, which settled the European powers' rivalry in North Africa and staved off the First World War by some nine years. This Roosevelt was a man of honor and decisive action, an individualist defying the constraints of international law and convention. His story merged in Milius's mind with a book by Edith Forbes called *The Sultan of the Mountain*. It tells how an Edwardian lady made her way into the Rif in North Africa and talked with a chieftain called the Raisuli. Slowly, the two elements came together—the chieftain and the woman, the president intervening in the world. It was a period of transition, when machine guns replaced swords of honor. It involved two legends—chieftain and president. And it offered an endless series of mirrors—American diplomats and Arab courtiers; the president and the Raisuli; the indulgent games of Roosevelt, such as his shooting practice with the Kaiser's head as the target, against the sultan's absurd games of polo on bicycles; the civilized talk of wine in a European garden against the exquisite gardens that the Raisuli has made for his desert fort. The vantage point was always to be that of a child: "When I was a kid," Milius says, "I'd have loved to have become a Berber and ridden with the Raisuli."

The problem was raising the money for such an ambitious film. He originally imagined the characters as an older woman, a grandmother, who would be kidnapped by the old Raisuli. Both would have the grandeur of age; it would make them appear awesome to the children and give them a common bond. Into that story would come the brash, new Theodore Roosevelt. It was not a commercial idea, and Milius realized that he must turn his characters toward cliché. Now the woman had to be young and beautiful, because that is what heroines are; and the Raisuli had to be romantic and virile, because that is what heroes are. Roosevelt became a more direct mirror of the Raisuli. "You have to make certain compromises," Milius says, "in order to get the damned things made."

United Artists showed interest but would not write the checks. "Everybody was out of money then," Milius says. "Columbia was deep in debt. MGM was changing; they'd handed over their distribution operation to United Artists. Eventually Columbia took the project, but they didn't want to pay for it all, so MGM came in as well." Milius claims ignorance of the exact mechanics of financing: "I never worry about where the money comes from. I just worry that it gets there on time." But the credits carry a clue. Production services are provided by Persky-Bright and Claridge Associates. Since Persky-Bright was the leading manager of tax shelter consortia—Columbia was staggering under its massive borrowings and crippling bills for interest, and MGM had limited funds of its own for film production—it seems likely that the main financier of *The Wind and the Lion* was the Internal Revenue Service.

What emerges is an elegy for times passed rather than an epic. Mrs. Pedecaris is an American woman in Morocco, kidnapped in the course of civil war by the Raisuli. Cultures clash most vividly in the first few minutes: Mrs. Pedecaris talks about the properties of red wine in an elegant garden, and suddenly Arab horsemen crash through the garden walls and fences. An army comes storming through the town, just as, when Mrs. Pedecaris is finally rescued, the first stage of an American invasion will be through the streets and souks. To save the woman and her children Roosevelt sends a gunboat and marines. But the Raisuli's many enemies—invading Americans, scheming European powers, the forces of the sultan, the brigands who infest the desert—do not count on the loyalty that has grown between Mrs. Pedecaris and her captor. She saves him. At the end the two central legends assess their position. The Raisuli is left framed against a sunset, talking of his time "drifting away in the wind." Roosevelt installs himself beneath the stuffed remains of a grizzly bear, his symbol for American virtues, and seems to regret the end of the power of a man who had, in reality, the life that Roosevelt finds only at play.

"Roosevelt sees an identification with the Raisuli,"

Milius says. "He, Raisuli, and the bear are the last of their kind. The world is about to move forward into an age of machine guns and complicated politics and legalities which are going to make it more difficult for high adventure to take place." Milius's regret is clear. But he laces it with a self-mockery that can be disconcerting. When Roosevelt is in full flight to a gaggle of newspaper reporters about the symbolic importance of the American grizzly bear, he breaks off to make sure they are spelling the difficult words correctly; when he leaves town on a whistle-stop tour, facing the bands and banners and crowds, he orders that the train move more slowly so that he can savor the moment. The Raisuli gives speeches that teeter uncertainly between poetry and pretension. Each one is deflated by the Raisuli's wry comments. "That," Milius says, "is part of me as well. I love to deliver great speeches and then mock it, because I don't take any of it too seriously. I don't take myself too seriously."

The film advances by a series of contrasts, between cultures and between characters. Roosevelt's gun talk while hunting bear matches the Raisuli's inquiries about rifles at a desert tourney. The past—desert duels, cooking meat killed that day, execution by sword, Berber warriors—is ousted by the future—diplomats and admirals discussing policy, marines with bayonets fixed, a tasteful birthday cake, an anticlimactic fading of characters once seen as strong. The film's weakness is a lack of dramatic tension; once Mrs. Pedecaris has been captured, we know that she is safe because we are told of the Raisuli's honor. Only when the Raisuli is himself betrayed, in the film's last minutes, does the narrative flow return. The film glorifies play and honor, the potent male sodality that comes from rivalry. The Raisuli's strong, clean code is seen as infinitely preferable to the soft luxury of the Moroccan court; Roosevelt is seen as a rough-rider of dignity, advised by overcautious, reasonable men like Hay. Yet neither world can continue. The Raisuli's world includes the power to order arbitrary death; that he shows mercy is Milius's device to hide the man's nearly despotic power. Roosevelt has to be controlled by Hay, lest he plunge the entire world into war. It is absolutely necessary that the time of high adventure should end, but Milius still mourns. By his sentiments he commits himself to an essentially rightist position, even to a glorification of feudal power. No New York television liberal, from the generation he despises, could make such a statement or such a movie.

Milius provides ravishing images throughout the film, but especially at the start. The Berbers come through the streets like a great wind, a force scattering the market people. The desert scenes have a sense of scale, of allowing characters to use the entire scope of the Panavision wide screen. Few of the scenes were story-boarded, although the battles were meticulously drawn out. Instead, Milius took devices from eclectic sources. From Kurosawa, his idol, he took the simple trick that makes the Berber invasion so powerful. "If you film horses in light," he says, "there is no sense of speed. They have to move from shadow to shadow so that the light flickers. Whenever forces are crossing the screen, there is usually something in front. It's like *The Seven Samurai*: When horses are riding along a fence, and the camera moves with them, it is the apparent movement of the fence which gives the sense of speed."

His other influence, clearest in the desert sequences, was David Lean and his *Lawrence of Arabia* in particular. From him Milius took the shifting planes of horsemen, battle, figures, and landscape within a single tracking shot. Relationships are always changing between the elements of an image, often with a triangular motion in which the camera stands back as characters approach each other and then comes close as they meet and confront each other.

The Wind and the Lion was not what critics had expected of Milius. It was not violent. It had no link with his claim that violence in film makes an audience feel a "wonderful courage," a mystical feeling whose closest parallel would be sexual climax. It had brisk, brief sequences of battle, and nothing was resolved through fights or killing. If anything, Milius had taken to the lyricism of John

Ford, just as he had earlier absorbed the power of the last line of the master's *The Man Who Shot Liberty Valance*: "Print the legend!" The romantic dominated the brute. But romanticism, with its indulgence and glorification of impulse, remained a sinister mainspring, even for the beautiful images of *The Wind and the Lion*.

After his excursion into the epic, Milius took two roads. The A-Team sign appeared again, this time on a one-story office block on Hollywood Avenue. Milius, with the producer of *Dillinger*, Buzz Feitshans, proposed to act as patron and producer. He planned to back the first film directed by the writer Paul Schrader, creator of *Taxi Driver* and Brian DePalma's *Obsession*. That plan fell through. "Maybe I'll back someone next year," he says, "maybe in ten years. It's a matter of passing something on, traditions, skills, like when I was taught to surf.

"The ultimate aim of A-Team is that it will become a company that makes lots of projects. I shall be the figurehead, and the father figure, and take a percentage; and I won't have to do anything except go off and direct my movie once every three years." It was not quite that easy, but Milius remains wedded to the idea. "In a deal, there's a matter of morality. People screw up careers because they do movies they don't want to do, for more money, or because they'd be working with somebody they think is more important. What matters most is the project and the desire to do a particular piece of work."

Milius set up his own film, *Big Wednesday*. This time, he aimed to move away from the legends he had filmed before. "*Dillinger* is all vicarious," he says, "and when the Raisuli does all those wonderful heroic things, it's what you expect him to do. In *Big Wednesday* I want to show men who, in the course of ordinary life, are asked to act in an extraordinary way." The film drew on the surfing culture with which Milius grew up and on his own ideas of honor and heroism. Again, he wanted to tell the story of "people becoming legends in their own time, and living past their time." The difference was that the central characters were not, this time, from history books. They act what Milius lived.

He cut *Big Wednesday* in editing rooms across a corridor from rooms where storyboards were assembled for Steven Spielberg's film *Hollywood '41*. Milius works with Spielberg, shoots with him, goes sometimes to parties with him; and Spielberg nudges him affectionately in the corridor. "You," Spielberg says, "you're just a producer now."

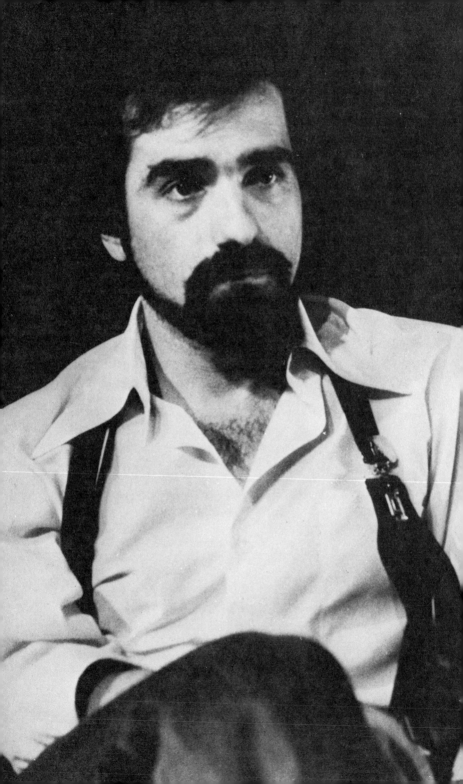

Martin Scorsese

Born 1942 in Flushing, New York, child of Italian immigrant parents who returned to live in Little Italy in New York City in the early fifties; father worked as clothes presser. Expelled from preparatory seminary, studied at Cardinal Hayes High School and Rhodes Academy. Failed to enter Fordham, the Jesuit university, and abandoned ambition to become priest. Studied at New York University, where he was later instructor in film. First feature *Who's That Knocking at My Door?* completed in 1969 after years of survival as film editor, maker of commercials in Icelandic, and a mail-order writer of tough guy dialogue for Dutch films. Later made *Boxcar Bertha*; became known for *Mean Streets*; became famous for *Alice Doesn't Live Here Anymore, Taxi Driver, New York, New York,* and *The Last Waltz.*

Martin Scorsese spent his growing years at the movies. "My father used to take me to see all sorts of films," he says. "From three, four, five years old, I was watching film after film, a complete range. I even saw *Duel in the Sun,* which was condemned by the Church when it came out." He was a child of Little Italy, ambitious to be a priest and learn from the Jesuits. He knew that as an asthmatic he could never make it in the other common occupation of his generation—the trade of a gangster. He still believes that was the essential choice he had to make.

Instead, he became the perfect child of Hollywood. His mind filled with a rich store of images from musicals, Westerns, and gangster films; for each he knew the date, the stars, and even the director. When he grew up, he could fix those images and use them for his own films. He learned to revere the shadowy figures who made them.

He talks of switching vocation between church and cinema, a direct equation between the call to be a parish priest and the desire to be a director. His Sicilian parents were not rich; there was no movie camera at home for him to use. Instead, he drew his own films, frame by frame, to flick through a pencil drawing of a movie screen. Sometimes they were CinemaScope epics, with every robe and pillar added; sometimes they were widescreen or Academy ratio, sepia horrors or even three-dimensional Westerns with cutout guns emerging from the screen. He abandoned three-dimension much when the industry did, because his parents thought he was cutting out paper dolls.

His parents were never strict in their religion, but they were proud that their son should want to be a priest. It was an accepted calling. Scorsese spent some years in a preparatory seminary. In his mind there are still grains of theology, but they appear more as superstition and ritual than as ordered ways of thought, for the substance of Catholic ritual has never left him. The Church, however, has. Martin Scorsese was expelled from the seminary for failing to concentrate on his studies.

In his growing years gangs wore leather jackets and played at Brando. There were girls in the street to distract the would-be priest. Crucially, there was the exploding force of rock 'n' roll. "That music was always very close to me," Scorsese says. "I am almost reverent to it. It expressed a lot of my feelings. I discovered rock 'n' roll in 1956—real rock 'n' roll, Little Richard, Fats Domino, Chuck Berry, Elvis, Screamin' Jay Hawkins. For me, it was a real revolution." The music haunts his films. Rock helps provide the structure for his early movies such as *Who's That Knocking at My Door?* and *Mean Streets*. It provided editing jobs to keep alive between his own films. It even, indirectly, provided the cash for *Mean Streets*, through a producer who had been road manager to Bob Dylan and the Band. His musical *New York, New York* plays brilliantly on the time of transition between big band music and 1950s bebop. His

documentary, *The Last Waltz,* completes the circle by looking at the last concert of the Band, the dissolution of a
great era of rock music. Scorsese's intuitive understanding of the links between music and drama, the style that
is often called operatic, was born in the days of the rock
revolution of the 1950s.

Scorsese was a failed priest. In his attempts to play
gangster, he was notorious for arriving late for gang activities. His skill as painter and graphic artist, his obsession
with the dreamland of the movies seem to lead logically to his time at film school; but, in fact, he first went to
Catholic college, wanted to go to Fordham University, and
was rejected because his grades were not good enough. "I
just wanted," he says, "to be an ordinary parish priest."
With that road blocked, he went to NYU and drifted into
courses on film history. It was his history, too, the experience of his childhood and adolescence. The questions that
faced him were how to use all that early experience of
street life and movie houses and how to value the movies
that had nourished him.

The revelation came when Andrew Sarris proposed his
American adaptation of the "politique des auteurs"—the
auteur theory. "They told us in film school that we had to
like only Bergman," Scorsese says. "Now Bergman's good,
but he isn't the only one. I discovered that I had liked most
of the films those auteurist guys were talking about. I found
there were many other things to do, that you didn't have to
reject totally the films you liked as a child. For three years I
hadn't looked at American movies. I found that very damaging. I had to catch up on TV. Now, you can't even get
prints of some of those films; it's a mess. But Sarris and the
'politique des auteurs' was like some fresh air. We knew
Hawks's name, but we didn't know how good he really was
—how good *Rio Bravo* is, how good *The Big Sleep* is. My
God, I found I liked practically three quarters of the man's
work."

With his New York colleagues Scorsese shares a basic
mix. They've learned the value of American cinema. But
they were also around when the first heady unveiling of

the French New Wave began, largely through the New York Film Festival. "We had the whole European influence," Scorsese says. "There were films showing in New York that never were shown on the West Coast. There was the theatrical tradition as well. And the way the city is situated, between Europe and the rest of America. In California you're cut off from everything, and that can be very destructive for a New Yorker." The European influences came from Resnais, Godard, and Truffaut; Scorsese's first short, *What's a Nice Girl Like You Doing in a Place Like This?*, starts its excursion into the comic territory of Carl Reiner and Mel Brooks with a two-minute reference to Truffaut's *Jules et Jim*. "I was really affected by Godard's early films, and it's an influence that stays with you, although it's not as if I would go out of my way to see them again. The Resnais influence stays with you too. And there are certain shots that Truffaut did which I will never get out of my system. There's a shot in *Shoot the Piano Player* when the girl is pressing the door button, carrying the violin case. He cuts three times, coming in closer each time. That shot's in every picture I make, and I don't know why."

His film school days had one use above all: an economic one. "The whole concept was to be able to get your hands on film and a camera and make a film." With his first short Scorsese remembers feeling his vocation switch from the Church to cinema. "The New York tradition was experimental. That doesn't mean underground films or avant-garde films but rough street films. Documentary was always the thing to try first." His second short, *It's Not Just You, Murray*, used the life of a minor gangster from 1922 to 1965; it was shot on location in Little Italy, a story of two friends who will steal each other's drink or girls. Its roots lay in the streets Scorsese knew; and it served as a sketchbook exercise for the later *Mean Streets*. It was meant to tell about the real life of his family. Later he cut together student footage about the 1970 march on Washington to protest against the Vietnam War; the film had been shot by students who spoiled $16,000 worth of NYU equipment in street brawls, and Scorsese was told, firmly, that he could keep his job as an instructor only if he could salvage a film that would justify the loss of cameras and stock. The result, *Street Scenes*, has only one scene of true power, the one directed by Scorsese; in it, the marching students' impotence and fury, their weekend liberalism, are surgically exposed. In the 1970s he contributed a film about his parents to a television series for the bicentennial about the immigrant threads in American culture. The film, *Italianamerican*, simply shows a dinner and a talk. But through it we glimpse a love story—the long, warm feelings of Scorsese's parents for each other. Even as he was working on *The Last Waltz*, he planned to complete a film on the life of his associate Steve Prince—a street story of guns, dope, and violence. "I believe in these 16mm films," he says. "They should be like chronicles of the period. They should be very rough, like oral history, magazine profiles, character studies. *Street Scenes* would be classified as one of those."

The documentaries about rock did more to pay the rent. Scorsese was the supervising editor on *Woodstock*, that chronicle of peace and love and music when all those terms meant rock and marijuana. He cut *Medicine Ball Caravan*, the staged pilgrimage of rock stars across America, and *Elvis on Tour*, a picture of Presley when the magic had utterly dimmed. Editing was his safety net as he set out into the industry.

Nobody hoped much at NYU, not for success in the mainstream commercial cinema. The students knew "we were facing a real problem in getting into the industry. We all had thoughts of making it, but what we were being taught, technically and economically, about the industry was changing already in the field as the professor was saying it." The New York schools did not teach technical gloss; they concentrated on ideas. "The Californian schools were much more proficient technically," Scorsese says. "We were less oriented to technique, just because our cameras were older."

After studying at NYU as an undergraduate, Scorsese

stayed at NYU as an instructor. There was little choice. The university supported his first two short films; he was in constant contact with the New York school of filmmakers and their ideas; he was influenced by the documentary-makers of the period who were making cinema-verité a common term, men like the Maysles Brothers for whom Scorsese worked as lighting man. His teaching, though, was erratic; he was tense and nervous, and his reticence would suddenly break. Then, he would embark on wildly funny monologues, quite beyond control. "People would come in off the corridors to listen," he says. His teaching load was fairly heavy. "I had one course in elementary film technique," he says. "You know the sort of thing—here's the camera, here's the film, you put the film in the camera this way. There was one other course I taught which was a little more involved; you'd have a script and you'd go out to shoot a three-minute film, and then work on the editing and the post-production. And I taught one course in film criticism."

"What matters to me," Scorsese says, "is that I get to make the pictures—that I get to express myself personally somehow." NYU was hardly likely to support his plans for a full-length feature, and he had no comfortable family resources to fall back on. Making the first feature took two years; and it took two more before the final version reached a public screen, known variously as *J. R.* and *Who's That Knocking at My Door?* The money was scraped together. Scorsese's father raised a few thousand dollars from a student loan; Scorsese's teacher, Hank Manoogian, tapped private sources for the rest, helped by an ex–film student named Joseph Weiler, a practicing New York attorney and the publisher of *Cahiers du Cinema* in English. It was a tiny budget, ludicrous even for a picture made outside union regulations on New York locations. The final total was $35,000. The crew assembled and shot whenever there was a chance; and the erratic schedule resulted in rough continuity, abrupt changes of hairstyle from shot to shot, and limited lighting which made the film more *gris* than the intended *noir*. It was shot partly in 16mm, partly in 35mm. Mike Wadleigh, later the director of *Woodstock*, shot the 16mm footage with Scorsese manhandling the dolly on which the camera was mounted. It was an awkward film full of references to Scorsese's love for John Ford—J. R., the central character, meets his girl by discussing Ford's *The Searchers* with her—and his respect for Godard. The characters' talk of film echoes French filmmakers rather than American ones; native cinema was rarely discussed in American movies then. Hero figures have to be "real bad" like Lee Marvin: "Ever see *Liberty Valance*?" The worst insult is: "Call yourself American? And aren't you ashamed you never saw a John Wayne picture?" But the loose structure, the improvisation all derive from the French New Wave. And taste in cinema helps define one gulf between the boy from Brooklyn, J. R., and the anonymous girl he meets on the ferry. She has books, jazz, an education, and her own apartment, and she likes European art movies. J. R. has rock and a room in his family's apartment, and he likes John Ford. Their meeting is a culture clash.

"We had freedom on that picture," Scorsese says, "up to a point. And that point was whether we wanted the film shown or not." *Who's That Knocking at My Door?* remained on the shelf for four years, a rough and vital film that nobody wanted to buy. Orthodox distributors frowned at its quality. "Sure, the film was so choppy," Scorsese says. "There was no way to take establishing shots because there was no money." It appeared at the Chicago Film Festival in 1967, but it did not find a buyer. Scorsese, expecting no better luck, left America.

"I was just messing around in Amsterdam," he says, "making strange sorts of commercials. We made them in Holland because it was a way of making them cheaper. They were unofficial. One was in Flemish. One was in Icelandic. There were a few British ones for Revlon; how I was making them, I don't know." He worked—"by mail," he says—for the Dutch filmmakers Pim De La Parra and Wim Verstappen, on a thriller called *Obses-*

sions. The Dutch needed tough American dialogue to match their dubious story about a voyeur who peers into his neighbor's flat to discover girl after girl in various stages of naked jeopardy. It was an ambitious project for a small company, and they wanted to sell it in America; but they could not offer Scorsese more work. His main patron was the extraordinary Jacques Ledoux, head of the Cinematheque in Belgium, who offered the money for a short. Scorsese took the offer and made *The Big Shave*. A man, in a white and clinical bathroom, starts to shave himself. His movements become more erratic. He shaves away his face and, finally, cuts his throat. Scorsese's original thought was to end the film on stock footage of Vietnam, to make his allegory of American self-destruction explicit. Happily, he decided that the film did not need the extra pointing.

Then Joseph Brenner intervened. He was a distributor of sexploitation films who had decided to deal in slightly more respectable goods on the side. "He was the only fellow who wanted to distribute *Who's That Knocking*," Scorsese says, "and he wanted a nude scene." Scorsese did not have the money to film in America; instead, he flew Harvey Keitel, the J. R. of the film, to Amsterdam. He shot an inconsequential erotic interlude with a naked girl who appears nowhere else in the picture, a naked Keitel, and a bed. "It was totally irrelevant," Scorsese says. "The only way we could do it was to stop the whole movie and put it right in the middle. As it is the screen goes white, everybody thinks the projector has broken. It's crazy." The segment's sole virtue is its accidental tribute to Godard: the girl is Anne Colette from Godard's *Tous les Garçons S'appellent Patrick*.

But the scene ensured that the film did appear; and it even made the columns of *Variety*, where it was briskly dismissed: "The film's obvious market, with the indicated type of promotion, is in the sexploitation field, where it should easily recover its costs." Years later *Variety* was still insisting that its irrelevant sex scene made it "the precursor of the sexpo tidal wave." That is a bizarre reading. Its real subject is the masculine street life of friends in Little Italy. J. R. is a self-portrait of Scorsese, a man who sees women as fitting one of only two possible categories—Madonna or whore. The girl he meets never has a name, and her tastes and class make her remote from him; but he rejects her and then actually "forgives" her for losing her virginity in a vicious rape. Her suffering is irrelevant; she is not a virgin, and therefore she is a broad. "You don't marry broads." The other side of J. R.'s system of values is the home, where a warm mother bakes under the watchful eye of the Madonna and the holy candles. J. R. refuses to make love to the girl under the eye of the Madonna; it is unthinkable in his culture. Women are never admitted to social life, except as ideals to be courted or broads to be clutched for quick sexual release. Social life revolves around male groups, playing cards, and discussing what to do next; and it can erupt into the threat of violence, toying with guns, and real fear in the faces of party goers. Scorsese uses slow motion to freeze the terror in the faces of the street kids as one of them menaces the others with a pistol. J. R. and his friends are trapped by sexism, Catholicism, violence, and class. They cannot escape to live independent lives like the girl J. R. courts; nor do they have the education that might help them escape their economic position. Little Italy seems bleak.

Scorsese's picture is full of sudden, surprising experiments. The camera swoops in displays of pyrotechnic shooting. Improvisation is allowed to stretch out scenes. The film is raw and vigorous and full of gimmicks, half-digested fragments of *nouvelle vague* technique. It serves as the second sketch for *Mean Streets*, another stage in refining Scorsese's portrait of his own home culture. But it also, valuably, served as a calling card to Hollywood.

It had taken four years to find a commercial outlet for *Who's That Knocking*. Scorsese kept alive with editing chores, working briefly on news film for CBS, cutting

Woodstock with his friend Mike Wadleigh, and working on documentaries. He had one disastrous brush with commercial feature production. He was hired to direct *The Honeymoon Killers*, completed the preproduction work, shot for a week, and was fired. The producers were worried about his complex camera work, his ambitious crane shots. They preferred to leave the project to its writer.

Scorsese left for Los Angeles to cut *Medicine Ball Caravan*, another rock documentary. He wanted to get back to making his own films, to being a director. When he reached the Coast, Roger Corman made contact with him through the William Morris agency. He had seen and liked *J. R.*, which was then the title of *Who's That Knocking at My Door?* He asked if Scorsese would be interested in making a sequel to *Bloody Mama*, Corman's superlatively bloody and perverse exploitation of gangster mythology. Scorsese agreed; Corman promised to call him within six months, when the script was ready; nine months later, Scorsese was on the point of giving up hope. But Corman keeps his word. Nine months after their discussion, the script for *Boxcar Bertha* arrived.

Strictly speaking, it was barely a sequel to *Bloody Mama*; the two films share little more than sex, violence, guns, a strong woman, and a Depression setting. *Boxcar* is not the satirical jibe at American motherhood, with a strong incestuous subplot, which AIP could promote with a billboard reminder that: "The family that slays together, stays together." This project had very different resonances. They fitted Scorsese's political interests as well as his desire to make film.

Boxcar Bertha is orphaned, penniless, and helpless when she embarks on an odyssey across America. Like thousands during the Depression years, she lived in the freight trains that offered free transport, if you could survive. She falls in with Big Bill Shelley, a labor leader of strict principle. Their love story becomes increasingly violent as Big Bill moves from strike leader against the railroad to social bandit, robbing the railroad to contribute to union funds. He confronts the rich railroad owners in their fancy homes to take their cash and jewels. His collision course ends in crucifixion on a boxcar by the railroad's hired thugs; that, in hideous fact, was the fate of some leaders of organized labor in the 1930s. As the train rides on, Bertha runs by its side. Big Bill has become a Christ, a martyr; his fate echoes the biblical quotations that he and the railroad chairman use in their confrontation.

Boxcar Bertha is exceptional in American cinema. It is a popular film; Scorsese says he designed it for "the boys on Forty-second Street," his friends at the big New York movie theaters before these theaters became a mix of porno houses and cruising places. But it deals seriously with the honor of organized labor. Big Bill is a heroic Robin Hood, a man without corruption; the conservative union bosses snarl at him for being a socialist; one bemused character who thinks him a Bolshevik has to admit: "You don't look like a spy. Spies wear glasses." Along with Bill, Boxcar Bertha acquires other companions who achieve heroism. The limp, Jewish cardsharp becomes an ally in the cause of social banditry. The black character ends the film with a blast of gunfire at the white machine that oppresses him. The love of Bertha and Bill transcends the brutishness of their economic position and gives them a lovely dignity; but we are not allowed to forget that "Depression is a word they've got for this empty feeling in the pit of my stomach. . . ."

Boxcar Bertha was made for Corman and by Corman's rules. "If I go back now and think of working on a Corman film in terms of independence," Scorsese says, "I wonder how I could possibly think I was independent at the time. Yet Corman did leave you alone, provided you played it within the genre and didn't get too crazy." His film proves the strength of the exploitation film—the sensational, popular, extreme film that was Corman's stock in trade. Given strong talent and a strong idea, the sheer energy and roughness needed to make a film with such low budgets and inadequate resources can make that film's statement stronger, simpler, and less compromised.

In *Boxcar Bertha* Scorsese delivers the requisite number of sexual encounters, gun battles, and scenes of mayhem; in return, he is free to slam home his political points. Nobody expects him to be moderate. He could make the film as he wanted, provided he spent no more than twenty-four days on location in Arkansas. "If I'd done okay the day before, I got to improvise the next day," Scorsese says. "You had to give and take a little bit."

Oddly, the limited locations actually add to the resonance of *Boxcar Bertha*. Big Bill is equated with Robin Hood, and to achieve that heroic status, his setting must be a little removed from reality. The film becomes a dream in which lumberyard, soup kitchen, brothel, and railroad recur. Scorsese had been intrigued by the idea of working within exploitation cinema, and he used the limitations and the visceral demands of the genre to drive home a statement about the economic and social oppression of the American working class. That did not count as a triumph over the exploitation rules; it worked better because of the exploitation rules.

Corman's next offers did not seem so attractive. One, *I Escaped from Devil's Island,* was a gratuitously sadistic answer to the big budget *Papillon.* The other seemed more interesting. It was called *The Arena* and it dealt with gladiators, as humans rather than objects. It told how they were recruited, trained, and killed. Scorsese was intrigued. But he had worked with John Cassavetes on *Minnie and Moskowitz* before making *Boxcar Bertha,* and now Cassavetes told him firmly that he should steer clear of exploitation and go back to more personal films, like, by implication, those that Cassavetes makes. Scorsese dug out an old script which he had begun with Mardik Martin, an Armenian classmate from NYU. It was to become *Mean Streets*.

Money pressure was pushing Scorsese back to Corman. He wanted to make his own films, but the chances of finding the cash to properly make *Mean Streets* seemed remote. It was not the sort of project that studios wanted to see. By luck, it was his rock contacts that saved him.

He went to dinner with Jonathan Taplin, the road manager for the Band and for Bob Dylan. Taplin was young, ambitious to make film, and he had a good contact for money named E. B. Perry. "What eventually happened," Scorsese says, "was that Taplin liked the script and we got to make the film, with the same Corman crew from *Boxcar Bertha.*" *Mean Streets,* the film in which Scorsese achieved a proper psychological distance from his adolescence in Little Italy, was shot, ironically, not in the New York where it was set but in Los Angeles.

It is Scorsese's story again, a mature version of *Who's That Knocking at My Door?* and *It's Not Just You, Murray.* The audience is hard put to tell, but the first line of the film—"You don't pay for your sins in church, but in the streets"—is spoken by Scorsese himself, before Harvey Keitel becomes the director's alter ego. Instantly, the Ronettes blast out with "Be My Baby," the music of the streets and of the rock 'n' roll revolution. The film is a rock opera, a recreation of Scorsese's adolescent world of rock, arbitrary violence, and urban fears; and it also represents the city's despair and claustrophobia. Daylight scenes seem out of place, just as the street punks seem absurd in the countryside in *Who's That Knocking.* Charlie, Scorsese's stand-in, belongs amid streets that beam with neon in the glinting interior of clubs. The red of the club lighting and the street lighting comes to signal a kind of inferno, an expressionistic device that links Scorsese to his idol, the British director Michael Powell, whose *Peeping Tom* and *Red Shoes* defied the staid naturalism of British cinema in the 1940s and 1950s. Charlie is a would-be saint who actually destroys the lives of others. His life belongs with his buddies; his woman, Teresa, is a private matter, an escapee from the constrictions of Italian-American culture whom Charlie will not fully follow. When she has an epileptic fit, Charlie leaves her to a neighbor; his main concern is his crazed, violent friend Johnny Boy. Violence is part of the macho loyalty between them. Johnny Boy, Teresa's cousin, fires his .38 caliber pistol from a rooftop toward the Empire

State Building and hits a kid who happens to pass him in the street. The narrative framework of the film concerns Johnny Boy's attempts to avoid repaying a debt to Michael, a hustler who wants promotion to minor racketeer; and the film ends with an explosion of violence in which the rules of the group are broken by a hired killer, Michael's method of revenge on Johnny Boy.

Charlie is trapped between families—the mob and the Church. He is seen at prayer, full of piety and love for the Madonna and mother; and he is seen working as debt collector for his uncle, a leading local racketeer. He is trapped by their codes. Teresa represents a possible escape, a halfway house to liberation, but Charlie has to fight on within the gun-toting, pietistic tradition of his families.

The color owes much to Powell; but the camera movement owes much to Samuel Fuller, the ex-newsman whose idiosyncratic action movies from the 1940s and 1950s have now earned critical acclaim. "Fuller's films taught me about emotional violence, which one mustn't confuse with physical violence," Scorsese has said. "Above all, that the emotional violence must be created by the camera, not only by the actor." In *Mean Streets* the handheld camera seems to join a pool hall fight as a participant. When Johnny Boy, the crazy boy, enters the club, there are long tracking shots of great emotional power, where the meaning is never spelled out but derives from the movement of the camera as much as from what is staged for the camera. What we see, how we see it, and how the camera moves in relation to its subject are all integrated perfectly. Sometimes the metaphors are in the images that Scorsese creates—the panthers in the backroom of Tony's club, for instance, are a particular fantasy of masculinity. More often, the camera movement, with the idea that can be written down, together make the point. Scorsese uses the whole language of film to exorcise his past. At the end he himself plays the hired killer who attacks Johnny Boy, and an apocalypse of violence follows. In Little Italy the choice between being a gangster or priest ends with Charlie playing gangster, but on his knees as though in prayer.

Ellen Burstyn was about to be a superstar. She had trained as a Method actress under Lee Strasberg at the Actors Studio; she made an honorable career in films like Bob Rafaelson's *The King of Marvin Gardens*; she had attracted notice with Peter Bogdanovich's *The Last Picture Show*. But until *The Exorcist*, she did not have the power of a star. Now that picture's dubious religion and worse taste gave her the influence to see that projects were made.

She had a personal interest in a script by Robert Getchell called *Alice Doesn't Live Here Anymore*. "She had an 'in' on the property with John Calley, president of Warner Brothers," Scorsese says, "and she had the power and the strength to get what she wanted on it." At dinner with Francis Coppola, she asked what young director could be trusted with the property. Coppola suggested Scorsese, and Ellen Burstyn went to see *Mean Streets*.

Scorsese, meanwhile, was caught in a familiar trap. After *Boxcar Bertha* it took ingenuity to escape exploitation movies. After *Mean Streets* he was offered only gangster scripts. *Alice Doesn't Live Here Anymore* represented something quite different. Women had always been invisible in his films, nameless characters or dispensable cripples like Teresa in *Mean Streets*. *Alice* was a film with a woman as its central character. Her world was utterly different from Scorsese's; she comes from New Mexico suburbs, he from New York backstreets. Her need to depend on someone, to live with someone, mirrors Scorsese's needs; but, beyond that, he knew he would have to stretch to make the film. The only violence is emotion; there are no guns. The women would be neither Madonnas nor whores, and they would answer back. "I wanted," Scorsese says, "to make a film which was completely different, and yet rough, the way I always like it. Rough in camera movement, rough in impact. But at the same time, I wanted to explore elements of the Douglas Sirk films and that whole early 1950s period. I'm interested in them but not fascinated by them. I'm just not interested in what happens in the stories. But I'm fascinated by the cult that surrounds them."

The "woman's picture" had the soft-centered story in which even the most independent woman finally crumbled for love. Douglas Sirk was the Danish-born director whose lush versions of, for example, *Imitation of Life* faced the melodrama head on, and transformed it. In place of cinematic flab, Sirk put muscle; that was Scorsese's inspiration. He opens on credits written across satin and a child singing "You'll Never Know How Much I Love You" from *Hello, Frisco, Hello* before a set which is a direct and expensive homage to William Cameron Menzies, the director and designer of *Things to Come* and *Invaders from Mars*. Scorsese had a mainly female cast and a mainly female crew—Sandy Weintraub, credited as associate producer, Toby Rafelson as set designer, and Marcia Lucas as editor. All three were with the film on location in Arizona, advising and helping. They commented on the reality of the woman's dialogue and behavior. "I tried to make the picture and relationships as real as they can be on screen," Scorsese said. "*Alice* is still, however, a movie about a woman directed by a man."

It opens on a perfect, russet backlot summer evening, an artifice from *The Wizard of Oz*. Alice as a child skips, singing, to her home. Scorsese indulged himself with $85,000 worth of set in order to establish Alice's dream of singing "just as good as Alice Faye." Abruptly, we leave dreamland for Socorro, New Mexico. Alice is trapped in marriage to a boorish truck driver, cooking the lamb "the way he likes it," trying to accept the man's distant approaches at warmth and his constant resentment of their overindulged son. The husband is killed in a truck crash, and Alice is left alone. She sells everything and sets out for Monterey, California, to try to be a singer again. Her monstrous, wisecracking twelve-year-old son goes along. Already the film is making compromises. Alice opts for freedom only when her husband is dead. Her marriage is sketched briefly, not, as Scorsese originally planned, shown and analyzed so that the boorish husband became more human, and Alice's position becomes more firmly rooted in social reality. On the road Alice finds a brief job as a singer; but it ends when she meets a psychopathic lover, listens to the tears of his wife asking for her support, and watches as he smashes into the motel room to threaten both women. Scorsese's camera is hand-held, a perfect example of camera movement containing emotional violence as potently as any violent action shown on the screen; it is a debt to Sam Fuller. Alice and son make their way to Tucson, Arizona, and there Alice works as a waitress; it evolves from being the job that she would never take while there was a hope of singing to the job she defends fiercely to her son: "What's wrong with being a waitress, then?" But the independence she wins at Mel's Cafe and the friendship that grows with her rough-tongued rival for the tips are finally thrown away; she meets a rancher, decides to try again to live with a man, and in effect admits her dependence. All the warmth of sisterhood that goes before dissolves in the face of Alice's overwhelming need to depend upon a man, however obvious his inadequacies.

This ending to a story of a woman surviving on her own is not quite as soft-centered as it seems; both Alice and the rancher are fully aware of all the likely problems ahead. They decide only to try life together. But the effect is to spoil the detail of Scorsese's earlier points. Alice and her neighbor giggle happily in suburbia about the size of Robert Redford's feet and its implications. Alice and her waitress rival have a heart-to-heart in the ladies' room or sun themselves by dusty trailers; when they talk, it is warm, supportive, and loving. But it will not, it seems, do. Alice is forced to be independent by the dramatic death of her husband; we are told there is virtually no money in the bank, so she must work. She cannot do what she most wants, which is to sing in

Monterey. When she finds sexual pleasure with the psychopathic cowboy on her terms—it is the film's one moment of equating sensuality and sexuality—the result is violence and destruction. Her cross-country journey is constantly spoiled or compromised by the needs of her male child.

The simplest sign of how far the film's women are subordinated to men is also its funniest reversal; it is when the third waitress, a sniveling, pathetic woman who always muddles the orders, is whisked off into the night on the back of a Hells Angels motorcycle. Because of the man who meets her, she changes from Olive Oyl to biker's old lady. Moreover, jobs for women are seen as expedients, necessities; the ideal is to escape work. Alice works because she has no choice; her waitress colleague works to buy prettiness for a buck-toothed daughter. When the film first appeared, its feminist pretensions—which were not Scorsese's—were properly dismissed.

The worst idealization happens in the film clips, as when Betty Grable sings in a segment from *Coney Island*, glimpsed on television. But Scorsese's working methods allow a heavy romantic tinge to settle around Alice. He improvises even more than usual, sometimes setting his camera to photograph talk face-on so that lengthy improvisations could be trimmed back later to brief incidents; the style of the confidential talk between Alice and her waitress friend in the ladies' room is studiously neutral, shot face by face so that any combination of shots would be possible in the final version. He made constant retakes, to construct performances line by line. Single phrases from improvisation were adopted for the script; and single intonations on those lines might work better than any other. Scorsese shot in order to use whatever fragments worked best. Rehearsal, retakes, and meticulous cutting all become equally important for the flow of the narrative.

But the process was exploded by Ellen Burstyn. She had the power in the project; she knew Scorsese was on unfamiliar ground; and she was a strongly mannered actress. She turned in the kind of bravura performance that wins Oscars for being noticeable. Improvisation, carefully controlled in *Boxcar Bertha* and *New York, New York*, here became a scatter shot of emotional effects. When Alice and her rancher have first made love, their talk in the kitchen afterward is private, indulgent, inaccessible, and long. It shows how the lack of strong scripting can defocus an entire scene and spoil what we know of a centrally important relationship. Alice, with all the stops pulled out, becomes the dramatic equivalent of a Mighty Wurlitzer—every effect, every color, every tone, and few of them under control.

Scorsese's compromises with Burstyn undermine the film. But he did do something that, at the time, was exceptional. He made a film for a major studio whose central character, however flawed, was a woman. After two decades of near invisibility, woman reappeared in American cinema. Those two decades, unsurprisingly, coincide with the homemaking ideology of suburbia at its peak. Families stayed home and used television as their fireside entertainment; women visited each other, not the cinema; the young went out to the movies in their cars. Community shaped the frontiers of people's lives. It was particularly difficult to affirm woman's identity and the range of possible roles a woman could play. Films simply reflected the attitudes of the men who made the investments, and those men read suburbia like this: men needed a sodality that the family does not offer; women and men over thirty hardly went to the movies anymore; since women play an active social role that is limited to their homes, apparently by choice, strong women will not be popular on screen; women are therefore not a proper subject for cinema, because woman's films have lost their audience. The logic evaporates half of the human race.

Taxi Driver was a labor of love. It was meant to be a personal, obsessive film that could be made on the strength

of some commercial success like *New York, New York.*
That is not how it worked. *New York, New York,* Scorsese's extraordinarily dark musical that derives from the films of the 1950s and personal pain in equal measure, ran into delays. It was shot after *Taxi Driver* and, when it appeared, it staggered around theater circuits, neither losing money nor becoming a manifest hit. *"Taxi Driver,"* Scorsese says, "was the labor of love. And that was the financial success."

Its making linked faith, determination, and money more intimately than usual. Paul Schrader wrote the screenplay out of his own experience—living in a bleak city, gobbling pills and spending nights at porno movies. He took his onetime history of personal violence and his Dutch Calvinist background with its obsessive sense of guilt and turned both into the story of a monomaniac— "a present day saint," as Scorsese says, "like Charlie in *Mean Streets.* He's a would-be saint, a Saint Paul. He's going to help people so much he's going to kill them." A year after the script was complete, Schrader showed it to Michael Phillips and Julia Phillips; they liked it, but the only commercial package they could find for its black and bloody story would have involved Jeff Bridges as the taxi driver, and Robert Mulligan, director of the adolescent agonies of *Summer of '42.* Schrader, who is bored to death by films about growing up, liked neither idea; and the Phillipses saw it as only a possible deal. But although they had produced *The Sting,* their power had limits. And although Schrader had launched his screenwriting career with a spectacular $300,000 deal for *The Yakuza,* a disappointing blend of Japanese and American codes of honor within a gangster film, he lacked the power to push a studio into financing the unappealing story of *Taxi Driver.* Moreover, *The Yakuza* had not been a success. If the only possible deal was Bridges and Mulligan, Schrader would have to agree. He wanted to see the film made.

By luck, Schrader saw *Mean Streets* and made the Phillipses see it too. The power of Scorsese and DeNiro was obvious; and DeNiro's violent, obsessive quality as Johnny Boy suggested that he could make the taxi driver a figure of terror. Both Scorsese and DeNiro liked the script, and the package was assembled. The problem now was to find a studio that would back so bleak a story. In essence, *Taxi Driver* is about the garbage on the streets of New York—about a man, Travis Bickle, who drives cabs, haunts porno films, lives on pills; who tries to make contact with a perfect blonde girl, but is rejected when he takes her to see a dirty film; who goes into awesome, almost monastic training with a fetishistic delight in guns; who veers away from an attempt to kill a political candidate, and channels his violence into helping an underage, junkie hooker by slaughtering her pimp and his associates. There is an appalling bloodbath and a coda in which Bickle seems to have emerged as a heroic figure, able now to reject the blonde girl in his turn and melt into the city streets. He is the anonymous threat in all city paranoia. But any studio signing the checks had to contend with a prostitute aged twelve, a scene of urban carnage that nearly won the film an American X rating, and a monocular vision that never opts for easy psychological explanations of Bickle's obsessions. Worse still, the ending seems to glorify Bickle's actions. It can be seen either as a continuation of Bickle's obsession, his own fantastic idea of how he would achieve heroism, or else as a confused attempt to turn him from maniac into hero and justify individual action against city filth to the point of murder. Nothing about the film was comfortable.

But Hollywood logic can be manipulated. The people in the package could disguise the apparent problems of the script. Schrader was hot after *The Yakuza*; money means power in the film business. The Phillipses had produced *The Sting*. Scorsese's *Alice Doesn't Live Here Anymore* was a success, with a performance that had won an Oscar; and Robert DeNiro had also won an Oscar for his performance as the young Vito Corleone in *The Godfather Part II*. Provided the team could stick together, some studio would have to bite. The catch was Columbia, interested in such a combination of talents for much less than their market price—a mere $1.3 million. "These guys," they reasoned, "want to take less money, so why not do the movie?"

The troubles started with delays. DeNiro came under fierce pressure to break away from *Taxi Driver*, which offered him only $40,000, to make another movie for $500,000. Scorsese was involved in the complex pre-production work for *New York, New York,* a musical that would give him a chance to work with a large budget and all the toys the studio playground can offer. The Phillipses had Spielberg's idea for *Close Encounters of the Third Kind* signed up, and Schrader was doing some preliminary work on that. The only way to make the film was for all four elements to stick together, and delay meant fearsome pressure to split apart. "We were almost at the point of suing each other," Scorsese remembers. "There we were, some of the oldest friends in the business and we were almost in court. Eventually we just said: 'Come on, let's make the picture.' "

The film remained, surprisingly for Scorsese, close to Paul Schrader's original script. "With Mardik the script is always loose," Scorsese says, "but with Schrader it's more succinct and direct and compact. I only improvised three or four scenes in the film." The effect is curious, a clash of influences. Schrader had written about Robert Bresson, and the Bressonian influence comes through the device of Bickle's diary, modeled on *Diary of a Country Priest* and *Pickpocket*. There is the attention to everyday life, the poetry of organizing mechanics like the arsenal Bickle assembles. There is no glib psychological analysis, so Scorsese forces the audience into Bickle's tunnel vision as Bresson does in *Mouchette*. There are even specific references to Bresson, such as Bickle's diet of bread soaked in apricot brandy and his fear he has cancer, a direct parallel to the country priest's diet of bread soaked in wine because he does, indeed, have cancer of the stomach. Arguably, the scenes of city night resemble the images of Bresson's *Four Nights of a Dreamer*.

But Scorsese has influences that are as strong, and they seem to clash with Schrader's vision and confuse it. The would-be saint, operating in the streets of New York, is Scorsese's repeated character—the man caught between being a priest and being a gangster. "His intentions may have been honorable, but look what he did," Scorsese says. "The pimps he kills didn't do anything to him; in fact, they're kind to him, they want him to have a good time. They're just doing their job, though it may be filthy and rotten." Bickle is "pure anarchy— and the negative side of anarchy. I think that's a real nightmare." To express his violence, Scorsese adopts the techniques of Samuel Fuller; when Bickle goes to murder the pimps, there is a long, rushed tracking shot from the shooting of Sport, the pimp, along the corridor to the room that the child-whore Iris uses. "The film that really taught me about violence was Fuller's *Park Row*," Scorsese says. "Remember that long tracking shot; they go into one office and wreck that, come out and crash into another place, start a fight which spills out of that place and a man gets beaten up under a statue of Benjamin Franklin down the road. All in one shot. I used to watch that on TV when I was eleven or twelve." And, like *Taxi Driver*, Fuller's films often fail to condemn the anarchy they contain, which can make them appear sinisterly individualistic tracts of the Right.

Taxi Driver is essentially a nightmare. It is a vision of urban squalor and paranoia. The world that Bickle sees is corrupt, soiled, hideous. A passenger orders him to stop outside an apartment block, points to a window where a woman is undressing, tells Bickle that the woman is his wife, and that she is having an affair with a black man. The passenger threatens to blow her vagina apart with a .44 Magnum. It is probably the ugliest single scene of misogyny that has been filmed. Its impact becomes stronger because the passenger is played by Scorsese himself. He says he took the part "because it was late in the schedule, and because the man I cast had broken his head and there was nobody else around that I could trust to do it." But nothing in the rest of the film suggests that

211

woman has a place in society. There is a whore in the taxi, unzipping the fly of a businessman client; and there is the child-whore Iris. And, across the Madonna-whore divide, there is the icy blonde whom Travis Bickle tries to date.

The taxi creeps and glides in slow motion, an unreal presence against the sordid, red-lit city. The film forces us to take Bickle's viewpoint, to share in his training for murder, to be implicated in his fetishistic handling of guns, in his holding his hands over flame to prove his will, in his obsessive monocular vision of the city and its evils. If the film remains nightmarish until the end, then it becomes an ugly warning, forcing an audience to accept Bickle's actions and see that they are possible from any psychopath out there among the city lights. Bickle believes he has become a hero at the end, although the heroism involves as much wish fulfillment as the buying of guns or training as a samurai. And Bickle is faded into the neon of New York, anonymous as only a taxi driver can be. The threat in the cities could come from anyone. The catch in that interpretation, which gives the film the poetic unity of a Céline rather than the Bernanos from whom Bresson draws, is very simple. Bickle kills people that most audiences despise. He prepared for the killing by the kind of discipline and training that audiences are accustomed to admire. He seems to aim for redemption through the act of murder, and he seems to emerge as a popular hero, his credibility enhanced by the icy blonde's new interest in him. If this reception continues Bickle's subjective vision, then *Taxi Driver* is a brutal, but coherent film. If it does not, then the end shows that Bickle has not been redeemed, that his violence is possible again, and that his actions were justified by the hope of redemption and the nature of his victims. The Bresson references suggest that Bickle is engaged in a spiritual quest that is to be seen as such. If so, the film becomes more than ugly. It becomes a vicious tract. Bickle is condoned in his lawless brutality.

The confusion is in the mind of Scorsese as well;

"Bickle," he says, "is somewhere between Charles Manson and Saint Paul."

The survival of the .44 Magnum scene says something about the nature of both British and American systems of rating. Scorsese was made to trim the pimp's sales talk for the child, to avoid the uncommercial American X rating; but neither British nor American censors took exception to the threat to destroy a woman through her sex. The American rating board also insisted that the makers cut a scene in which a black man is beaten, even though he is already dead; and, most absurdly, it made Scorsese overlay the final bloodbath with a chemical tint so that it would look less realistic. The black-red gore turns out to be almost more powerful than the splattered ketchup of the original. Scorsese certainly thinks it is worse.

The compromises were kept to a minimum by the low budget—$1.9 million in the end—and the cooperative power of the filmmakers. But they were under constant pressure to finish. "We wanted another week," Scorsese says. "I always wanted just one more day. Finally, they pulled the plug on us, and we had to finish. I had a lot of tension fighting the studio system." Perhaps the central problem was the horror of the film's picture of Bickle as a victim of America. It is Schrader's own line that Bickle is the existential hero who would commit suicide if he could understand that the problem is his own existence. Instead, he turns his aggression and doubt outward and focuses it elsewhere. Schrader blames "the immaturity and youngness of our country." He never blames Bickle.

Stage 29 at MGM is where *An American in Paris* was shot. It is the heart of the playground. It was the only place to confect the ultimate expression of the movie brats' philosophy, *New York, New York*.

Scorsese planned a conscious pastiche of the musicals of the late 1940s and early 1950s, but, unlike the mechanical reproduction of Bogdanovich's filming-by-numbers in *What's Up, Doc?*, this pastiche was used to a purpose.

Through the stylistic cleverness come the fears, obsessions, anxieties, and loves of its creators. The musical was always intended to have a dark side and to be a love story in which both partners had equal weight; but it was also meant to be fun. "It turned out," Scorsese says, "to be one of the most personal films I've ever made." The mixture is immensely potent, perhaps the most extraordinary of all the films that Hollywood's children have made within the studio machine —a film that was made in the playground, with a careful knowledge of all the games that had gone before.

It was meant to be a highly commercial package. Its story was simple: singer meets sax player and they love and marry. Sax player takes over a big band and the singer becomes the star. The band dims as the star rises. The sax player retreats to his music and opens a nightclub; the singer goes to Hollywood and becomes a superstar. Later they meet, but all the sparks have gone. *New York, New York* is about a period of musical transition, from big band and swing to the belting torch songs and Modern Jazz Quartet experimentation of the 1950s; and it is about the films from that period and their framing and style; and it is an adult, heterosexual love story, something surprisingly rare in a Hollywood that constantly deals with love as a plot device and does not dare deal intelligently with the gay implications of male bonding.

The film was built on producers Chartoff and Winkler's relationship with United Artists, and it was essentially a project that depended on the packagers' credibility. The title and story had been touted in the trade papers; at one time, Barbra Streisand and Ryan O'Neal were considering it. Scorsese loved the idea from the start. When New York itself has been the central force in so many of his movies, he could hardly resist the title; his constant use of music to build the structure of his films made him eager to try a full-fledged musical. Even *Taxi Driver* takes much of its doom and sense of dream from the music of Bernard Herrmann and its economic, precise use.

But Scorsese was only one possible part of a package. Nothing in this game is fixed until everything is fixed.

Scorsese had already suffered troubles over launching *Taxi Driver*; and there was an uncomfortable time working with Marlon Brando and the Indians on a project to film the battle of Wounded Knee and the destruction of Indian culture. Scorsese, from an underprivileged immigrant family, had found himself treated by the Indians like an overprivileged East Coast WASP. And, as *New York, New York* became more of a reality, his first meeting with Liza Minnelli was not a good omen. "It's going to be really interesting doing this film," she said. "Especially with James Caan." Scorsese cleared his throat and corrected her. "It got worse as it went along," he says. "I asked her if she'd seen *Mean Streets*, I reminded her DeNiro was in that, and she said: 'Is he the guy with the suit all the time?'" (That is Charlie, Scorsese's alter-ego, and the actor is Harvey Keitel.)

The money riding on the package was, by Scorsese's standards, gigantic. The film was finished for more than $9 million, $2 million over its original budget; before that, Scorsese had never been able to spend as much total as he overspent on *New York, New York*. Big money changed the rules of the game. Scorsese had to learn how to take advantage of the star system. "For instance, why should Liza be in any film where her part is nothing? That's an economic consideration. But at the same time, what's the sense of doing a love story if it's all one-sided and just the man? And I really wanted to make a film with two central characters. *Taxi Driver* has one, *Alice* really only has one." And the simple fact of rebuilding the heart of the dream machine, the studio stages at MGM, was a fantasy realized. "Just to watch the sets being built, to see things going up— that was really something." His only disappointment was the backlot at MGM. Time had rotted the standard railroad station set—the one where Astaire, wistfully, decides to be "by myself, alone" in *The Band Wagon*. The exteriors had to be shot at Twentieth Century-Fox, where the New York of *Hello, Dolly!* still stood, and at Burbank Studios. That was further from the heart of the dream.

The soundstages, though, were the ones where MGM musicals were created. Liza Minnelli inherited the dressing room her mother had used; she remembered, with a startled shock, the chandelier. Barry Primus played the big band's pianist in a suit once worn by John Garfield; MGM's wardrobe had kept some of its historic relics. Jack Haley, the Tin Man from *The Wizard of Oz*, had a cameo part. Lionel Stander, resident cynic of the '30s movies and a veteran of the first version of *A Star Is Born* in 1937, played Minnelli's agent. The directors of MGM's great days, Vincente Minnelli and George Cukor, appeared on set to help and advise and discuss. Minnelli's less candy-floss musicals and the somber tone of Cukor's 1954 *A Star Is Born* were profound influences on Scorsese's ambition to make a musical with tones rather than froth. The studio machine was grinding back into action, to do what the studios always did best, to create a separate world on soundstages.

Scorsese prepared for the film like a scholar. He looked again at the darker films of the 1940s, like Raoul Walsh's *The Man I Love*, and noted carefully how shots were composed, how the films were cut, and how action was framed. "The pictures I ran were not artistic in any sense," he says. "They were the low budget pictures, shot by directors who weren't major, or pictures by major directors that weren't very good. I was looking for how they made the hall look so big or the use of color; and where do they cut people off in two-shots. It's usually below the knee, not above; they never came in really tight, except for love scenes or their equivalent. So throughout *New York, New York* Jimmy Doyle and Francine Evans are always in the same frame together whether they like it or not. They're stuck together." Scorsese's meticulous preparation did not mean stealing sequences; "I've never taken out just one element." But it did include a direct act of homage to the films of the 1940s. The New York skyline behind the credit titles at the start is taken directly from *The Man I Love*. "We reprinted that," Scorsese says, "and repainted it."

One basic had changed since the 1940s and, unlike color, it was not possible to reproduce. The shape of screens had changed from a ratio of 1:1.33 to 1:1.66. Few cinemas can still project in the old ratio instead of the more usual widescreen, and it proved economically impossible to shoot in "Academy ratio." "But we could still frame within that ratio," Scorsese says, "and we did."

The film took its tone from the more dramatic musicals of the period. The ideal was the drama of a film like *Blues in the Night*. Liza Minnelli developed her part from the passive, patient June Allyson in *The Glenn Miller Story*, the woman in the corner whose thoughts we never knew; Cukor's *A Star Is Born* influenced color, the story of shifting show business fortunes, and the sense of drama; and *Pal Joey* helped shape many of the club and ballroom sequences. The key difference is that "there is marvelous stuff in *Pal Joey*, but the fact is that they go off into the sunset together at the end," says Scorsese. "That was what I didn't want."

What the musical gives Scorsese is a chance to take his stylization, his supersaturated colors and artificial sets, to an extreme, and do so with the license of those earlier films to which he pays homage, such as the fleeting moment from *On the Town* when a sailor and his girl dance, perfectly, in the flickering lights of the elevated railway. He stages drama like musical numbers. Jimmy Doyle first meets Francine Evans during the V-J Day celebrations in New York; their game of courtship and rejection is played with the hand gestures, the physical cues that cry out for a song. Jimmy and Francine are reconciled in the snow before a forest of sepia cutout trees; their movements echo, indirectly, the courtship of Astaire and Rogers in another studio snow scene in *Swing Time*. More remarkable is Scorsese's use of music to dramatic effect. When Evans, pregnant and a little drunk with drinks to celebrate her recording contract, advances on the stage where Jimmy Doyle is playing, the horns and sax turn on her and drive her back. Music shows Doyle's aggression. When she is rising as a star, and the band itself is in difficulty, the tensions appear at musical rehearsals; Jimmy and Francine dispute who gives the beat and the orders. Francine Evans first becomes real to Doyle in an audition where she dictates his musical style to fit what the prospective employer wants. The integration of music, stylization, and drama is, exactly, operatic. It is no accident that Visconti's *The Leopard,* with its great, operatic ballroom sequence, gave Scorsese clues on how to stage the V-J celebrations at the Waldorf-Astoria.

The emotions are bleak. The two lovers grow apart. The birth of a child brings no companionship. At the end neither partner is equipped with a simple alternative, but they know there is simply no point in meeting again. Scorsese puts realism, not romanticism, into his love story; he aims for the pessimism of the *film noir.* He made his actors expose their feelings as he did. Much of the material was improvised in advance, videotaped, and examined critically as the screenplay was reshaped; even when the film was finished, Scorsese was not happy with its shape. The thin book took blood from its performers. Only on the soundstages were the camera positions fixed and the acting drilled into precision even with two cameras rolling. Shooting within studio artifice took twenty-two grueling weeks, something Scorsese says he will never do again.

Scorsese does not attempt to be impersonal. When Doyle goes to the hospital to see his wife after childbirth, the white walls and the gloomy expression lead us to believe the child is stillborn; and the scene between Doyle and Evans is shot entirely from the man's viewpoint, showing his trouble in handling the reality of a child. There is no comfort for the woman. "While I was making the film, my wife was pregnant," Scorsese says. "The DeNiro character reacts as I was reacting from the pressures around me. His art was on the line and so was mine. I was always working on the film, living in the studio; things got a little rough. And perhaps it is easier for us to express personality in each of our films—easier than it was for a Hawks or a Ford who were studio directors."

The film had begun, for Scorsese, with the muddled memories of his uncles coming home from war in uniform and the musicals his father took him to see in New York.

It remained personal in all its substance, an elegant use of conventions that manages to explode every one of them by sheer force of feeling. If Scorsese had been able to lean on a studio system, the final version of the film might have been more palatable to a general public; as it was, "when we saw the film wasn't drawing an audience," he says, "I realized I did have a commitment toward United Artists in terms of the money. Also, I was involved in the picture and its success." He trimmed the film, and now he feels unable to see it again. He will ignore it until the time comes to make such technical adjustments as television requires. The film's producers had control of the final cut, and they gave Scorsese that privilege; but he still had to change the film. Out there, people expected something different from DeNiro and Minnelli, expected a grand production number and perhaps a happy ending. There was too much in *New York, New York* that was strong and dark. To see Minnelli and DeNiro fighting is ugly and painful. Doyle's rejection of his child is confused and selfish and cruel. The mixture is rich, extraordinary; but it is not predictable.

Scorsese left *New York, New York* behind, concentrating his energies on assembling the footage for *The Last Waltz*, his account of the Band's last concert. With DeNiro he planned a film about prizefighting in New York, territory where people expect Scorsese and DeNiro to be at home, with street wisdom and violence. Minnelli left to perform *The Act*, the story of a Francine Evans–type ten years on as she prepares to appear in Las Vegas; Scorsese, unhappily, directed the show until a week before its Broadway opening. Everyone returned to what was expected of them, leaving behind a tragedy—a tragedy because so few people, barely enough to make the film pay, were interested in the brilliant novelty that is the essence of Scorsese's apparent homage to American cinema. It is sad to think there is only a limited audience for one of the most cine-literate, and moving, films of our times.

Steven Spielberg

Born 1948 in Ohio; raised in New Jersey and Scottsdale, Arizona. Obsessed with film as teenager, but failed to enter University of Southern California film school; majored in English at California State University, Long Beach. Shot drama *Amblin'*, which won him seven-year contract with MCA-TV at the age of twenty-one. For them, made *Something Evil* and *Duel* as well as series episodes. First theatrical feature was *The Sugarland Express* in 1974, followed by *Jaws* and *Close Encounters of the Third Kind*.

S uburbia is home to Steven Spielberg. He grew up there, in New Jersey and Arizona. His first film, a stagecoach robbery that lasted three and half minutes, was shot on 8mm film for a budget of ten dollars; it was made when Spielberg was young enough to want a Boy Scouts' photography badge. From that first attempt he progressed to science fiction on 16mm film. He made a two and a half hour film called *Firelight,* a story of scientists investigating strange lights in space and the National Guard battling monsters from space. It may well be, he says, the worst film the world has ever seen.

That self-mocking humor keeps Spielberg from the arrogance of the wunderkind. For even *Firelight* was a commercial success; his father hired the local Scottsdale cinema to show it and recouped the $500 production costs in one night. Before he was twenty-one Spielberg had a seven-year contract to make films for MCA-TV, the sister company to Universal Pictures. His second feature film, *Jaws*, was the most profitable film of all time for a few years, before *Star Wars* overtook it. By then Spielberg had been entrusted with $19 million and the future of an entire studio on *Close Encounters of the Third Kind*. He was almost thirty when that film appeared.

His school grades were not good enough to take him to film school. The University of Southern California was oversubscribed, and even Spielberg's 16mm experience was not enough to win him a place. As compensation he immersed himself in movie lore. He watched every film on late night television, memorizing names and faces, recalling shots or credits at will. He became a scholar of film. While he was studying at California State University at Long Beach—his major was English—he spent a year shooting, directing, and cutting a short film about hitchhikers called *Amblin'*. It won prizes at the Atlanta and Venice film festivals. He began to work out which films he most admired, an eclectic list that ran from the accepted classics—John Ford's *The Searchers*—to the downright unfashionable—Robert Wise's thriller about parapsychological phenomena, *The Haunting*. He had made himself into a graduate of the school of Hollywood.

As Spielberg tells it, he put on a sober suit, walked into the offices of Universal, found an empty office, and persuaded the switchboard to list his name. He invaded a set where Alfred Hitchcock was working and was thrown out; but in the labyrinth of the studio, nobody thought to question the presence of a serious young man in a side office. That is the myth. The record shows, more prosaically, that Sidney Shainberg, head of television films for Universal/MCA, saw *Amblin'*, liked it, and offered Spielberg a contract. On Spielberg's first day at official work, he was assigned to direct the aging icon Joan Crawford in a sharp short story for the television series "Night Gallery." In it Crawford is a woman of great wealth who is blind. She uses her riches to buy the eyes of a man and gain sight for twelve hours. But for all those twelve hours, the power fails, and there is no light. She never sees anything. With awe, the unit publicist remembers Spielberg's apparent command of the set from the beginning. "It was extraordinary," he says, "this kid in complete control of a star like Crawford."

The show itself is reputedly extraordinary, full of visual invention. It does not seem to have suited MCA. For a year Spielberg was left to cool his heels and wait for work. But the television machine grinds out a vast amount of product, and contract directors will always find some job to do. Spielberg made episodes for "The Psychiatrist," "Marcus Welby, M.D.," "The Name of the Game," and for the more distinguished series "Columbo." His working life was spent among the all-purpose, anonymous streets of Universal backlot sets, where any suburb can be dressed in a few hours using the basic houses and the basic stores. He saved his ambition for making a real film.

His chance came with *Duel*. It was designed as a Movie of the Week for ABC television. By anybody's standards it was an exceptional film for television; and when Universal brought the film to theaters in Europe, critics hailed it as an exceptional film in its own right. It is common for television films to appear in European theaters, but usually they are low budget affairs that quickly disappear. They are among the few films cheap enough to play as second features on double bills. For *Duel*, the British critics clamored so loudly that the film was brought back into central London cinemas on the strength of the notices. In Europe as a whole it grossed $6 million. Given that the fees from the American network would have given Universal its production costs and a profit, the film became a phenomenon.

The story, by Richard Matheson, is simple enough. Mr. Mann is driving toward a business appointment along an anonymous Californian freeway. He realizes that the giant truck behind him is not just following him. It is stalking him. It means to kill. The ordinary road becomes a jungle. Car and truck, driver and driver, are engaged in a deadly and apparently irrational duel. The truck becomes alternately wolf, shark, tank, or prehistoric monster; it has a set of strategies from patient waiting to sudden strikes. It is the doom of Mr. Mann.

"The hero of *Duel* is typical of that lower middle-class

American who's been insulated by suburban modernization," Spielberg has said. "A man like that never expects to be challenged by anything more than his television set breaking down and having to call the repair man." The film follows a clear line from suburbia to anarchy. It opens on black screen, which turns out to be the driver's viewpoint as he leaves his garage, clears the driveway, negotiates a suburban street, and makes for the tunnel that leads him to the freeway. The first shot that is not from the driver's viewpoint is framed, menacingly, by strands of barbed wire.

Slowly, we discover two things. The first is the malevolence of the truck, teasing Mann to overtake it in the path of an oncoming car, waiting behind him until it can pass Mann's car with a blast of the horn. The second is the terrible insecurity of Mann's manhood. His reactions to danger are deadened. He thinks he is no longer really head of his family, although he is the man of the family. When he calls his wife from a Laundromat, he apologizes to her; and she, in the debris of a suburban home, complains bitterly that he did nothing the night before when a man "practically tried to rape me in front of other people." Mann has no answer to that. He asks himself: "What did she expect me to do? Duel?"

Mann talks to himself a great deal; that device makes the plot line clear, but weakens the force of Spielberg's efficient exposition. The truck grows in menace as Mann drives on. It tries to force him off the road; we see, repeated, the road signs that forbid passing. The rules are all gone. "Here you are," Mann says to himself and us, "right back in the jungle again." At a roadside cafe he tries to spot the truck's driver among the men drinking at the bar. He challenges the wrong man and narrowly escapes a beating. He is close to hysteria. Along the road he sees a school bus stalled on a corner. Mann tries to help, but he does not have the power. The truck waits for him at the end of a tunnel, its lights like animal eyes. Mann loses face before the kids; he worries, petulantly, that they will scratch the hood of his car; and the truck finally turns back to help the bus. Then it comes to kill Mann.

By now the social roles that define and support Mann have all collapsed. He does not rule his family, protect his wife, fight for himself, or help the children on the school bus; he lacks potency. He is deadened by his suburban life and aspirations. He becomes open prey—nudged onto a railway line in front of a train, trapped in a snake farm, allowed a brief respite by the roadside while he imagines the truck has gone on. But it has not. Mann tries to confront it; he stalks toward it in the classic manner of a Western hero, and later snaps on his seat belt as though it were a six-shooter and gunbelt. He tries to enlist support, but the nice old couple in their battered car do not want trouble; they drive off. As Mann flees, the truck and a passing locomotive exchange hoots of solidarity from which he is excluded. The duel reaches its climax.

Everything, now, shows signs of meticulous story-boarding. The car belches smoke and the truck seems likely to catch it on a downward slope. Spielberg cuts between the car gauges, the face of Mann shot through a slightly distorting lens to emphasize his panic, the car pouring smoke, and long-racked focus shots of the truck—that is, close-ups taken from a distance with a telephoto lens—that have the disconcerting effect of making it seem giant and close and yet unreal. Mann dives off the road and gibbers defiance at the truck. He entices it, in its last charge, to fall over a cliff and hang there, burning. He is left, a curious echo of *THX-1138*, framed against sunset, a quasi-hero.

Duel uses a classic suspense structure: a man is brought lower and lower until nothing worse can happen. Then something worse happens; and he escapes. The story's development is ingenious, but Spielberg's exposition is even better. The truck's articulation suggests animal metaphors. (When Spielberg was offered *Jaws* he worried in case the shark would be compared with the truck in *Duel*.) It can be a snake or a stalking animal. Its bulk becomes some impersonal force, unstoppable and beyond control. It would be amusing to read the film as a parable of a man denying his sexuality and its implacable force; perhaps even a man denying his homosexuality, since truckers,

225

boots, and cruel game-playing have a disproportionate importance in the commercial American gay culture. But what faces Mann is more than the breakdown of the rules that allow him to handle suburban life. Anarchy strikes and he is unprepared. The whole giant weight of trivial problems is rolled together into one homicidal machine. We know Mann is anxious about a contract and worried about his job; we see the fragility of his relationship with his wife; there are hints of economic anxiety and over-protectiveness about possessions like his car. Under such pressure a man's identity becomes uncertain; he can be forgiven the paranoid fantasy that the truck represents.

He has become "an ordinary man in extraordinary circumstances." That is Spielberg's constant theme. His central characters may be the suburbanite Mr. Mann; the dim girl on the run in *The Sugarland Express* who suddenly becomes a celebrity; the peaceful seaside community in *Jaws*, no more greedy or corrupt than any other tourist town but still menaced by the great white shark; or the country people and the lumpen proletariat in *Close Encounters of the Third Kind*, the ones who are called to meet the aliens. The theme is always the same: how the ordinary person transcends the limitations he expects to find and becomes a hero, a martyr, an adventurer. It is at once a glorification of suburbia and a pointer to escape routes from that class. (Richard Dreyfuss has said that Spielberg has a love affair going with the suburban middle class. "I don't share his fascination," Dreyfuss said, "but Steven could do whole movies about block parties if he wanted to.") It expects identification from the audience. That may be why certain Spielberg films have so extraordinarily wide an appeal. They show the way out of most people's lives.

Even in the machine of MCA-TV, there could be alarming lulls. In the year of idleness that Spielberg suffered, waiting for his second television assignment, he worked on his chance to make a feature film. He knew it would have to be a chance that he created. Although he made *Duel* and a second television film about demonic possession, *Something Evil,* the television business allowed him only to make unordinary films that went unnoticed in America. He had a seven year contract at the studio, but he began to tout ideas to other companies.

Richard Zanuck and David Brown were still at Twentieth Century-Fox, months away from the explosion that would blow them clear across Hollywood to find refuge at Warners. Spielberg offered them a script he had cowritten, *Ace Eli and Rodger of the Skies,* a saga of early pilots and early planes. "We liked the script," Zanuck says, "but Spielberg wanted to direct it. We ran everything that he had done, and when I say everything, there wasn't that much. There were a couple of shorts and a few television shows. And although we bought the script, we didn't get Steven to direct it."

Zanuck and Brown left Fox for Warners, and, after eighteen months, they opted out for a generous deal at Universal. In effect, they were charged with taking the studio back into the business of commercial, mainstream cinema. They would be independent producers, but their films would go only to one studio. They prepared to move into one of the bungalows that were then the essential privilege of all favored partners in the MCA empire. And they began to scout for stories and ideas. "A week before we moved," Zanuck remembers, "we met with Steven's agent. We were trying to find out what was happening, what projects were around. The agent told us: 'You guys like Steven Spielberg. Well, he's got a project at Universal called *The Sugarland Express,* but he can't get it off the ground. What he really needs is a heavyweight production team who can launch it some place.' "

Spielberg had, by now, caught up with the class of '67 at USC, for the script for *The Sugarland Express* was the work of Hal Barwood and Matt Robbins. The members of that class were to become his closest associates in the film world. He would work from the same office building as John Milius; offer to share second unit duties on films by George Lucas; dream, with the others, of some final retreat to "Shangri-Coppola," where films are made without moguls or studios or interfering executives. Now, however, his problem was the powerful Mr. Wasserman, head of MCA and Universal. "We read the script," Richard Zanuck says, "and we instantly liked it. But we had to tell Steven's agent that there was a real problem. It looked as though we were going to form an alliance with Universal, and if the studio had already turned down the project, that could be very awkward for us." After some thought Zanuck and Brown decided that they would back the project; but they cautiously buried it in their first batch of proposals along with more obviously commercial fare like *The Sting*.

The confrontation with Wasserman was polite and diplomatic. "We think Steve has a great future," he told Zanuck and Brown. "But I have to tell you we do not have any faith in the project." Wasserman took the view that the American appetite for anarchy had been saturated after *Easy Rider*, that the brief years of the so-called "youthquake" were over. He admitted the script was good, and he was reluctant to refuse a low budget film to his newly acquired star producers. "Make the film, fellows," he said. "But you may not be playing to full theaters."

"It was a kind of rebirth for us," Zanuck says. He stayed with Spielberg and the crew while they were on location in Texas, protecting the film from studio interference, sometimes involved in a curious reversal of roles between producer and director. It would be Spielberg who offered compromises to make the film more commercial. It would be Zanuck who tried to persuade him to make the film he had first planned.

The result is an astonishingly accomplished first film, if, after Spielberg's television experience, it is right to call it a first film at all. The surprise, after the clever, mechanical craft of *Duel*, is the range of emotion, the warmth. Spielberg was to become associated with wonders on screen—the technical difficulties of shark attacks on *Jaws* and the coming of the unidentified flying objects in *Close*

Encounters of the Third Kind. In his first feature film he showed that he had no need of those obvious firework displays to make his subtle points.

The film is based on incidents that happened in Texas in 1969. A determined woman helped her husband escape from jail. Both set off across country to rescue their baby from its new foster parents. Their journey became a cavalcade, a carnival. They became popular heroes. Their anarchic celebrity ended in death, because gunfire was the only way left for the authorities to stem their embarrassment and humiliation.

In Spielberg's version of the story the strong central figure is the woman, Lou Jean, played by Goldie Hawn. She makes her husband escape the Prerelease Center of the Texas Department of Correction; in a hurried sexual interlude in the men's room he is threatened that this good time will be "the last time" if he does not escape. To the man's horror she takes over the gun and kidnaps a Texas ranger and his car to start their journey to Sugarland and Baby Langston. At the end it is she who makes the husband Clovis walk to the white-painted house where Baby Langston has his new home; and it is she who is, indirectly, responsible for the furious hail of bullets that kills Clovis. To his embarrassment it is Lou Jean who takes the most delight in the headlines that follow them, the rapturous reception in small towns, the gifts of teddy bears for the baby. She is the film's mainspring.

Lou Jean is less than bright. She is an inarticulate woman who cannot cope with the Welfare, the machine that has taken away her baby, but she is prepared to fight the machine head on. The couple who have Baby Langston are respectable and middle class, with a detached house and a neat lawn and dressers full of china; Lou Jean and Clovis are from what sociologists call the lower working class, the lumpen proletariat. Both have drifted round the fringes of crime. Spielberg never compromises on the class position of his heroine or the alliance of police, surrogate parents, and authority that opposes her. Lou Jean's defiance of the middle-class machine is what brings the peo-

229

ple in small towns out onto the streets to welcome the captured police car and the long procession that follows it. Gun happy snipers come roaring out of suburban garages to deal with the couple; they are unwanted volunteers who blast away at the used-car lot where Lou Jean, Clovis, and their captive ranger have spent the night. They drive a car with a back window sticker that says: "Register Communists, Not Firearms." Only the fatherly marshal who leads the police campaign to persuade Lou Jean and Clovis to surrender breaks the pattern of class antagonism; he wants to save life, to find a compromise. Otherwise, the shutters come down on the bourgeois home; it becomes a fortress with rifles at each window. Lou Jean and Clovis are the threat of anarchy.

As the rubberneckers join the procession across Texas, Spielberg choreographs his line of cars with evident skill. That is what he is expected to do best—manipulate machines. But he also achieves a depth of characterization and a variety of emotion that is remarkable. The opening scenes are efficient, crisp; Lou Jean arrives on the dusty road by the prison and makes her way through the bleak perimeter to the checkpoint. A tricky, twisting, tracking shot follows her progress past the guards, as she flirts, faces, and hides her real intentions. There is an equation between the character's duplicity and the camera's unexpected movement. When the journey starts there is downright farce: Lou Jean loves giveaway trading stamps at gas stations, and she manages to take so many that she is cocooned in them; edgy humor: the slowly loosening relationship with the captive Texas ranger, as he realizes his survival is tied to theirs; resentful pride: when Clovis speculates about becoming a ranger, or when he refuses to be called a mentally disturbed suspect in the rangers' radio code; terror: when the bullets of the farcical group of volunteer snipers become all too real; bleak fear: when the bourgeois couple watch their home become a guardpost to protect their possession of a child they are learning to love; and tragedy: after Clovis is shot and the car plunges off the road, the final shot is the Texas ranger, head hung down, sitting by water in a state of shocked misery. The death of Clovis is not in proportion to his actions.

None of the violence in *The Sugarland Express*, such as there is, ever appears casual. It is terrifying. The contrast is the procession, the counterpoint to the couple's emotions and preoccupations. The endless line of cars pile into each other like cartoon characters; at times they fare as badly as the coyote in the Road Runner cartoons. This convention allows Spielberg to explore the feelings of his characters while providing a mechanical ballet as light relief. "Steve is a very emotional director," as Ned Tannen says. "His trademark is getting in and getting in." As in *Duel*, his characters are the ordinary folks put into extraordinary circumstances—Lou Jean and Clovis are small-time casualties of American society, but they become celebrities. The theme prefigures *Close Encounters*. "I've discovered," Spielberg said, "I've got this preoccupation with ordinary people pursued by large forces."

The Sugarland Express did not, in the end, lose money. With television sales it cleared its costs and made a tiny profit. But something was wrong in the chemistry. Zanuck and Brown bought the idea believing, they say, that it had "action, humor, international appeal—all the calculations a producer usually doesn't admit when a film is not a hit." Spielberg offered compromises that the producers refused; he thought it might help the film's chances at the box office if the couple both survived their journey. When the film was complete, it was difficult to find a simple selling line. "We all realized we were in trouble," Zanuck says, "when we had so much trouble coming up with an ad campaign. We couldn't get any one visual idea that would express what the picture was."

Despite Mr. Wasserman's initial doubts, Universal took no joy in the film's troubles. "Contrary to what people seem to think about studios, they did not try to force any campaigns on us," Zanuck says. "They experimented endlessly. They would take whole cities and create new ad campaigns." In some places the studio itself hired cinemas to play the film—in industry jargon, they "four-walled" it. After *Jaws* they rereleased it, hoping to capitalize on Spielberg's name. It never, yet, has reached the audience it deserves. And David Brown, it co-producer, still wonders if the reason is the unglamorous couple at its center. If they had been more articulate, more bright, then a mass audience might have been more prepared to identify with them. It is possible.

Before work had started on *The Sugarland Express*, Spielberg had casual conversation with producer Michael Phillips about unidentified flying objects—UFOs. Both took an interest in the phenomenon. As *Sugarland Express* advanced, Michael Phillips and Julia Phillips were also on the Universal lot, producing *The Sting* for Zanuck and Brown. The vague and general talk about UFOs now crystallized into a specific idea—the plot line that Spielberg later developed into *Close Encounters of the Third Kind*. Both Michael Phillips and Julia Phillips were admirers of *Duel;* it was, to them, the best film ever made for television, and proof that Spielberg could make something remarkable out of the mechanics of a UFO story. Before *The Sugarland Express* was complete, they shook hands on a deal. The papers were formally signed in the autumn of 1973, when *The Sugarland Express* was complete.

Before the Phillipses could begin hunting the considerable cash they knew would be needed for *Close Encounters*, a manuscript landed on the desks of Zanuck and Brown. Steven Spielberg, paying a social call, picked it up and took it away to read. Its title was *Jaws*.

Bruce the shark was made of polyurethane, measured twenty-four feet, weighed one and a half tons, cost more than $150,000, and sank when he was first launched. When the technical crew pushed the brute out to sea again, he exploded. When Spielberg wanted him to look menacing, his jaws clamped together and his eyes crossed. Bruce alone put some $3.5 million onto the budget of *Jaws* by his awkward behavior; and he was only one of the technical troubles that the film faced. The great white sharks off the Great Barrier Reef proved less impressive than they should have been; to compensate, an anxious midget was exposed to their wrath in a reinforced steel cage. Off Martha's Vineyard, the wind and tides made shooting conditions chaotic. Universal set impossible deadlines for finishing the film; an actors' strike was threatened.

The worst fears of the film's producers seemed well founded. They had bought *Jaws* as a manuscript, against stiff competition. Now, their problem was fundamental: "We had," they say, "absolutely no idea of how to make the movie."

What happens in *Jaws* is simple to summarize. A seaside town lives off tourists; a great white shark settles in its waters and lives off townsfolk and tourists alike. At first the authorities conceal the horrors in the interests of the summer season. But they cannot hide panic. An ancient mariner, an ichthyologist, and a sea-scared police chief set off in pursuit of the shark; finally, after a chase and a heart-tearing moment when the monster leaps onto their boat, the shark is literally exploded. Blood smears the screen. The two surviving hunters swim home.

The book was not like that. It had sex, allegedly introduced by the American publishers to make the book more successful; and it had an element of class antagonism. The wife of the gross police chief made love to the upper-class ichthyologist. Both elements were removed from the screenplay. The film is stripped down to the menace of the shark and a series of rollercoaster devices that inspire fear rather than suspense. A child's fake fin causes panic on the beach; the audience is left to doubt what it will see next. For most of the film the shark is unseen; it is represented by a series of growling, bass chords and a zigzag underwater motion of the camera, as though from the shark's point of view. It is the menace that permeates every shot of the waters, undefined and even, at times, allowed to seem unreal. A girl is torn apart, a crowd is scattered, a body is found; but the villain, the reason, the cause is invisible. When the adversary in the hunt finally appears, the shots are extraordinary. Technically they are of astonishing complexity, needing both careful story-boarding and great cunning; to make a polyurethane shark leap into a boat and savage a man requires either crude cheating or extreme sophistication, and Spielberg does not cheat. The problems of shooting, indeed, are obvious; sea, tide, and light are very rarely matched from shot to shot.

Jaws was promoted as a horror that would be, literally, beyond the wildest dreams. Radio commercials proclaimed that "none of men's fantasies of evil can compare with the reality of *Jaws*." Until the shark appears, we can project whatever we want into the waters around the town of Amity. The poster shows a great, phallic head rising toward a girl who is swimming; the first death is a girl who has been playfully enticing a boy into the water after a beach party. *Jaws* plays with sexual anxieties. It could, also, stand for unnamed fears of what a government can do; it appeared after the Watergate break-in was fully exposed and an American president had seemed vulnerable to criminal charges. But its summertime success suggests that it works most effectively because of a much more general thread in American political consciousness—a decade of consumerism had taught that companies, townships, and governments would sell almost anything for profit and, unless checked, would take almost any risk with human life. The threat in the seas could be any of those that had been exposed, month by month, by careful investigation—an ill-considered drug, a dangerous car, an airplane with a fatal flaw, a killing industrial process. Americans had become used to the idea that such horrors can be concealed if the profit motive is strong enough. It was a political training for accepting the literal reality of the tactics that the mayor and townspeople of Amity use; and it was reason to think the threat in the seas might be unnameable, awful, and unimaginable.

The novel proved an enormous success when it appeared; MCA could congratulate Zanuck and Brown on their shrewdness. But they now had to find the right person to film it. "We talked with one distinguished action director," Brown says, "but the negotiations faded out. He kept talking about 'the whale.'" There was a temptation to find a "safe" director. Zanuck and Brown started to wonder if, perhaps, it might be appropriate for so young and inexperienced a director as Spielberg to take on the project, but Spielberg's response was cool. "I just don't know," he told the producers. "After all, it's only a shark story."

He had sweatshirts made with "Jaws" blazoned across them; and then he returned a week later, to announce that he could not possibly make the picture. It was too big. It scared him. He did not know how to handle the shark. The shark would be compared with the truck in *Duel.*

Zanuck and Brown invited him over to their office and put on the "Jaws" sweatshirts to greet him. "It was a simple strategy," they say. "We shamed him into staying on the project."

Peter Benchley's script was, as the producers had asked, a virtual transcript of his novel. Spielberg, Zanuck, and Brown were all disappointed. The story needed to be restructured. "We were all, for various reasons, in the South of France at the Hotel de Cap," Zanuck says. "He was wavering again. I remember sitting there in the cabana and working out the story line that was the basis of the film. The fat, incompetent policeman in the book became a guy from New York who was trying to escape the city. We took out the whole sexual relationship. The ichthyologist became not some Tab Hunter character, but more the Richard Dreyfuss kind, not that we had thought of casting Dreyfuss at the time."

The few days in France settled matters. Spielberg would make *Jaws.* His extraordinary cool was paying off. Even while the shark film was being rebuilt, Spielberg's agent rang the hotel to announce that Paul Newman wanted Spielberg to direct a project called *Lucky Lady*, a saga of rum-running in which Liza Minnelli, Gene Hackman, and Burt Reynolds later sank without trace. "I marveled at the kid," Zanuck says. "He had only one picture behind him, and that had not been released yet. He shared an agent with Paul Newman. And there he was, telling the agent,

Freddie Fields, that he might do *Lucky Lady*, but not with Newman. He was twenty-four years old, and he turned down Paul Newman like he swatted a fly."

The final script of *Jaws* was a collaborative effort. Carl Gottlieb shares screen credit with Peter Benchley; but Howard Sackler, the author of *The Great White Hope* and a knowledgeable seaman, was also involved; and the speech in which the ancient mariner Quint tells of the shark attack on the struggling survivors of the shipwrecked Indianapolis was rewritten by John Milius. Since the story outline was prepared by Spielberg, Zanuck, and Brown in the comfort of their cabanas, the film serves as an object lesson in the essential unreality of assigning authorship to a film. In this case at least seven people made major contributions to the script alone.

After the long filming at Martha's Vineyard, the selling of *Jaws* began. Eight months before the film opened, Zanuck, Brown, and Benchley were busily touring chat shows on television and radio to promote the book and the plot, and the menace of the great white shark. One month before the release, even the film's editor Verna Fields— her swimming pool had been an uncredited location for the film—was on tour to promote what the studio now called "*Jaws*-consciousness." Then, three days before the film opened in the summer of 1975, the studio sprang its last trick. It financed a three-day advertising campaign that saturated the airwaves with sharks, screams, and horror film voices talking of fantasies of evil and the horrid reality of *Jaws*. The campaign covered any television or radio station near the 464 cinemas where the film was to open. The selling of *Jaws*, like the selling of *The Godfather*, was designed to make the film into an event.

The publicity worked more effectively than anyone dreamed. The book had been a success; it had sold more than 7.6 million paperbacks before the film opened. But the film achieved staggering figures. In its first six weeks, one person in eight of the entire American population had seen it. The promotional budget, well over $2.5 million, brought in anxious holidaymakers. Saturation booking in seaside resorts helped. "Never before," said an MCA advertisement, "have so many people seen one movie, in just thirty-eight days."

The campaign featured a strong and simple poster—the shark rising to the girl. It provided copy and ideas for newspapers during the silly season. Styrofoam shark fins went on sale, to alarm fellow swimmers; ice cream appeared as Finnilla, Jawberry, and Sharkalate; official licensees touted T-shirts, beach bags, knee stockings, plastic cups, and pajamas with the Jaws motif. Johnny Carson made drear jokes about the need to book seats in the shallow end of the theater. A discotheque called "Jaws" opened near New York. Cartoonists seized gratefully on the shark and swimmer as an infinite source of political metaphor: Ronald Reagan bared his teeth at a placidly swimming Gerald Ford; oil profiteers menaced the Consumer; the Energy Crisis threatened Government Ineffectiveness; the CIA attacked the Statue of Liberty; and inflation loomed below a worried-looking figure marked The Consumer. Universal counted at least thirty-five nationally syndicated cartoons that parodied the poster. MCA took space in the *Wall Street Journal* to remind people that "It is a movie too."

The transformation of film into event through clever manipulation of the media is probably the single most interesting fact about *Jaws*. Pop newspaper psychologists speculated why it should have happened: did the audience, they asked, identify with shark or victims? In doing so, they contributed to the event. The text of the film itself is rather more disconcerting. It is an enormously efficient fear machine, a series of awful incidents in which the natural and unfamiliar intrude abruptly on the familiar social structures of a small town and its politics, the holidaymakers and their pleasures, and the exurbanite police chief and his family. The policeman, like Mann in *Duel*, is a man with deadened responses and uncertain resources who is pushed into an extraordinary situation. The film offers individual heroism—the mythic if grotesque figure of Quint, the social outcast who alone has the magic to defeat the monster; and, at the end, Quint's death and the brave achievement of the police chief and ichthyologist tend to reassure the audience that ordinary people can triumph against the monster as well. *Jaws* plays cleverly with the expectations of "ordinary" people. But it also, curiously, seems to outlaw and punish sexuality. The first victim of the shark is a woman behaving seductively; after that first death, and a handful of family scenes, women are virtually excluded from the film. It is, literally, man against shark. Film and poster together imply that some of the film's success lies in its use of castration anxiety and man's fear of woman.

There is an ironic footnote to this success. While Zanuck and Brown were puzzling over the technical problems of the film, they approached Peter Gimbel. His film, *Blue Water, White Death,* is a documentary about hunting the great white shark off Australia; it has graphic footage of the monster and its victims. Gimbel first wanted to direct the film; Zanuck and Brown demurred. But they did, casually, offer him a chance to produce it. "It was," Zanuck says, "potentially one of our greater errors." Had Gimbel agreed, Zanuck and Brown would have given away their share of what was for a long time the most successful film ever made.

Close Encounters of the Third Kind was a surprising project for Columbia. The corporation was convalescing after a nearly fatal financial crisis. It had long depended on a bank consortium that kept open a revolving credit of $120 million. It worked with any independent producer who could bring decent films to the studio by raising tax shelter money; the studio itself had strictly limited resources. Now it suddenly seemed flush. Its balance sheet was healthier as the profits from distribution flowed in, and relatively little capital had to be put out on making movies. Columbia bought itself a pinball machine company. It also agreed to make Spielberg's gigantic special effects movie, a film that would predictably cost more than the glories of *2001: A Space Odyssey*. Since Kubrick's film is said to have taken seven years of theatrical release to recoup its costs, the attractions were not obvious.

The project did have its own built-in logic by the standards of Hollywood. It had Steven Spielberg after *Jaws* and Julia Phillips and Michael Phillips after the success of *The Sting* and the less predictable success of *Taxi Driver* for Columbia; and it had UFOs as a subject when 15 million Americans, including President Carter, had claimed to have seen them. It was quite another thing for Columbia to find the $19 million, even after their few, brief years of profitability.

The cash came in in three ways. First, the British conglomerate EMI had made a great deal of money in the United States with its body scanner devices, medical aids to diagnosis; and its show business interests included film and records. With some of the body scanner profits, EMI bought Columbia's music publishing. As partial payment it agreed to cofinance three films, of which *Close Encounters* was one. In place of a taxable capital gain, Columbia got help on a project that would earn money for its distribution arm. And EMI, for a fixed investment, retained a fixed percentage of profit even when Spielberg's budget grew. Next, Time Incorporated put money into the film. Time has a history of brief flirtations with film—a minority stake, less than 5 percent, in MGM, held in association with Samuel Bronfman and his family trust KMPC; and a television division that handles documentary and classic material, often from Britain, for American television stations. Last, the Germans still allowed individuals to shelter their incomes from taxation by investment in film. As the Internal Revenue Service shut off the privilege to Americans, Columbia could find additional capital in West Germany. Those three factors, along with Columbia's evident recovery, made the film possible.

The nature of the investment matters because it explains why Steven Spielberg did not have to answer the same objections to science fiction that George Lucas and Gary Kurtz were facing at Twentieth Century-Fox. However fascinated the American public might be with the possibility of alien life, the arithmetic was against a multimillion dollar investment in those dreams. With a production cost of $19 million, bankers would calculate that the distributor needs to receive nearly $50 million to make a profit, and the public has to be persuaded to buy tickets worth $133 million. The only justification for a gamble on that scale is that Columbia could lay off sizeable parts of its risk and attract investors who did not need to be certain of profit.

Spielberg, like Lucas, was careful to avoid the label of science fiction; he preferred to talk of an "adventure thriller." Unlike Lucas, he spent so much on creating his fantasy that the studio had to sell the film as an event. The pressure on cinemas was harsh from the start. In New York, theaters were asked to put up $150,000 each as a minimum guarantee; this was for the privilege of showing a film that the theater owners could not see because it was being reshaped until the last few days before its premiere. Out in New Jersey the going rate was $50,000 for each theater. The cinemas had to promise to run the film for at least twelve weeks. Never before had theaters been formally asked for so much money in advance when a film was to open in so many theaters across the country simultaneously. Fifty thousand dollars brought no guarantee of exclusivity. On top of the guarantees Columbia demanded a check for $2,000 from each theater, to go toward the cost of promoting the film.

In Chicago the studio used slightly different tactics. It wrote to theaters telling them that "the amount of the guarantee will have great significance in most cases in the ultimate award of this film. It should reflect your enthusiasm and projection of the movie's potential in your theaters." Before opening, Columbia hoped to recoup $24 million in advance payments. It was more than the cost of making the film itself, but not nearly enough to make the project profitable. The money did roll in; the film had become an event through Columbia's giving the distinct impression that cinemas should be privileged to compete for the honor of showing the film. With such pressure it would be a brave theater owner who could be certain that this unseen film was not, indeed, the film of his dreams.

The film was offered to theaters—"bid"—in August. The prices seemed ironic in October, when two uninvited journalists crept into a sneak preview in Texas. Their uncomplimentary reviews made investors jittery; the future of Columbia was seen, all too clearly, to be riding on Spielberg's film. "It will either be the best Columbia film," John Milius said drily, "or it will be the last Columbia film."

The ingredients seemed bizarre. The crew retreated to a gigantic disused aircraft hangar in Mobile, Alabama; whatever they were doing, it was evidently too large for any soundstage in the world. Spielberg closed the set and spent his nights in a trailer, screening alternately cartoons and *2001*. François Truffaut was hired and confessed to understanding nothing of what was going on; he took the part as a kind of laboratory experiment, to help him with a book on actors and acting. "I was there a lot," he said. "But, like Greta Garbo, I can only say I had the feeling of waiting."

Spielberg was quoted on his fears that audiences might "expect *Star Wars* in terms of visual battle action and special effects." In the stills that were released, the only spectacle was blinding white light. Spielberg's cryptic explanation of the film's theme made it sound like any of his other works: it was, he explained, about "extraordinary encounters in middle-class suburbia."

That did prove the key to *Close Encounters*, although along the way it pays homage to Hitchcock's *North by Northwest*, William Cameron Menzies's *Invaders from Mars*, Walt Disney's *Bambi*, *Pinocchio*, and *Fantasia*, and especially the invention of the sequence set to Mussorgsky's *Night on Bare Mountain*. The film proved the ultimate statement about suburbia, about the death of the ideology that killed the old system of Hollywood. It is appropriate that the diagnosis should be made by one of the children of Hollywood, for *Close Encounters* ends with the millennium, and Steven Spielberg is its prophet; and the implications, for the dying ideal of suburbia and the ideology of plenty, are extraordinary.

We have argued that the social and industrial context of films is as important to their understanding as the less quantifiable aesthetic categories; and we have tried to examine film as a product consumed by millions—just as these millions choose to own cars, form social relationships, listen to rock music, love their parents, buy a freezer, and go to church. Film is inextricably involved with the society in which it is produced and consumed and the industrial process that produced it. Spielberg's film about the first contact between man and alien life makes the point almost too well.

Close Encounters draws on film history. In it a house is besieged by light as a UFO hovers outside; the sense of menace within the home parallels Hitchcock's *The Birds*. A child perceives the aliens and goes toward the light with an expression of joy; it is a child who sees the spacecraft land in Menzies's *Invaders from Mars*, outside his bedroom window, and it is children who can spot the pods in human form in *Invasion of the Body Snatchers*. When UFOs hurtle round the roads of Indiana, they strongly resemble the Road Runner in Chuck Jones's cartoons. When the child runs off to see the spacecraft pass, his mother pursues him through a studio woods that strongly resembles the forest in *Bambi*; when aliens and man communicate through the five-note musical theme, there are almost absurd echoes of the "April Showers" number in the same film. At the end of the film the mother ship of the alien race was to have whirled into space, its human adventurers aboard, to the strains of "When You Wish upon a Star" from *Pinocchio*; the tune remains earlier in the film, played by a musical box. When the electricity lineman and the housewife-artist, Everyman and Everywoman, are scrambling toward their rendezvous with the aliens at

242

Devil's Tower, Wyoming, their frantic climb is paralleled by Pinocchio's escape from Pleasure Island and Cary Grant and Eva Marie Saint hanging, in great peril, from the noses of presidents on Mount Rushmore in *North by Northwest*; they are menaced by a low-flying helicopter, spraying anesthetic gas, just as Grant was menaced by a low-flying crop-duster in that film. Even the casting of François Truffaut, apparently the whim of an admirer, has resonances from other films. *Close Encounters* deals with communication between man and alien; Truffaut plays the man who devises the means of communication and works with it patiently. Spielberg has said that he cast Truffaut because of his performance in *The Wild Child*, where Truffaut plays a doctor who struggles to find some way of communicating with a child raised in the forest.

But the system of references, based on Spielberg's encyclopedic knowledge of film, is not surprising. The implications of the film, on the other hand, are. If the power of its theme were matched by the power of its execution, it would be a masterpiece. Unfortunately, the abiding impression it leaves is one of great technical skill devoted to making every mystery overexplicit. It begins with a startling effect: the screen stays black while the noise of a mighty wind builds on the sound track. Suddenly, the screen lightens. We are in a sandstorm in the desert; figures advance, asking "Are we the first?" There is a sense of mystery and terror. But that feeling is rapidly dissipated. We are shown a mother and child in a house surrounded by alien light; the child is taken by the aliens. We meet a lineman who is sent out to repair the damage done by the UFOs traveling overhead; he comes close to the aliens, and, like the mother, his mind is planted with a five-note musical theme and the image of a strange mountain. He becomes obsessed with modeling the mountain until his wife and children leave him, panicked. The mother, meanwhile, distraught over the loss of her child, is drawing the same tower shape. Together with others they feel called to the mountain; and there, the clouds boil and the aliens descend in ships of light and perspex.

243

Everyman, the electricity lineman, goes aboard the alien ship to voyage into the unknown.

The story is full of cheating. A police helicopter is silent until it lands so that we may momentarily think it is a UFO. While Everyman models the tower, a TV set in the corner of the screen shows that same mountain; there is a contrived moment of suspense while we wait for him to look at the television and recognize his obsession. The first alien to leave the ship is a shadow, spreading its arms in apparent benediction; it is an image of great grace and beauty and wonder. Immediately, it is spoiled by sledge-hammer cutting to reaction shots that tell us to feel wonder, by the overliteral score of John Williams, and by an insistence on taking us close to the alien so that mystery dissipates in simple appreciation of technical skill. Spielberg is overly literal throughout *Close Encounters*. When all the humans taken by the aliens over the decades return to Earth from the mother ship, each recites his name and is struck off a list on a board. The adventurers who go with the aliens at the end go through the motions of preparing for a standard NASA mission; and while this would be clever irony if it were played against true mystery, it goes for nothing when it is intercut with the literal presentation of the alien race. Monsters, and aliens, are usually better sensed than seen.

But there is a reason for showing the alien's face. On the surface the film is playing with anxieties about contact with alien cultures, with suspicion that the government is suppressing information—either about aliens or about some dubious activities of its own. Actually the film subverts the familiar paranoia of science fiction made during the Cold War. The alien must be clearly seen in order to banish fear. It is simply unfortunate that the creature simpers as though it had come to replace Mary Pickford as America's sweetheart.

Alien life in films of the Cold War period is always malevolent. Scientists were monomaniacal, cold, and impractical, unlike the warm, humanistic figure that Truffaut presents. Science could destroy mankind; it was the time of greatest anxiety about atomic threats. We, meaning America and all those who consumed American film, had to be constantly on our guard against the coming of invaders, outsiders, enemies. If they did come, only guns and the military could help. Action, not thought; practical men, not dreamers; men who give orders, not men who ask questions would be our salvation. In Howard Hawks's *The Thing from Another World* (Brit.: *The Thing*), made in 1952, a flying saucer lands near an Arctic military base. There are no lights and wonder, only a sinister silhouette under the ice, from which comes what a serviceman flippantly dubs an "intellectual carrot." It is vegetable life that absorbs human cells to live. It has to be killed. The scientists want to investigate it; the military know it must be destroyed. Its death saves the Earth, and the film ends on an anxious voice: "Watch the skies, America!" Similar themes are common. In *The War of the Worlds* Martians in ships with lethal tendrils blast the Earth with green dayglo light. In *Them* scientists unleash mutated giant ants that the army stops as they advance on Washington. The system of values is not hard to disentangle.

By the time of *Close Encounters* nothing was quite so simple. Armies had been seen to destroy. Even Eisenhower leaving office in 1961 had warned of the "military-industrial complex" that the great films of paranoia set out to glorify. Scientists were not always considered malevolent or unthinking. Destruction was not the only possible reaction to alien cultures. When the alien ship lands in Spielberg's film, the audience has been led to associate it with kidnapping a child, terrorizing his mother, and apparently making the Everyman figure insane. Yet when the alien appears it brings love. Aliens can be friends.

There are other curiosities. The central sympathetic figure of Spielberg's film is a scientist who resists all military schemes to harm the handful of human beings called by chance to meet the aliens. Yet he is never seen as a scientist. When someone has to translate the figures beamed from space into a location on Earth, the answer is found by the scientist's interpreter, who happens to have been a cartographer. The scientist is more shaman than laboratory worker. He is full of wonder, not calculation. And although the five-note theme from space is heard in India, the chosen few who see the tower are all Americans. The scientist may be French and the journeys of the UFOs may take them round the globe, but the meeting place of man and alien is America, and the chosen adventurers are American. It is more than a curiosity, this exact placing. The lineman who sees the UFO at close quarters is a man forbidden to use his initiative when he goes out on a job, a man who is fired without courtesy of an explanation; this Everyman has an exact social location in the lower working class with no hope of escape or promotion or change. He is at the poor end of suburbia. The woman whose child is taken is also placed in an economic position that denies her hope. The figures who stand along the road to watch the UFOs pass could come from *Tobacco Road*; they are the derelict, the fragile, the lost America. They are, in short, the people to whom the myth of the millennium has always mattered most, whether in Cromwellian England or thirteenth century Munster or the Wyoming and Indiana of Spielberg's imagination. They are the dispossessed.

Whatever innocent enthusiasm drew Spielberg to the theme of UFOs in the first place, the text of the film points clearly to the hopeless Americans who share the myth and wonder of UFOs. These wheels of light careering through the sky have their historic parallels: the visions of the prophet Ezekiel, the idea of the chariot of God, the mandalas of Jung. The fiery clouds of biblical texts become the boiling clouds and blinding light of Spielberg's film. Intervention from above, bringing hope at last, is a constant theme at times of social crisis and change. Some God must save us, because we cannot save ourselves. And if God is an alien, with lights and wonder and color and music, then God is prettier than we thought.

For it has changed. The postwar self-confidence that bred the suburban life-style has gone. The GI's won their degrees but their children cannot work without a doctorate. The homes were built, but suburban developers noticed that they shrank in size as years went by. Certain employment gave way by 1976 to an 8 percent unemployment rate, and 6 percent in 1978, when recession receded. Material goods did not arrive in such great profusion that class became irrelevant. Possessions did not salve the wounds of the dispossessed—the women, the working class, and the racial minorities of America. The ideology of liberalism failed because goods did not do good. Self-reliance was an empty idea to black, native American, Puerto Rican, and Chicano households within America. And when the liberals failed, the new conservative majority that opinion polls diagnosed, based largely on the inherent conservatism of organized labor, was most bitterly betrayed by its much touted savior, Richard Nixon. In disillusion, all that is left is the dream of the millennium. It took a suburban child, able to make films because of the industry troubles provoked by the failure of studios to recognize the new suburban ethic, to encapsulate the death of suburban ideals. That is the significance of *Close Encounters of the Third Kind.*

Social historians have analyzed the growth of millennial dreams and the coming of some blinding revelation from above. They have not yet paid such detailed attention to the ideology of film. We suggest that film succeeds most when it responds most to the needs that people feel but may not yet have articulated. We suggest:

Watch the screens, America!

Filmography

Francis Coppola

Features

1962: DEMENTIA 13
(British title: *The Haunted and the Hunted*)
Director: Francis Ford Coppola. *Producer*: Roger Corman.
Screenplay: Francis Ford Coppola. *Director of Photography*: Charles Hannawalt. *Editor*: Stewart O'Brien. *Music*: Ronald Stein. *Art Direction*: Albert Locatelli.
Cast: William Campbell (Richard Haloran), Luana Anders (Louise Haloran), Bart Patton (Billy Haloran), Mary Mitchell (Kane), Patrick Magee (Justin Caleb), Eithne Dunn (Lady Haloran), Peter Read (John Haloran).

1966: YOU'RE A BIG BOY NOW
Director: Francis Ford Coppola. *Producer*: Phil Feldman.
Screenplay: Francis Ford Coppola, based on the novel by David Benedictus. *Director of Photography*: Andy Laszlo.
Editor: Aram Avakian. *Music*: John Sebastian. *Art Direction*: Vassele Fotopoulos.
Cast: Peter Kastner (Bernard Chanticleer), Elizabeth Hartman (Barbara Darling), Geraldine Page (Margery Chanticleer), Julie Harris (Miss Thing), Rip Torn (I. H. Chanticleer), Tony Bill (Raef), Karen Black (Amy).

1968: FINIAN'S RAINBOW
Director: Francis Ford Coppola. *Producer*: Joseph Landon.
Screenplay: E. Y. Harburg and Fred Saidy, based on their

musical play. *Director of Photography*: Philip Lathrop. *Choreography*: Hermes Pan. *Editor*: Melvin Shapiro. *Sound*: M. A. Merrick and Dan Wallin. *Production Design*: Hilyard M. Brown.
Cast: Fred Astaire (Finian McLonergan), Petula Clark (Sharon McLonergan), Tommy Steele (Og), Dan Francks (Woody), Barbara Hancock (Silent Susan), Keenan Wynn (Judge Billboard Rawkins), Al Freeman, Jr. (Howard).

1969: THE RAIN PEOPLE
Director: Francis Ford Coppola. *Producers*: Bart Patton and Ronald Colby. *Screenplay*: Francis Ford Coppola. *Director of Photography*: Wilmer Butler. *Editor*: Blackie Malkin. *Music*: Ronald Stein. *Art Direction*: Leon Ericksen. *Sound*: Nathan Boxer.
Cast: James Caan (Kilgannon), Shirley Knight (Natalie), Robert Duvall (Gordon), Marya Zimmet (Rosalie), Tom Aldredge (Mr. Alfred), Laurie Crews (Ellen).

1972: THE GODFATHER
Director: Francis Ford Coppola. *Producer*: Albert S. Ruddy. *Screenplay*: Mario Puzo and Francis Ford Coppola, based on the novel by Mario Puzo. *Director of Photography*: Gordon Willis. *Production Design*: Dean Tavoularis. *Editors*: William Reynolds and Peter Zinner. *Music*: Nino Rota. *Sound*: Christopher Newman.
Cast: Marlon Brando (Don Vito Corleone), Al Pacino (Michael Corleone), James Caan (Sonny Corleone), Richard Castellano (Clemenza), Robert Duvall (Tom Hagen), Sterling Hayden (McCluskey), John Marley (Jack Woltz), Richard Conte (Barzini), Diane Keaton (Kay Adams), Talia Shire (Connie Rizzi), Gianni Russo (Carlo Rizzi), John Cazale (Fredo Corleone), Al Martino (Johnny Fontane).

1974: THE CONVERSATION
Director: Francis Ford Coppola. *Producer*: Francis Ford Coppola. *Co-Producer*: Fred Roos. *Associate Producer*: Mona Skager. *Screenplay*: Francis Ford Coppola. *Director of Photography*: Bill Butler. *Production Design*: Dean Tavoularis.

Supervising Editor and Sound and Montage Re-Recording: Walter Murch. *Editor*: Richard Chew. *Music*: David Shire. *Cast*: Gene Hackman (Harry Caul), John Cazale (Stan), Allen Garfield (Bernie Moran), Frederic Forrest (Mark), Cindy Williams (Ann), Michael Higgins (Paul), Harrison Ford (Martin Stett), Robert Duvall (The Director), Elizabeth MacRae (Meredith).

1974: THE GODFATHER PART II
Director: Francis Ford Coppola. *Producer*: Francis Ford Coppola. *Co-Producers*: Gary Frederickson and Fred Roos. *Screenplay*: Francis Ford Coppola and Mario Puzo, based on the novel *The Godfather* by Mario Puzo. *Director of Photography*: Gordon Willis. *Editors*: Peter Zinner, Barry Malkin, and Richard Marks. *Music*: Nino Rota (conducted by Carmine Coppola). *Production Design*: Dean Tavoularis. *Art Direction*: Angelo Graham.
Cast: Al Pacino (Michael Corleone), Robert Duvall (Tom Hagen), Diane Keaton (Kay Corleone), Robert De-Niro (Vito Corleone), John Cazale (Fredo Corleone), Talia Shire (Connie Corleone), Lee Strasberg (Hyman Roth), Michael V. Gazzo (Frankie Pentangeli), G. D. Spradlin (Senator Pat Geary), Morgana King (Mama Corleone).

Collaborations

1960: Director, *Ayamonn the Terrible* (short).

c. 1960: Director, *The Peeper, The Wide Open Spaces*.

1962: Director, additional sequences for *The Belt Girls and the Playboy*.

1962: Re-edited and dubbed the Russian film *Sadko-C*, released in the U.S. as *The Magic Voyage of Sinbad*.

1962: Re-edited and dubbed the Russian film *Nevo Zovet*, released in the U.S. as *Battle Beyond the Sun*.

251

1962: Assistant Director to Roger Corman on *The Premature Burial*.

1962: Dialogue Director, *Tower of London*.

1963: Sound and Second Unit Director, *The Young Racers*.

1963: Associate Producer and Second Unit Director, *The Terror*.

1965: Co-Screenwriter, *Is Paris Burning?*, with Gore Vidal, directed by René Clément.

1966: Co-Screenwriter, *This Property Is Condemned*, with Fred Coe and Edith Sommer, directed by Sydney Pollack.

1970: Co-Screenwriter, *Patton*, with Edmund H. North, directed by Franklin J. Schaffner.

1971: Executive Producer, *THX-1138*, directed by George Lucas.

1973: Co-Producer, *American Graffiti*, with Gary Kurtz, directed by George Lucas.

George Lucas

Shorts

1967: ELECTRONIC LABYRINTH: THX 1138:4EB
A fifteen-minute award-winning student film.

1968: FILMMAKER
A forty-minute documentary on the making of *The Rain People*.

Features

1971: THX-1138

Director: George Lucas. *Producer*: Lawrence Sturhahn. *Executive Producer*: Francis Ford Coppola. *Screenplay*: George Lucas and Walter Murch, from a story by George Lucas. *Directors of Photography*: Dave Meyers and Albert Kihn. *Editor*: George Lucas. *Art Direction*: Michael Haller. *Music*: Lalo Schifrin. *Sound Montages*: Walter Murch. *Titles and Animation*: Hal Barwood.

Cast: Robert Duvall (THX), Donald Pleasance (SEN), Maggie McOmie (LUH), Don Pedro Colley (SRT), Ian Wolfe (PTO).

1973: AMERICAN GRAFFITI

Director: George Lucas. *Producer*: Francis Ford Coppola. *Co-Producer*: Gary Kurtz. *Screenplay*: George Lucas, Gloria Katz, and Willard Huyck. *Visual Consultant (Supervising Cameraman)*: Haskell Wexler. *Editors*: Verna Fields and Marcia Lucas. *Sound Montage and Re-Recording*: Walter Murch. *Design Consultant*: Al Locatelli. *Art Direction*: Dennis Clark.

Cast: Richard Dreyfuss (Curt), Ronny Howard (Steve), Paul Le Mat (John), Charlie Martin Smith (Terry), Cindy Williams (Laurie), Candy Clark (Debbie), Mackenzie Phillips (Carol), Wolfman Jack (Disc Jockey), Harrison Ford (Bob Falfa), Bo Hopkins, Manuel Padilla, Jr., Beau Gentry (The Pharaohs).

1977: STAR WARS

Director: George Lucas. *Producer*: Gary Kurtz. *Screenplay*: George Lucas. *Director of Photography*: Gilbert Taylor. *Special Photographic Effects Supervisor*: John Dykstra. *Special Production and Mechanical Effects Supervisor*: John Stears. *Editors*: Paul Hirsch, Marcia Lucas, and Richard Chew. *Production Illustration*: Ralph McQuarrie. *Costume Design*: John Mollo. *Art Direction*: Norman Reynolds and Leslie Dilley. *Sound*: Derek Ball, Don MacDougall, Ray West, and Bob Minkler. *Music*: John Williams. *Production Design*: John Barry.

253

Cast: Mark Hamill (Luke Skywalker), Harrison Ford (Han Solo), Carrie Fisher (Princess Leia Organa), Peter Cushing (Grand Moff Tarkin), Alec Guinness (Ben Kenobi), Anthony Daniels (C3PO), Kenny Baker (R2-D2), Peter Mayhew (Chewbacca), David Prowse (Lord Darth Vader), Alex McCrindle (General Dodonna), Eddie Byrne (General Willard).

Brian DePalma

Shorts

1960: ICARUS

1961: 660124, THE STORY OF AN IBM CARD

1962: WOTAN'S WAKE
Cast: William Finley

1966: THE RESPONSIVE EYE

Features

1964: THE WEDDING PARTY
Direction, Production, Screenplay, and Editing: Brian DePalma, Cynthia Munroe, and Wilford Leach. *Director of Photography*: Peter Powell. *Music*: John Herbert McDowell.
Cast: Jill Clayburgh (Josephine Fish), Charles Pfluger (Charlie), Valda Setterfield (Mrs. Fish), Raymond McNally (Mr. Fish), Jennifer Salt (Phoebe), Robert DeNiro (Cecil).

1968: MURDER À LA MOD
Director: Brian DePalma. *Producer*: Ken Burrows. *Screenplay*: Brian DePalma. *Directors of Photography*: Bruce

Torbet and Jack Harrell. *Editor*: Brian DePalma. *Music*: John Herbert McDowell. *Sound*: Robert Fiore.
Cast: Margo Norton (Karen), Andra Akers (Tracy), Jared Martin (Christopher), William Finley (Otto), Jennifer Salt (First Actress).

1968: GREETINGS
Director: Brian DePalma. *Producer*: Charles Hirsch. *Screenplay*: Charles Hirsch and Brian DePalma. *Director of Photography*: Robert Fiore. *Editor*: Brian DePalma.
Cast: Jonathan Warden (Paul Shaw), Robert DeNiro (Jon Rubin), Gerritt Graham (Lloyd Clay), Megan McCormick (Marina), Ashley Oliver (Secretary), Allen Garfield (Pornographer).

1970: DIONYSUS IN '69
Directors: Brian DePalma, Robert Fiore, and Bruce Rubin. *Director of Stage Production*: Richard Schechner. *Directors of Photography*: Brian DePalma and Robert Fiore. *Editors*: Brian DePalma and Robert Fiore.
Cast: The Performance Group—William Finley (Dionysus), William Shepherd (Pentheus), Joan MacIntosh (Agave), Judith Allen, Remi Barclay, Samuel Blazer.
Filmed during a performance of the play as produced in the Performing Garage in Greenwich Village, New York.

1970: HI, MOM!
Director: Brian DePalma. *Producer*: Charles Hirsch. *Screenplay*: Brian DePalma, from a story by Brian DePalma and Charles Hirsch. *Director of Photography*: Robert Elfstrom. *Editor*: Paul Hirsch. *Music Composed and Conducted*: Eric Kaz.
Cast: Robert DeNiro (Jon Rubin), Charles Durnham (Superintendent), Allen Garfield (Joe Banner), Abraham Goren (Pervert in Movie Theater), Lara Parker (Jeannie Mitchell), Jennifer Salt (Judy Bishop), Gerritt Graham (Gerrit Wood), Nelson Peltz (Playboy).

1970: GET TO KNOW YOUR RABBIT
Director: Brian DePalma. *Producers*: Steven Bernhardt

and Paul Gare. *Executive Producer*: Peter Nelson. *Screenplay*: Jonathan Crittenden. *Director of Photography*: John Alonzo. *Editors*: Frank Urioste and Peter Colbert. *Music*: Jack Elliott and Allyn Ferguson.
Cast: Tom Smothers (Donald Beeman), John Astin (Mr. Turnbull), Suzanne Zenor (Paula), Samantha Jones (Susan), Allen Garfield (Vic), Katharine Ross (Girl), Orson Welles (Mr. Delasandro).

1973: SISTERS
(British title: *Blood Sisters*)
Director: Brian DePalma. *Producer*: Edward R. Pressman. *Screenplay*: Brian DePalma and Louisa Rose, from a story by Brian DePalma. *Director of Photography*: Gregory Sandor. *Music*: Bernard Herrmann. *Documentary Footage*: Jay Cocks. *Editor*: Paul Hirsch.
Cast: Margot Kidder (Danielle Breton), Jennifer Salt (Grace Collier), Charles Durning (Joseph Larch), Bill Finley (Emil Breton), Lisle Wilson (Phillip Woode), Bernard Hughes (Magazine Editor).

1974: PHANTOM OF THE PARADISE
Director: Brian DePalma. *Producer*: Edward R. Pressman. *Executive Producer*: Gustave Berne. *Screenplay*: Brian DePalma. *Director of Photography*: Larry Pizer. *Production Design*: Jack Fisk. *Editor*: Paul Hirsch. *Music*: Paul Williams.
Cast: Paul Williams (Swan), William Finley (Winslow Leach, the Phantom), Jessica Harper (Phoenix), George Memmoli (Philbin), Gerritt Graham (Beef), Jeffrey Comanor, Archie Hahn, Harold Oblong (The Juicy Fruits, The Beach Bums, The Undead).

1976: OBSESSION
Director: Brian DePalma. *Producers*: George Litto and Harry N. Blum. *Executive Producer*: Robert S. Bremson. *Screenplay*: Paul Schrader, from a story by Brian DePalma and Paul Schrader. *Director of Photography*: Vilmos Zsigmond. *Editor*: Paul Hirsch. *Music*: Bernard Herrmann. *Portraits*: Barton DePalma.

Cast: Cliff Robertson (Michael Courtland), Genevieve Bujold (Elizabeth Courtland/Sandra Portinari), John Lithgow (Robert LaSalle), Sylvia "Kuumba" Williams (Judy), Wanda Blackman (Amy Courtland).

1976: CARRIE
Director: Brian DePalma. *Producer*: Paul Monash. *Screenplay*: Lawrence D. Cohen, based on the novel by Stephen King. *Director of Photography*: Mario Tosi. *Editor*: Paul Hirsch. *Music*: Pino Dinaggio. *Art Direction*: William Kenny and Jack Fisk. *Stunt Coordinator*: Richard Weiker.
Cast: Sissy Spacek (Carrie White), Piper Laurie (Margaret White), Amy Irving (Sue Snell), William Katt (Tommy Ross), John Travolta (Billy Nolan), Nancy Allen (Chris Hargenson), Betty Buckley (Miss Collins).

John Milius

Features

1973: DILLINGER
Director: John Milius. *Producer*: Buzz Feitshans. *Executive Producers*: Samuel Z. Arkoff and Lawrence A. Gordon. *Associate Producer*: Robert Papazian. *Screenplay*: John Milius. *Director of Photography*: Jules Brenner. *Music*: Barry Devorzon. *Editor*: Fred Feitshans, Jr. *Sound*: Don Johnson and Kenny Schwarz. *Art Direction*: Trevor Williams. *Special Effects*: A. D. Flowers.
Cast: Warren Oates (John Dillinger), Ben Johnson (Melvin Purvis), Michelle Phillips (Billie Frechette), Cloris Leachman (Anna Sage), Harry Dean Stanton (Homer Van Meter), Steve Kanaly (Lester "Pretty Boy" Floyd), Richard Dreyfuss (George "Baby Face" Nelson), Geoffrey Lewis (Harry Pierpont), John Ryan (Charles Mackley), Roy Jenson (Samuel Cowley), John Martino (Eddie Martin), Read Morgan (Big Jim Wollard), Frank McRae (Reed

Youngblood), Jerry Summers (Tommy Carroll), Terry Leonard (Theodore "Handsome Jack" Klutas), Bob Harris (Ed Fulton).

1975: THE WIND AND THE LION

Director: John Milius. *Producer*: Herb Jaffe. *Screenplay*: John Milius. *Director of Photography*: Billy Williams. *Camera Operator*: David Harcourt. *Production Design*: Gil Parrondo. *Sound*: Roy Charman. *Editor*: Bob Wolfe. *Special Effects*: Alex Weldon.

Cast: Sean Connery (The Raisuli), Candice Bergen (Eden Pedecaris), Brian Keith (Theodore Roosevelt), John Huston (John Hay), Geoffrey Lewis (Gummere), Vladek Sheybal (The Bashaw), Steve Kanaly (Captain Jerome), Simon Harrison (William Pedecaris), Polly Gottesman (Jennifer Pedecaris).

Collaborations

1968: Co-Screenwriter, *Devil's Eight*, with James Gordon White and Willard Huyck, directed by Burt Topper.

1971: Co-Screenwriter, *Evel Knievel*, with Alan Caillou, directed by Marvin Chomsky.

1972: Screenwriter, *The Life and Times of Judge Roy Bean*, directed by John Huston.

1972: Co-Screenwriter, *Jeremiah Johnson*, with Edward Anhalt, directed by Sydney Pollack.

1973: Co-Screenwriter, *Magnum Force*, with Michael Cimino, directed by Ted Post.

Martin Scorsese

1969: WHO'S THAT KNOCKING AT MY DOOR?
Director: Martin Scorsese. *Producers*: Joseph Weill and Betzi and Hank Manoogian. *Screenplay*: Martin Scorsese. *Directors of Photography*: Michael Wadleigh (*16mm*), Richard Coll (*36mm*), and Max Fisher (*erotic sequence*).
Cast: Zina Bethune (The Girl), Harvey Keitel (J. R.), Anne Colette (Girl in Erotic Sequence), Lennard Kuras (Joey), Michael Scala (Sally Gaga), Catherine Scorsese (The Mother of J. R.).
First title (1965)—*Bring on the Dancing Girls*. Second version (1967)—*I Call First*.
1969: Distributed in New York as *Who's That Knocking at My Door?*
1970: Distributed in Los Angeles as *J. R.*

1970: STREET SCENES
Production Supervisor and Post-Production Director: Martin Scorsese. *Producer*: New York Cinetracts Collective.

1972: BOXCAR BERTHA
Director: Martin Scorsese. *Producer*: Roger Corman, for James H. Nicholson and Samuel Z. Arkoff. *Production Assistant*: Julie Corman. *Screenplay*: Joyce H. and John William Corrington, based on the book *Sister of the Road* (1937), the autobiography of Boxcar Bertha Thompson, as told to Dr. Ben Reitman. *Director of Photography*: John Stephens (and Gayne Rescher, noncredited). *Visual Consultant (and Art Direction, noncredited)*: David Nichols. *Editor*: Buzz Feitshans (and Martin Scorsese, noncredited). *Music*: Gib Guilbeau and Thad Maxwell (conducted by Herb Cohen). *Sound*: Don Johnson.
Cast: Barbara Hershey (Boxcar Bertha), David Carradine (Big Bill Shelley), Barry Primus (Rake Brown), Bernie Casey (Von Morton), John Carradine (H. Buckram Sartoris), Victor Argo and David R. Osterhout (The McIvers), Martin Scorsese (Client in Brothel).

1973: MEAN STREETS
Director: Martin Scorsese. *Producer*: Jonathan T. Taplin. *Screenplay*: Martin Scorsese and Mardik Martin, from an idea by Martin Scorsese. *Director of Photography*: Kent Wakeford. *Visual Consultant (and Art Direction, noncredited)*: David Nichols. *Editor*: Sid Levin (and Martin Scorsese, noncredited). *Sound*: Don Johnson.
Cast: Harvey Keitel (Charlie), Robert DeNiro (Johnny Boy), David Proval (Tony), Amy Robinson (Teresa), Richard Romanus (Michael), Cesare Danova (Giovanni), Victor Argo (Mario), David Carradine (The Drunk), Robert Carradine (The Young Killer), Catherine Scorsese (Neighbor on Staircase), Martin Scorsese (Shorty, the Killer in the Car).

1974: ALICE DOESN'T LIVE HERE ANYMORE
Director: Martin Scorsese. *Producers*: David Susskind and Audrey Maas. *Executive Producer*: Larry Cohen. *Associate Producer*: Sandra Weintraub. *Screenplay*: Robert Getchell. *Director of Photography*: Kent Wakeford. *Music*: Richard LaSalle. *Art Direction*: Toby Carr Rafelson. *Editor*: Marcia Lucas. *Sound*: Don Parker.
Cast: Ellen Burstyn (Alice Hyatt), Kris Kristofferson (David), Alfred Lutter (Tommy), Harvey Keitel (Ben), Diane Ladd (Flo), Lelia Goldoni (Bea), Jodie Foster (Audrey), Valerie Curtin (Vera), Billy Green Bush (Donald), Lane Bradbury (Rita), Vic Tayback (Mel).

1976: TAXI DRIVER
Director: Martin Scorsese. *Producers*: Michael and Julia Phillips. *Screenplay*: Paul Schrader. *Director of Photography*: Michael Chapman. *Visual Consultant*: David Nichols. *Art Direction*: Charles Rosen. *Supervising Editor*: Marcia Lucas. *Editors*: Tom Rolf and Melvin Shapiro. *Music*: Bernard Herrmann.
Cast: Robert DeNiro (Travis Bickle), Cybill Shepherd (Betsy), Albert Brooks (Tom), Peter Boyle (Wizard), Harvey Keitel (Sport), Jodie Foster (Iris), Leonard

Harris (Palantine), Steven Prince (Gun Salesman), Martin Scorsese (Man in Taxi).

1977: NEW YORK, NEW YORK
Director: Martin Scorsese. *Producers*: Irwin Winkler and Robert Chartoff. *Screenplay*: Earl MacRauch and Mardik Martin, from an original scenario by Earl MacRauch. *Director of Photography*: Laszlo Kovacs. *Supervising Editors*: Irving Lerner and Marcia Lucas. *Original Songs*: John Kander and Fred Ebb. *Choreography*: Ron Field. *Art Direction*: Harry R. Kemm. *Production Design*: Boris Leven.
Cast: Liza Minnelli (Francine Evans), Robert DeNiro (Jimmy Doyle), Lionel Stander (Tony Harwell), Barry Primus (Paul Wilson), Mary Kay Place (Bernice), Georgie Auld (Frankie Harte), George Memmoli (Nicky), Diahnne Abbott (Singer in Harlem Club), Dick Miller (Owner of the Palm Club).

Collaborations

1968: Co-Screenwriter, *Obsessions*, directed by Pim De La Parra and Wim Verstappen.

1968: Pre-production work, one week as director on *The Honeymoon Killers*, completed by Leonard Kastle.

1969: Supervising Editor and Assistant Director (noncredited), *Woodstock*, directed by Michael Wadleigh.

1971: Supervising Editor and Post-Production Associate, *Medicine Ball Caravan*, directed by François Reichenbach.

1972: Editing Supervisor credit on *Elvis on Tour*, directed by Pierre Adidge and Robert Abei, disowned by Martin Scorsese.

1973: Supervising Editor, *Unholy Rollers*, directed by Vernon Zimmerman.

1973: Assisted with editing *Minnie and Moskowitz*, directed by John Cassavetes.

Steven Spielberg

Shorts and Television

At 13 he won a film contest with a forty-minute war film, *Escape to Nowhere*. At 16 he made a science fiction film, lasting over two hours, *Firelight*.

1969: *Amblin'* (twenty-four minutes) won him a contract with Universal. He directed episodes of the following television series: "Night Gallery," "Columbo" (pilot), "Owen Marshall," "Marcus Welby, M.D.," "The Name of the Game" (science fiction episode called "L. A. 2017"), and "Psychiatrist."

1971: DUEL
Director: Steven Spielberg. *Producer*: George Eckstein. *Screenplay*: Richard Matheson, based on his published story. *Director of Photography*: Jack A. Marta. *Editor*: Frank Morriss. *Sound*: Edwin S. Hall. *Music*: Billy Goldenberg. *Art Direction*: Robert S. Smith.
Cast: Dennis Weaver (David Mann), Jacqueline Scott (Mrs. Mann), Eddie Firestone (Cafe Owner), Lou Frizzell (Bus Driver), Gene Dynarski (Man in Cafe), Lucille Benson (Lady at Snakerama), Tim Herbert (Gas Station Attendant), Charles Seel (Old Man), Shirley O'Hara (Waitress), Alexander Lockwood (Old Man in Car), Amy Douglass (Old Woman in Car), Dick Whittington (Radio Interviewer), Cary Loftin (The Truck Driver), Dale Van Sickle (Car Driver).

1971: SOMETHING EVIL

1972: SAVAGE

He also wrote the story for *Ace Eli and Rodger of the Skies* (1973).

Features

1974: THE SUGARLAND EXPRESS

Director: Steven Spielberg. *Producers*: Richard D. Zanuck and David Brown. *Screenplay*: Hal Barwood and Matthew Robbins, from a story by Steven Spielberg, Hal Barwood, and Matthew Robbins. *Production Executive*: William S. Gilmore, Jr. *Director of Photography*: Vilmos Zsigmond. *Editors*: Edward M. Abroms and Verna Fields. *Music*: John Williams (Harmonica Solos by "Toots" Thielemans). *Sound*: John Carter and Robert Hoyt. *Art Direction*: Joseph Alves, Jr. *Stunt Coordinator*: Cary Loftin. *Special Effects*: Frank Brendel.

Cast: Goldie Hawn (Lou Jean Poplin), Ben Johnson (Captain Tanner), Michael Sacks (Maxwell Slide), William Atherton (Clovis Poplin), Gregory Walcott (Mashburn), Steve Kanaly (Jessup).

1975: JAWS

Director: Steven Spielberg. *Producers*: Richard D. Zanuck and David Brown. *Screenplay*: Peter Benchley and Carl Gottlieb, based on the novel by Peter Benchley. *Production Executive*: William S. Gilmore, Jr. *Director of Photography*: Bill Butler. *Live Shark Footage*: Ron and Valerie Taylor. *Underwater Photography*: Rexford Metz. *Production Design*: Joseph Alves, Jr. *Editor*: Verna Fields. *Music*: John Williams. *Special Effects*: Robert A. Mattey. *Set Decoration*: John M. Dwyer.

Cast: Roy Scheider (Martin Brody), Robert Shaw (Quint), Richard Dreyfuss (Hooper), Lorraine Gary (Ellen Brody), Murray Hamilton (Vaughn), Carl Gottlieb (Meadows), Jeffrey C. Kramer (Hendricks), Susan Backlinie (Chrissie), Jonathan Filley (Cassidy), Ted Grossman (Estuary Victim), Chris Rebello (Michael Brody), Jay Mello (Sean Brody), Lee Fierro (Mrs. Kintner), Jeffrey Voorhees (Alex

Kintner), Craig Kingsbury (Ben Gardner), Dr. Robert Nevin (Medical Examiner), Peter Benchley (Interviewer).

1977: CLOSE ENCOUNTERS OF THE THIRD KIND
Director: Steven Spielberg. *Producers*: Julia and Michael Phillips. *Screenplay*: Steven Spielberg. *Director of Photography*: Vilmos Zsigmond. *Photography, Additional American Scenes*: William A. Fraker. *Photography, Special Sequences, India*: Douglas Slocombe. *Additional Photography*: John Alonzo, Laszlo Kovacs. *Editor*: Michael Kahn. *Music*: John Williams. *Special Effects*: Douglas Trumbull. *Technical Advisor*: Dr. J. Allen Hynek. *Art Direction*: Dan Lomino.
Cast: Richard Dreyfuss (Roy Neary), François Truffaut (Claude Lacombe), Teri Garr (Ronnie Neary), Melinda Dillon (Jillian Guiler), Bob Balaban (David Laughlin), Lance Hendriksen (Robert), Warren Kemmerling (Wild Bill), Cary Guffey (Barry Guiler).

Bibliography

We list here those sources of particular importance to our argument, as well as those from which we have taken direct quotations. For reasons of space we do not acknowledge fully our debt to the files of *Variety*, *Film Daily*, the *Sunday Times* (London), *The New York Times*, the *Washington Post*, the *Los Angeles Times*, *Time*, *Newsweek*, the *London Daily Mail*, and *Screen International*. Much material in these newspapers and magazines was invaluable. We have added to this basic bibliography a note on publicly available American material that bears on film history as we have told it. Outside the scope of this listing, but seminal to the thought in this book, were: E. J. Hobsbawm's *Bandits* (London, 1969); Norman Cohn's *The Pursuit of the Millennium* (London, 1970); Keith Thomas's *Religion and the Decline of Magic* (London, 1968); and the work of Jacques Lacan whose *Ecrits* (London, 1977) is now translated.

On basic economic data, we drew on the extensive historical tables in the *Economic Report of the President*, 1977; the NBC research material reproduced annually in the *TV Fact Book*; and material made available by Michael Linden, head of research for the Motion Picture Association of America. Key economic indicators in this MPAA material appear annually in the *International Motion Picture Almanac*. For clarifying the correlation between television's rise and the apparent fall of Hollywood, and for his meticulous analysis of competition outside an orthodox price framework, we are grateful to an unpublished work by Henry Williams: "Economic Changes in the Motion Picture Industry as Affected by Television and Other Factors"

(Ph.D. thesis, University of Indiana, 1968). This cleared away a great deal of theoretical underbrush.

Motion picture companies file annual reports, like other corporations, with the Securities and Exchange Commission in Washington; and the outline of any film corporation's history can usually be traced through the Department of Corporations in any major California city. This material is, at best, skimpy; it does not reveal investments in individual films, nor the structure of film deals. More useful are the prospectuses issued when shares are issued or mergers consummated. These summarize corporate history reliably and briskly. Individual directors may propose deals that require them to reveal their financial status and business interests; we derive the figures for *The Godfather Part II* from documents filed by Francis Coppola with the Federal Communications Commission in Washington, D.C., when he bid for radio station KMPX in San Francisco.

In this list *AJS* = *American Journal of Sociology*
    ASR = *American Sociology Review*
    Annals = *Annals of the American Academy*
    Journal = *Journal of the Producers Guild of America*
    TIBG = *Transactions of the Institute of British Geographers*

Allen, Tom: on Steven Spielberg. *Village Voice*, June 23, 1975.

Arkoff, Samuel Z. "Myths of the Movie Business." *Journal*, June 1971.

Balio, Tino. *United Artists, the Company the Stars Built.* Madison, Wisconsin, 1975.

Balio, Tino, ed. *The American Film Industry*. Madison, Wisconsin, 1976.

Barnouw, Eric. *Tube of Plenty*. New York, 1977.

Bensman, Joseph, and Vidich, Arthur J. *Metropolitan Communities*. New York, 1975.

Berry, Brian J. L. "The Geography of the United States in the Year 2000." *TIBG*, November 1970.

Bluem, A. William, and Squire, Jason E. *The Movie Business*. New York, 1972.

Bogardus, Emory S. "A Television Scale and Television Index." *ASR* 17:220.

Broeck, John: on Bernard Herrmann. *Film Comment* 12:5 (Sept.-Oct. 1976).

Carlos, Serge. "Religious Participation and the Urban-Suburban Continuum." *AJS* 75:742.

Christie, Ian; Hardy, Phil; and Petit, Chris: on Brian DePalma. *Film Directions* 1 (1977).

Ciment, Michel, and Henry, Michael: on Martin Scorsese. *Positif*, June 1975.

Clarke, Alfred C. "The Use of Leisure and Its Relation to Levels of Occupational Prestige." *ASR* 21:301.

Coleman, J. S. "Adolescent Subculture and Academic Achievement." *AJS* 65:337.

Cook, Bruce: on Steven Spielberg. *American Film* 3:2 (November 1977).

Coppola, Francis: attorneys' submission to FCC, 1975, file KMPX San Francisco.

Coppola, Francis: memo on American Zoetrope. *Esquire*, November 1977.

Cressey, Paul G. "The Motion Picture Experience as Modified by Social Background and Personality." *ASR* 3:516.

Duncan, B.; van Arsdol, M. D., Jr.; and Sabagh, C. "Patterns of City Growth." *AJS* 67:418.

Elder, Grant H., Jr. *Children of the Great Depression*. Chicago, 1974.

Fara, Sylvia Fleis. "Suburbanism as a Way of Life." *ASR* 21:34.

Farber, Stephen: on *The Godfather*. *Sight and Sound*, Autumn 1972.

Feigenbaum, K., and Havinghurst, R. J. "Leisure and Life-Style." *AJS* 64:396.

Flynn, Charles, and McCarthy, Todd. *Kings of the B's*. New York, 1975.

French, Philip. *The Movie Moguls*. London, 1969.

Gelmis, Joseph. *The Film Director as Superstar*. London, 1974.

Gorsch, Martin, and Hammer, Richard. *The Luciano Testament*. London, 1976.

Gottlieb, David. "Neighborhood Tavern and the Cocktail Lounge." *AJS* 62:559.

Havinghurst, R. J. "The Leisure Activities of the Middle-Aged." *AJS* 63:152.

Hess, John: on *The Godfather Part II*. *Jump Cut*, May-July 1975.

Higham, Charles. *Hollywood at Sunset*. New York, 1972.

Hodenfield, Chris: on Martin Scorsese. *Rolling Stone*, June 16, 1977.

Hodenfield, Chris: on Steven Spielberg. *Rolling Stone*, January 26, 1978.

Hodgson, Godfrey. *In Our Time*. London, 1977.

Horton, D., and Strauss, A. "Interaction in Audience Participation Shows." *AJS* 62:579.

Howe, A. H. "A Banker Looks at the Picture Business." *Journal*, June 1971.

Hulett, J. E., Jr. "Estimating the Net Effect of a Commercial Motion Picture upon the Trend of Local Public Opinion." *ASR* 14:263.

Huyck, Willard; Katz, Gloria; and Lucas, George. *American Graffiti*. New York, 1974.

Komarovsky, Mira. *Blue Collar Marriage*. New York, 1967.

Koszarshi, Richard: on Francis Coppola. *Films in Review* 19:9 (Nov. 1968).

Lang, Gladys Engel, and Lang, Kurt. "The Unique Perspective of Television and Its Effect." *ASR* 18:3.

Maas, Peter. *The Valachi Papers*. London, 1969.

Mead, Margaret. "The Pattern of Leisure in Contemporary American Culture." *Annals* 313:11.

Metro Goldwyn Mayer: prospectus for bond issue, July 12, 1974.

Milius, John. *The Wind and the Lion*. New York, 1975.

Reisman, David. "The Suburban Dislocation." *Annals* 314:124.

Rosen, Marjorie: on Martin Scorsese. *Film Comment* 11:2 (March-April 1975).

Scanlon, Paul: on George Lucas. *Rolling Stone*, August 25, 1977.

Schnore, Leo F. "The Functions of Metropolitan Suburbs." *AJS* 61:453.

Schnore, Leo F. "Metropolitan Growth and Decentralization." *AJS* 63:171.

Schnore, Leo F. "Municipal Annexations and the Growth of Metropolitan Suburbs 1950–1960." *AJS* 67:406.

Smith, J. S. "Conventionalization and Control, an Examination of Adolescent Crowds." *AJS* 74:172.

Snider, Burr: on John Milius. *Esquire*, June 1973.

Soule, George. "The Economics of Leisure." *Annals* 313:16.

Taylor, John Russell: on Francis Coppola and *Finian's Rainbow*. *Sight and Sound*, Winter 1968–69.

Thompson, Richard: on John Milius. *Film Comment* 12:4 (July-August 1976).

Thompson, Richard: on Paul Schrader. *Film Comment* 12:2 (March-April 1976).

Toeplitz, Jerzy. *Hollywood and After* (Nowy Film Amery-kanski). London, 1974.

Warner Brothers: prospectus for merger with Kinney National, May 16, 1969.

Will, D., and Willerman, P., eds. *Roger Corman*. Edinburgh, 1970.

About the Authors

Michael Pye is a staff writer for *The Sunday Times* (London) and former film critic for *The Scotsman* in Edinburgh. He holds a First in modern history from St. John's College, Oxford, is a Fellow of the Royal Anthropological Institute, and is a "mainline movie addict."

Lynda Myles is the director of the Edinburgh Film Festival. She has been a script writer for Scottish Television, worked for the BBC in radio and television, and done freelance broadcasting. She is a graduate of the University of Edinburgh, where she earned an honors degree in philosophy.